Vampola

INSANITY AND IDIOCY IN MASSACHUSETTS

This volume is published as part of a long-standing cooperative program between Harvard University Press and the Commonwealth Fund, a philanthropic foundation, to encourage the publication of significant scholarly books in medicine and health.

INSANITY AND IDIOCY IN

MASSACHUSETTS: *Report of*

the Commission on Lunacy, 1855
by Edward Jarvis

with a critical introduction by Gerald N. Grob

A Commonwealth Fund Book

Harvard University Press, Cambridge, Massachusetts, 1971

© 1971 by the President and Fellows of Harvard College

All Rights Reserved

Distributed in Great Britain by Oxford University Press, London

Library of Congress Catalog Card Number 72–134950

SBN 674-45480-4

CONTENTS

ACKNOWLEDGMENTS

I should like to thank Dr. Barbara Rosenkrantz of Harvard University and Professor Tilden Edelstein of Rutgers University, both of whom gave me the benefit of a careful and critical reading. Mr. Richard Wolfe of the Countway Medical Library of the Harvard Medical School proved of inestimable help in calling material to my attention. I should also like to thank the staffs of the American Antiquarian Society, the Houghton Library of Harvard University, the New York Public Library, and the Massachusetts State Library for their gracious and kind help. Over the years Professor Roger Bibace of Clark University has shared with me his insights into and knowledge of the field of mental health and mental illness; I owe him a debt of gratitude that can never be adequately repaid. I should also like to express my thanks to the National Institute of Mental Health, United States Public Health Service (HEW), which has supported my work with Grants 12743 and 17859.

Gerald N. Grob
Rutgers University
New Brunswick, New Jersey
February 20, 1970

Author's Note

In this introduction I have used the word "psychiatrist" even when referring to practitioners during the first half of the nineteenth century, when they were known either as hospital superintendents or alienists. I have also used the terms "insane" and "insanity" as well as "mentally ill" and "mental illness." Although the first two terms have acquired an odious reputation, they were perfectly respectable and valid *medical* usage during the nineteenth century. Using them here is a historical convenience and does not imply any derogatory connotation. It is quite probable, after all, that the term "mental illness" will in the future be looked down upon with the same disfavor and hostility as "insanity" is at present.

G.N.G.

INTRODUCTION

Mental illness, along with cancer and heart disease, ranks in the minds of many as one of the foremost health problems facing the American people. Statistics on the prevalence of mental disease are quite striking. At least half, if not more, of all hospital beds in the United States are now occupied by mental patients. A recent study of one area in New York City concluded that less than 20 percent of the population was mentally well.[1] Aside from the human misery, the financial costs are staggering, for the direct and indirect costs stemming from mental illness run into the billions.

By 1955 the problems arising out of mental disease had become so vast that the Congress unanimously endorsed the establishment of the Joint Commission on Mental Illness and Health, empowering it to analyze the needs and resources of the mentally ill and to make recommendations for a national policy. Like many individuals within the mental health professions, the Commission began with an assumption about the past: namely, that American society had never allocated sufficient resources to extirpate or control mental illness and its consequences. Its final report, completed in 1961, opened with the strong and unequivocal assertion that the institutional system caring for the mentally ill in the United States was an abject and dismal failure. "Viewed either historically or currently," it charged, "the care of persons voluntarily admitted or legally committed to public mental hospitals constitutes the great unfinished business of the mental health movement."[2]

[1] "In terms of Mental Health Rating II [the scale developed for the Midtown Manhattan Study] . . . less than one-fifth of the population is well, about three-fifths exhibit subclinical forms of mental disorder, and one-fourth shows some impairment and constitutes the clinical or morbid range of the scale." Thomas S. Langner and Stanley T. Michael, *Life Stress and Mental Health* (New York: Free Press of Glencoe, 1963), 76.

[2] *Action for Mental Health: Final Report of the Joint Commission on Mental Illness and Health 1961* (New York: Basic Books, 1961), 4.

Yet nearly a century earlier the Commonwealth of Massachusetts had also become increasingly disturbed by the social and medical problems arising out of mental illness. Like the Congress in 1955, it too authorized the establishment of a commission to study the problem and offer recommendations. The result was the publication in 1855 of the *Report on Insanity and Idiocy in Massachusetts, by the Commission on Lunacy, Under Resolve of the Legislature of 1854*, perhaps the most extensive and influential study of its time. Not only did this report provide an exhaustive analysis of conditions among the mentally ill within one state, but it also offered a series of recommendations to guide the legislature in developing a comprehensive policy toward this alarming malady. Indeed, the parallels between the analysis of the Joint Commission and the *Report on Insanity* were quite striking. Both had been based on impressive and comprehensive research; both had approached the problem within the broad context of public policy toward mental illness; both had analyzed existing conditions; and both had suggested the outlines of a new policy that would, if implemented, presumably upgrade institutional care and therapy.

The background of the Massachusetts study did not differ fundamentally from the one authorized by Congress a century later. In 1818 the McLean Asylum (a division of the Massachusetts General Hospital) had opened its doors. A private institution that catered largely to those individuals and families who could afford the high costs of protracted hospitalization, it could not and did not meet the needs of lower- and middle-class patients. In 1830, therefore, the Massachusetts legislature passed a law authorizing the establishment of a State Lunatic Hospital. The fight in the legislature was led by Horace Mann, then embarking on his noted career as a humanitarian reformer. Indeed, the entire episode reflected the larger current of reform that played such a significant role in American society in the 1830's and 1840's.

In 1833 the new institution, located in Worcester, received its first patient. Under the leadership of Dr. Samuel B. Woodward (also the first president of what is today the American Psychiatric Association), the Worcester hospital gained a national reputation and served as a model for other states as a result of its early therapeutic successes. By the 1840's, however, the hospital was beginning to face all of the problems that have been endemic to mental institutions generally. Crowding, declining curability rates, an influx of lower-class groups—to cite only a few examples—all combined to reduce sharply the effectiveness of the hospital as a therapeutic (as opposed to a custodial)

institution.[3] In 1848 the legislature provided for the establishment of a committee to study the problems related to mental
illness and to offer recommendations. Out of this study came a
second state hospital at Taunton, which opened its doors in the
spring of 1854.

The opening of a second public institution, however, did little
to improve conditions within the Bay State. The number of
mentally ill persons seemed to increase faster than the general
population. Moreover, the Worcester hospital, once a model
institution, had deteriorated to the point where its trustees
described it as "one of the poorest, if not the very poorest, in the
country." The Committee on Public Charitable Institutions of
the legislature, when informed of substandard conditions at
Worcester, decided that the problems growing out of mental
illness were so complex that an impartial and exhaustive
analysis was required that would provide the basis for a more
intelligent and enlightened policy. The legislature concurred,
and the stage was set for one of the most significant investigations of mental illness in the nineteenth century. Largely the
work of Dr. Edward Jarvis, the *Report on Insanity* would lay down
guidelines that helped to mold public policy toward mental
illness not only in Massachusetts, but in the United States as
well.

In retrospect it is clear that the *Report on Insanity* failed to
achieve the goal of meeting the challenges growing out of
mental illness. Had it been successful, there probably would
have been little necessity a century later to establish a national
commission to study the problem anew and offer alternative
policies. It would be easy, of course, to dismiss the *Report on
Insanity* as the product of an age that lacked a "scientific psychiatry" or as a document produced by individuals operating in
an intellectual and scientific vacuum. Most individuals, after all,
like to feel that somehow their age is wiser and better informed
than past generations, and that they are better equipped to
"solve" age-old problems. The historian, on the other hand,
cannot be so confident of the present nor so harsh about the
past. Countless generations have often seen their dreams
frustrated and their vaunted knowledge seemingly incapable of
comprehending all of the factors that influenced events.

To understand fully the *Report on Insanity* requires not only a
knowledge of the immediate circumstances that gave rise to this

[3] I have treated the history of the Worcester hospital and the development of
public policy toward mental illness in Massachusetts in *The State and the Mentally
Ill: A History of Worcester State Hospital in Massachusetts 1830–1920* (Chapel Hill:
University of North Carolina Press, 1966). Some of the material in this book has
been used in the present study with the kind permission of the Press.

particular study, but also an awareness of the larger society in which it was written. For it is abundantly clear that neither psychiatry nor mental hospitals reflected solely the dominant scientific and medical currents of a particular period. On the contrary, both developed out of the interaction of complex social, economic, and intellectual forces, and frequently reflected the unique characteristics of their indigenous environment.

Public mental hospitals, for example, performed a variety of roles, some of which were thrust on it by a society that lacked effective means of accomplishing certain ends. Mental hospitals were not only entrusted with the function of caring for sick individuals; they often accepted the aged and indigent as well as others whose behavior was deemed socially disruptive by the community. Moreover, care and treatment were frequently functions of individual and group values not directly related to scientific or medical considerations. Above all, the care and treatment of the mentally ill was inextricably tied to economic factors, in part because of the large cost of protracted hospital-ization and in part because such a high proportion of institu-tionalized patients came from lower-class and ethnic minorities. Neither American psychiatry nor the mental hospital, then, can be studied solely in medical terms; both must be viewed within an institutional framework related to the broader problems of welfare and indigency. Before examining the specific circum-stances that led to the *Report on Insanity,* we must understand the external factors that influenced the development of American psychiatry and mental hospitals during the first half of the nine-teenth century.

II

The colonists who migrated to the New World in the seven-teenth and eighteenth centuries brought with them institutions and patterns of thought characteristic of their places of origin. This is of crucial importance in understanding the context in which psychiatry developed, for fundamental changes were taking place in Europe during the seventeenth and eighteenth centuries. Until the seventeenth century deranged individuals generally remained with their families or friends; the com-munity accepted responsibilty only in those extreme cases where behavior became dangerous or socially disruptive. Moreover, it was common for harmless lunatics to wander about at will, and no effort was made to segregate them from society in special institutions. Hospitals existed during the Middle Ages, but their role and purpose were quite different from our own concep-

tions of such institutions. Medieval hospitals were often under
the control of the Church and were as much related to religious
notions of charity and philanthropy as anything else.

As European society began to shift away from an ecclesiastical
and religious base, the role of the hospital began to undergo a
radical transformation. The development of the hospital was
influenced by the emerging secular state, which found itself
confronted with the necessity of providing in some manner for
the indigent, the sick, the aged, the mentally ill, and even the
unemployed. Mercantilist statesmen and thinkers who placed
a premium on such virtues as thrift, ambition, and efficiency,
were attempting to create an administrative and financial
structure that would be capable of maintaining a high degree
of order so as to strengthen the emerging nation-state. Consequently, problems involving health and indigency for the first
time began to fall within the normal activities of government.[4]

During the sixteenth and seventeenth centuries, governments
began to construct a variety of institutions to cope with the
mounting problems arising out of health and indigency. Poverty,
inferior diet, and substandard sanitation led to disease, and
disease often furthered poverty by sharply diminishing pro-
ductivity. The state, therefore, had a vested interest in developing effective mechanisms to deal with health-related
problems. There was no serious effort to separate health from
indigency; both were viewed as different sides of the same coin.
England, for example, with the Elizabethan Poor Law Act of
1601, adopted the principle that society had a corporate responsibility for the support of the poor. The Act, a codification of
previous practices and statutes, attempted to combine public
responsibility with private charity so as to make certain that
vagrancy and other forms of idleness—whether voluntary or
involuntary—were contained within certain limits. Along with
corporate responsibility went a series of institutional reinforce-
ments, including the development of workhouses and houses
of correction. These institutions, designed originally to deal
with impoverished lower-class groups, became involved ultimately in the more general problem of health. In France a
similar situation prevailed. The Hôtel Dieu cared for the sick,
while the Hôpital Général cared for the aged, the mentally ill,
and those individuals afflicted with venereal diseases. Over a
period of years these institutions came to perform many

[4] One of the best brief discussions of the origins of the modern hospital is
George Rosen's essay "The Hospital: Historical Sociology of a Community Insti-
tution," in *The Hospital in Modern Society*, Eliot Freidson, ed. (New York: Free
Press of Glencoe, 1963), 1–36.

different tasks, combining the characteristics of jail, asylum, workship, and hospital.[5]

By the eighteenth century contemporary thinkers had begun the task of drawing all of the threads together and formulating a national policy to cope with the problems of health and indigency. This was done by linking the health of the population with the well-being of the nation-state. The result was a broad-based movement led largely by members of the middle class (especially merchants, physicians, clergymen) to help control the ravages of disease by establishing hospitals in major urban areas. In general, these hospitals, supported by both public and private sources, were intended to care for sick persons, particularly those in indigent straits, rather than caring for unfortunates of all kinds (as medieval institutions had done). The development of hospitals was also given impetus by the scientific revolution of the sixteenth, seventeenth, and eighteenth centuries, which opened the door to the application of science to medical care. By the eighteenth century surgery and obstetrics had already benefited from the dissection of human bodies, while newer concepts of disease, based on observation and study of clinical symptoms, contributed to the growth of the hospital as a functionally important social institution. In turn, the application of techniques of measurement and observation intensified the need for hospitals, since an adequate supply of clinical material for research and training depended on the existence of such institutions.

Within this context the mental hospital began to mature, particularly during the latter half of the seventeenth and especially in the eighteenth century. Such hospitals (and oftentimes its forerunner was a local institution such as a jail, a workhouse, a poorhouse) had a dual purpose. They protected the community against individuals who ostensibly threatened its security and well-being; and they also were entrusted with the responsibility of providing therapeutic care for some patients and humane custodial care for others. The hospital thus owed allegiance to the community and to the individual patient. Such divided allegiance was to give the mental hospital an ambivalent charac-

[5] See W. K. Jordan, *Philanthropy in England 1480–1660: A Study of the Changing Pattern of English Social Aspirations* (London: George Allen & Unwin, 1959), and George Rosen, "Social Attitudes to Irrationality and Madness in 17th and 18th Century Europe," *Journal of the History of Medicine and Allied Sciences,* 18 (July 1963), 220–240. The development of attitudes toward mental illness and the rise of the mental hospital in Europe are explored in a collection of the essays of George Rosen entitled *Madness in Society: Chapters in the Historical Sociology of Mental Illness* (Chicago: University of Chicago Press, 1968), and Michel Foucalt's thought-provoking work *Madness and Civilization: A History of Insanity in the Age of Reason* (New York: Random House, 1965).

ter, for it was by no means unusual to find the two roles in
conflict with each other.

The origins of the mental hospital, then, lay rooted not merely in contemporary medical or psychiatric definitions of mental illness, but also in the social, cultural, and economic fabric of a society moving into the modern era. Indeed, it must be emphasized that the mental hospital, at least in its beginnings, was an institution having as one of its major functions the protection of the community and the care of groups unable to provide for themselves because of their illness. It is significant, too, that the mentally ill were originally classified with indigent and dependent groups of all varieties, including vagrants, criminals, the unemployed, and the aged. While the mental hospital had already taken its modern form by the mid-nineteenth century, it would never completely outgrow its early character as an undifferentiated welfare institution.

III

The development of the mental hospital in the United States was in many respects similar to that of England and the continent. The mental hospital here fulfilled not only a medical role, but a welfare role as well, since the overwhelming majority of its patients came from low socio-economic groups concentrated in urban areas. Indeed, the origins of the American mental hospital were closely related to the emergence of an urban-industrial society in the nineteenth century. That such institutions appeared initially in an urban rather than a rural setting is understandable. Urbanization was responsible for a heightened social sensitivity toward deviant behavior and mental illness; it had also caused informal mechanisms for the care of mentally ill persons to break down. Consequently, there were demands that special provision be made for the mentally ill not only to protect the general public, but to provide as well for the care and welfare of such persons. Moreover, pressure for institutionalization probably came from lower-class immigrant families who were unable to care for their mentally ill members. (Whether or not the level of tolerance of abnormal behavior varied by class or ethnic group is a problem that is difficult to answer because of the paucity of source material bearing on this subject.)

The individuals who founded mental hospitals in the United States were recruited, as they were abroad, from the ranks of the middle class and included not only physicians, but clergymen and reformers active in a variety of occupations. The close interconnection between these reformers and Protestantism, particularly middle-class Protestantism, was especially evident. By this time a number of Protestant thinkers had developed a theology based on the doctrines of the free individual and a moral universe, which, when applied to society, resulted in the transformation of Evangelical Protestantism into a radical social force seeking the abolition of the restraints that bound the individual and hindered his self-development. All persons, they forcefully argued, were under a moral law that gave them a responsibility for the welfare of their fellow man.[6] As a result of their teachings and agitation, virtually dozens of reform movements appeared during the first half of the nineteenth century, including movements to better the condition of the insane, the inebriate, the blind, the deaf, the slave, the convict, and other unfortunate members of society. Some of these reform movements were intended to help individuals and groups powerless to change their condition; others had broader social and humanitarian goals, including the abolition of war, the remaking of society by establishing model utopian communities, and the founding of a free universal system of public education.[7]

[6] This theme is especially evident in the careers of the Rev. Louis Dwight, secretary of the Boston Prison Discipline Society (an organization that helped to focus attention on the confinement of deranged individuals in jails and poorhouses); Dorothea L. Dix, who was instrumental in helping to establish numerous state mental hospitals between the 1840's and the 1870's; Samuel B. Woodward, who served as the first president of what is today the American Psychiatric Association; and Samuel Gridley Howe, who was active in a variety of reform movements. For Dwight's views see William Jenks, "Memoir of Rev. Louis Dwight," in *Reports of the Boston Prison Discipline Society* (3 vols.: Boston, 1855), I, 5–41, and the *Annual Reports* of the Society, 1–29 (1826–1854). Dix's attitudes are revealed in her famous memorials to the legislatures of well over a dozen states. Two typical examples are the *Memorial Soliciting a State Hospital for the Insane, Submitted to the Legislature of Pennsylvania, February 3, 1845* (Harrisburg, 1845), and the *Memorial Soliciting Adequate Appropriations for the Construction of a State Hospital for the Insane, In the State of Mississippi, February, 1850* (Jackson, 1850). For Woodward's career see Gerald N. Grob, "Samuel B. Woodward and the Practice of Psychiatry in Early Nineteenth-Century America," *Bulletin of the History of Medicine*, 36 (September-October 1962), 420–443, and the Woodward Papers in the American Antiquarian Society, Worcester, Massachusetts. On Howe, see his article "Insanity in Massachusetts," *North American Review*, 56 (January 1843), 171–191. The Howe papers are in Houghton Library, Harvard University, Cambridge, Massachusetts; there is also an excellent biography by Harold Schwartz entitled *Samuel Gridley Howe: Social Reformer 1801–1876* (Cambridge, Mass.: Harvard University Press, 1956).

[7] Recently, some historians have begun to reinterpret the nature of reform movements in American history by arguing that their basic objective was a form of social control of lower-class and minority groups. Michael Katz, *The Irony of Early School Reform: Educational Innovation in Mid-Nineteenth Century Massachusetts* (Cambridge, Mass.: Harvard University Press, 1968), hints at this in his important and insightful study by arguing that reform was very often "imposed" on lower-class groups by middle- and upper-class groups. Also within this newer tradition are Clifford S. Griffin, *Their Brothers' Keepers: Moral Stewardship in the United States, 1800–1865* (New Brunswick, N.J.: Rutgers University Press, 1960), and Roy Lubove, *The Professional Altruist: The Emergence of Social Work as a Career*

Many of the intended beneficiaries of reform, it should be noted, were either from the lower classes or else included a disproportionately high percentage of lower-class members. Responsibility for the welfare of these groups was generally entrusted to more fortunate individuals, if only because of the inability of dependent groups to change significantly the conditions under which they lived. The slave, for example, was in no position to effect his own liberation. Nor could mentally ill individuals agitate for the establishment of therapeutic and custodial institutions. Moreover, reformers had to have both leisure time and an income base that would permit them to pursue careers as social activists. Reform movements, therefore, drew much of their inspiration and personnel from the ranks of the middle class and well-to-do. The reform movements of this period were imbued with a middle-class outlook; reformers, rejecting most radical proposals, worked to eliminate the more glaring evils in a society whose basic framework they accepted without major reservations.

In many respects mental hospitals, which were among the fruits of early nineteenth-century reform, reflected the values and aspirations of their supporters. So long as they accepted a homogeneous group of patients their structure and inner workings fulfilled the functions for which they had been established. When, however, patient populations became more heterogeneous and began to include a large proportion of individuals coming from lower-class and minority ethnic backgrounds, mental hospitals found themselves beset by problems for which there were few precedents and for which their staffs were largely unprepared. Consequently, their growth and development occurred in ways that were alien to the ideals of those individuals and groups responsible for founding such institutions.

Between 1800 and 1860 institutions providing care and treatment for the mentally ill began to proliferate rapidly. In 1820 there were fewer than ten mental hospitals in the United States; of these, some were private institutions intended largely for patients from relatively affluent circumstances. By the Civil War virtually every state had one or more public institutions that catered largely to one group or another.

1880–1930 (Cambridge, Mass.: Harvard University Press, 1965). Obviously, all institutions to some extent perform the function of social control. That their establishment came about because of a desire to institute controls is less obvious. Moreover, institutions serve a variety of purposes, and to single out one in particular (especially when it is by no means certain that this purpose is of primary significance) and deprecate others is an unjustifiable technique that more often than not arises out of an activistic and moralistic commitment on the part of the historian.

Oddly enough, the growth of the mental hospital actually preceded the emergence of psychiatry as both a "scientific" discipline and a profession. This is a fact of paramount importance, for it meant that psychiatric thought and practice were not dominant factors in shaping the structure and functions of institutions. On the contrary, psychiatry to a large extent was molded and shaped by the institutional setting within which it was born and grew to maturity. Indeed, many of the dominant characteristics of psychiatric ideology were simply rationalizations of existing conditions within mental institutions as well as popular attitudes. And since the mental hospital, at least during its formative years, was an institution created by society to cope with abnormal behavior and to provide care and treatment for a variety of dependent groups, the result was that psychiatry, although a scientific and medical discipline, would in large measure reflect the role assigned to it by society. This is not in any way to imply that psychiatrists *consciously* or *deliberately* attempted to define their discipline within such a context or to justify institutionalization on other than medical grounds. It is only to say that psychiatry, perhaps because of the philosophical and scientific complexities posed by the very concept of mental illness and the difficulties of providing adequate definitions, was shaped by external social, psychological, economic, and intellectual influences.

Consider, for example, some of the dominant currents in early and mid-nineteenth century American psychiatric thought.[8] Although assuming that mental illness was a somatic illness—usually involving lesions of the brain (which was regarded as the organ of the mind)—psychiatrists had considerable difficulty in providing empirical evidence to prove this assertion. Consequently, they identified mental illness by observing a person's outward behavioral symptoms. To identify mental illness in terms of outward behavioral symptoms, however, created some difficulties. In some cases the criteria for diagnosing cases of mental illness seemed clear. Hallucinations, smearing of feces, dramatic neurological symptoms associated with advanced cases of syphilis—to cite only a few examples—

---

[8] Norman Dain's book, *Concepts of Insanity in the United States, 1789–1865* (New Brunswick, N.J.: Rutgers University Press, 1964), is the most authoritative recent discussion of American psychiatric thought. The classic work on the mentally ill in the United States is Albert Deutsch's *The Mentally Ill in America: A History of Their Care and Treatment From Colonial Times* (New York: Doubleday, Doran, 1937), a work that still remains one of the best single surveys on the subject, despite the fact that its perspective is somewhat dated. There is some useful information in J. K. Hall *et al., One Hundred Years of American Psychiatry* (New York: Columbia University Press, 1944), although this book suffers because most of its contributors were psychiatrists who lacked a sense of history.

seemed to place the individual clearly within a category of illness. Other types of abnormal behavior, however, were less
clear and distinct, and here the normative standard of the
psychiatrist at times became of considerable significance, if
only because it entered into his relationship with the individual
under his care. And the normative standard of psychiatrists, as
we shall see, was not only a physical one that involved proper
organic functioning; in some respects it was a culturally defined
standard that often placed a premium on middle-class, Protestant, and agrarian values. Such values were to play a significant
internal role in mental institutions, particularly since these
institutions catered to heterogeneous groups coming from quite
different social, economic, and cultural backgrounds.

To define mental illness in terms of outward behavioral
manifestations and yet to claim that it was organic in nature
created serious theoretical problems. Yet these problems did not
pose insurmountable barriers. On the contrary, American psychiatrists, borrowing heavily from European and English intellectual traditions, constructed an imposing theoretical model
of mental illness that minimized internal contradictions.

The model of mental illness held by early and mid-nineteenth
century American psychiatrists was an interesting blend of
ideas. It included sensationalist and associationist psychology,
phrenology, and behaviorism, as well as ideas borrowed from
the Scottish Common Sense school of philosophy. Most psychiatrists began with Lockean assumptions; they believed that
knowledge came to the mind through sensory organs. If the
senses (or the brain) became impaired, false impressions would
be conveyed to the mind, leading in turn to faulty thinking and
abnormal behavior. Phrenology, which gained a firm foothold
in the United States after being imported from Europe in the
1820's and 1830's, in turn provided a means of connecting mind
and matter. The mind, according to phrenological theorists,
was not unitary, but was composed of independent and identifi-
able faculties, which were localized in different regions of the
brain. To this theory phrenologists added the postulates of a
behavioristic psychology and a belief that individuals could
deliberately and consciously cultivate different faculties by
following the natural laws that governed physical development
and human behavior. From phrenology psychiatrists took the
idea that the normal and abnormal functioning of the mind was
dependent on the physical condition of the brain.[9]

[9] The best discussions by American psychiatrists on the nature of mental illness are to be found in the annual reports of mental hospitals (the *American
Journal of Insanity*, which began publication in 1844, was for many years the only

Such reasoning provided psychiatrists with a medical model of mental illness that still permitted them to account for psychological or environmental factors. Such a model was by no means unique to psychiatry, for it was widely accepted by a variety of "empirics" enjoying considerable popularity during these decades. Mankind, reasoned many psychiatrists, was governed by certain immutable natural laws that provided a guide to proper living. If an individual followed these laws, a healthy mind and body would result. If these laws were violated, however, the physical organs would not develop or function normally. In other words, mental illness, though somatic in nature, could have psychological as well as physical causes. Thus it was the abnormal behavior of the individual (who possessed free will) that was the primary cause of insanity, leading as it did to the impairment of the brain (the organ of the mind). Mental illness, therefore, was in some respects self-inflicted; by ignoring the laws governing human behavior the individual placed himself on the road to disease.

Such a model of mental illness appeared, at least superficially, to be neutral insofar as socio-economic factors were concerned. But when psychiatrists took up the problem of etiology, their own values became clear. In hundreds of reports, books, articles, and speeches, they listed what they believed to be the leading causes of disease. These included intemperance, overwork, domestic difficulties, striving after wealth, and above all, the pressures of an urban, industrial, and commercial civilization (which was not natural to the human organism) upon the individual. Psychiatrists, in other words, saw mental illness as the inevitable consequence of behavior that represented a departure from their own normative model. Like many Ameri-

---

periodical of its kind). For typical examples of concepts of mental illness see the following: Amariah Brigham, "Insanity and Insane Hospitals," *North American Review*, 44 (January 1837), 91–121; Worcester State Lunatic Hospital, *Annual Report*, 7 (1839), 65–66; *ibid.*, 10 (1842), 64–65 (Samuel B. Woodward); John M. Galt, *The Treatment of Insanity* (New York, 1846); Edward Jarvis, "Causes of Insanity," *Boston Medical and Surgical Journal*, 45 (November 12, 1851), 289–305; New Jersey State Lunatic Asylum, *Annual Report*, 6 (1852), 22–28 (H. A. Buttolph); Butler Hospital for the Insane, *Annual Report* (1853), 11–29 (Isaac Ray); Maine Insane Hospital, *Annual Report*, 14 (1854), 25 (Henry M. Harlow); Northern Ohio Lunatic Asylum, *Annual Report*, 1 (1855), 12 (L. Firestone); McLean Asylum for the Insane, *Annual Report*, 42 (1859), in Massachusetts General Hospital, *Annual Report* (1859), 26–31 (John E. Tyler); Alabama Insane Hospital, *Annual Report*, 2 (1862), 20–22 (Peter Bryce); Utica State Lunatic Asylum, *Annual Report*, 21 (1863), 34–40; *ibid.*, 27 (1869), 16–23; *ibid.*, 29 (1871), 62–63; *ibid.*, 32 (1874), 23–24 (John P. Gray). John D. Davies, *Phrenology: Fad and Science: A 19th-Century American Crusade* (New Haven: Yale University Press, 1955), is a superior study dealing with the relationship of phrenology to American society in the antebellum decades.

cans during the first half of the nineteenth century, they held a romantic and sentimental ideal of mankind, an ideal that seemed threatened by developments that augured ill for the future. Thus they extolled agrarian virtues and denigrated urban life. "We find," wrote Thomas S. Kirkbride, one of the most influential psychiatrists of his time, "as was always believed, that no life is so generally conducive to health as one that, like agriculture, gives active exercise in the open air, that none is so likely to be troubled with nervous affections, and none so generally to be preferred for those who are constitutionally disposed to this class of infirmities."[10] Above all, psychiatrists saw a clear relationship between the advance of civilization and the incidence of mental illness. As Isaac Ray, the most dominant figure in American psychiatry in the mid-nineteenth century, put it, mental illness was "the price we pay for civilization."[11] In many ways the beliefs of most mid-nineteenth century psychiatrists were not fundamentally dissimilar from other critics of American society whose own values were hostile to social and economic change and who bitterly resented the newly emerging urban-industrial social order. A substantial part of psychiatric theory, therefore, was but a reflection of a particular social ideology, presented as empirical fact.

Before 1850, however, most psychiatrists did not necessarily draw pessimistic conclusions from their view of the causes of mental illness. Influenced by the optimism and faith in progress that was characteristic of their generation, they believed that mental illness could indeed be conquered. From their theoretical model they drew the conclusion that mental illness was as curable as, if not more curable than, other somatic illnesses. If derangements of the brain and nervous system produced the various types of insanity, it followed that the removal of such causal abnormalities would result in the disappearance of the symptoms and therefore the disease. The prognosis for insanity

[10] Pennsylvania Hospital for the Insane, *Annual Report*, 22 (1862), 15. For a similar statement by John S. Butler, superintendent of the Connecticut Retreat for the Insane, see Connecticut Retreat for the Insane, *Annual Report*, 24 (1848), 16–17.

[11] Butler Hospital for the Insane, *Annual Report* (1852), 19. For similar expressions of opinion see the following: Connecticut Retreat for the Insane, *Annual Report*, 22 (1846), 24 (John S. Butler); Indiana Hospital for the Insane, *Annual Report*, 1 (1849), 15 (Richard J. Patterson); Edward Jarvis, "On the Supposed Increase of Insanity," *American Journal of Insanity*, 8 (April 1852), 363–364; South Carolina Lunatic Asylum, *Annual Report* (1853), 16 (Daniel H. Trezevant); Virginia Eastern Asylum, *Report* (1853–1854/1854–1855), 18–23 (John M. Galt). See also the discussion of this issue at the sixteenth annual meeting of the Association of Medical Superintendents of American Institutions for the Insane in the *American Journal of Insanity*, 19 (July 1862), 47–81.

was thus quite hopeful (provided that the mentally ill were treated before the disease had entered the chronic stage).

Along with an optimistic view about the prognosis of mental illness went a well-defined and carefully thought-out thera-peutical system. In general, the treatment of insanity in mental hospitals during the first half of the nineteenth century fell into two broad categories: medical and moral (i.e. psychological). Since most psychiatrists adhered to a medical model of mental disease, they relied on a variety of medicinal agents. Subscribing to the ancient axiom of a sound mind in a sound body, alienists believed that it was important to strengthen the patient's bodily condition, which was related to his mental state. Tonics and laxatives, therefore, were used with a high degree of frequency. In addition, most psychiatrists were strong advocates of drug therapy. Where behavior was particularly active and violent, narcotics like opium and morphine were administered in order to quiet patients and make them more amenable to other forms of therapy. Other medicines commonly used included Dover's powder, digitalis, hyoscyamus, calomel, antimony, Ipecac, and Actea Racemosa. Moreover, both warm and cold baths, cold head compresses, and special diets were often part of the medical regime.

Medical treatment of mental illness, however, was but a pre-lude to what was known in the nineteenth century as moral therapy (which corresponds somewhat to contemporary milieu therapy). While susceptible to many interpretations, moral therapy meant kind, individualized care in a small hospital with occupational therapy, religious exercises, amusements and games, and in large measure a repudiation of all threats of physical violence and an infrequent resort to mechanical restraint. Moral therapy in effect involved re-educating the patient in a proper moral atmosphere. Hospitalization was an indispensable feature of moral treatment, for it separated the patient from his former environment and placed him in an institution controlled by the psychiatrist, who presumably could provide all the beneficient influences that would promote recovery.[12] The doctor-patient relationship in moral therapy, however, was not one between equals, for while the psychiatrist clearly played a benevolent and kindly role, he also exercised his power within an authoritarian framework.

Such was the theoretical and therapeutic outlook of the young psychiatric profession. Its optimistic views about the nature of mental illness and its hopeful prognosis seemed to be confirmed

[12] Fuller discussions of moral treatment can be found in Dain, *Concepts of Insanity, passim,* and Grob, *The State and the Mentally Ill,* 43–79.

by the actual results achieved in a number of mental hospitals.
During these years the patient population tended to come from the same background and environment as psychiatrists. Most mental hospitals accepted relatively few lower-class immigrants and minority ethnic groups, if only because as late as 1840 such groups constituted a very small percentage of the total population. The fact that hospital populations, especially in the 1830's and 1840's, remained relatively small also contributed to the maintenance of an internal therapeutic atmosphere. In addition, many of the individuals then prominent in American psychiatry had entered the field out of their humanitarian and religious convictions. In their eyes a hospital superintendency was no different than the calling that led some to enter the ministry or others to spend their lives furthering the elimination of institutional evils. Many early superintendents brought to their vocation, therefore, personalities that often promoted beneficent personal relationships with patients. Consequently, the feelings between physician and patient were often harmonious and trusting. The recovery rates of this period—even by the best of contemporary standards—were indeed imposing. Hospital superintendents claimed that up to 90 percent of recent cases (defined as cases of less than one year's duration) were curable, given prompt and proper treatment. One follow-up study, which took nearly twenty years to complete and included nearly twelve hundred patients, demonstrated that 58 percent of those discharged as recovered remained well until their death and never again required treatment in a mental hospital. It is therefore possible to infer that the internal environment of many institutions, both private and public, coupled with the kind, humane, and optimistic attitudes of many psychiatrists toward their patients, produced a psychological climate that had a beneficial impact upon inmates.[13]

For a short span of time, therefore, the character of some mental hospitals seemed to be undergoing a sharp transforma-

---

[13] The follow-up study of patients discharged as recovered can be found in the *Annual Reports* of the Worcester Lunatic Hospital, 47 (1879), 14–15; 49 (1881), 12–14; 50 (1882), 13–14, 57; 51 (1883), 14, 59; 52 (1884), 59; 53 (1885), 63; 54 (1886), 64; 55 (1887), 64; 61 (1893), 70.

Recent studies have emphasized the importance of the attitude of both the therapist and the environment of the patient in successfully treating the mentally ill. See the following: Milton Greenblatt *et al., From Custodial to Therapeutic Patient Care in Mental Hospitals* (New York: Russell Sage Foundation, 1955); J. Sanbourne Bockoven, "Moral Treatment in American Psychiatry," *Journal of Nervous and Mental Disease*, 124 (August–September 1956), 167–194, 292–321; *Action for Mental Health*, 36–37; Jerome D. Frank, "The Dynamics of the Psychotherapeutic Relationship," *Psychiatry*, 22 (February 1959), 17–39, and *Persuasion and Healing* (Baltimore: Johns Hopkins Press, 1961); Karl Menninger *et al., The Vital Balance: The Life Process in Mental Health and Illness* (New York: Viking Press, 1963).

tion. This is not to imply that social and class factors played no role within mental hospitals or that such institutions had abandoned completely their custodial and welfare character. Clearly, the organization of hospitals reflected to some degree the social and class structure of American society. At public mental hospitals it was not at all uncommon to classify patients on the basis of socio-economic differences and then to separate them physically and to give individuals with a higher status more privileges and better care.[14] Indeed, few Americans questioned the practice of providing more affluent individuals with superior care. It was the general practice of the majority of public institutions to either exclude or else to provide separate (but unequal) facilities for insane persons who were black. To most psychiatrists the thought of treating blacks and whites as equals was never seriously entertained. With some exceptions, many hospitals prior to 1860 would not accept black patients at all, since separate facilities had not been provided for by the state legislatures.[15]

[14] As one superintendent remarked: "It is certainly exceedingly unpleasant, to be almost compelled to associate with those whose education, conduct and moral habits, are unlike and repugnant to us. Because persons are insane, we must not conclude that they always lose the power of appreciating suitable associates, or are insensible to the influence of improper communications. This is by no means true. It is among our greatest perplexities here, to know how to quiet the complaints of those whose delicacy is shocked, whose tempers are perturbed, and whose quietude is annoyed by improper and unwelcome associates." [Eastern] Kentucky Lunatic Asylum, *Annual Report* (1845), 24. Such sentiments, which were widespread among hospital officials, usually led to differential care and therapy based on class and status. For evidence on this point see the following: Worcester State Lunatic Hospital, *Annual Report*, 7 (1839), 89; *ibid.*, 12 (1844), 88–89; *ibid.*, 15 (1847), 33; *ibid.*, 26 (1858), 60; *ibid.*, 36 (1869), 73, 83; South Carolina Lunatic Asylum, *Annual Report* (1871), 27–29; Taunton State Lunatic Hospital, *Annual Report*, 15 (1868), 14–15; Vermont Asylum for the Insane, *Annual Report*, 24 (1860), 12; Insane Asylum of Louisiana, *Annual Report* (1866), 5; Massachusetts Board of State Charities, *Annual Report*, 10 (1873), 19.

[15] For the policy of some states before the Civil War regarding the treatment of black insane persons see the following: American Freedmen's Inquiry Commission Mss. Collection, Houghton Library, Harvard University, Cambridge, Massachusetts; Charles H. Nichols to Thomas S. Kirkbride, April 14, 24, 1855, Kirkbride Papers, Institute of the Pennsylvania Hospital; Kentucky Eastern Lunatic Asylum, *Biennial Report*, 33/34 (1856/1857), 24; Maryland Hospital for the Insane, *Annual Report* (1851), 7–8; Mississippi State Lunatic Asylum, *Annual Report*, 4 (1858), 11–12; *ibid.*, 5 (1859), 24; South Carolina Lunatic Asylum, *Annual Report* (1844), 5; *ibid.* (1850), 12; *ibid.* (1851), 8–9; *ibid.* (1858), 12; *ibid.* (1860), 13; Tennessee Hospital for the Insane, *Biennial Report*, 1 (1852/1853), 21; Virginia Western Lunatic Asylum, *Annual Report*, 17 (1844), 26–27; *ibid.*, 18 (1845), 7–8, 29–30; *ibid.*, 21 (1848), 4–5, 32–34; Virginia Eastern Asylum, *Annual Report* (1848), 23–29; *ibid.* (1849), 5–6.

The segregation in or exclusion of blacks from mental hospitals was by no means unique. A study of other welfare institutions would show much the same pattern. Witness, for example, the following description of conditions among black inmates at the New York City Almshouse in 1837: "In the Building as-

Nevertheless, because class differentials in the United States were far less than in Europe in the early nineteenth century, the mental hospital began to de-emphasize somewhat its older and more traditional role as a custodial and undifferentiated welfare institution. Swept up in their enthusiasm to extend the benefits of hospitals to all Americans irrespective of their background, lay reformers such as Dorothea L. Dix, Horace Mann, Samuel Gridley Howe, among others, set to work to convince their fellow citizens that the founding of an extensive system of public mental hospitals was a highly desirable object. These individuals were committed to the extirpation of the restraints that prevented mankind from realizing its essential humanity. In fighting for an expansion of public facilities in Massachusetts in 1843, for example, Samuel Gridley Howe articulated the convictions that dominated his life as well as the lives of others like him. "Let all then, who, by word or deed, can command any influence," he told not only the residents of the Bay State, but all Americans,

exercise it to discharge this duty, and to confer this blessing upon those whom misfortune has made dependent upon them. Let them visit the almshouses and prisons, and see for themselves the deplorable condition of their brethren; their visits will at least have the effect of causing greater vigilance, cleanliness, and attention on the part of the keepers. There is room here for all to work, women as well as men. Come, then, ye whose bosoms heave with just indignation at the oppression of man in distant lands; here are victims of dreadful oppression at your very doors. Come, ye who lament the heathenish customs of ignorant pagans, and would fain teach them Christianity; here are worse than heathenish customs in our very towns and villages. Come, ye who are filled with sickly sentimentality, who weep over imaginary sufferings of imaginary beings, who sigh for some opportunity of doing heroic deeds, who are speculating upon human progress; here are realities to be grappled with, here is misery to be alleviated, here is degraded humanity to be lifted up.

---

signed to colored subjects, was an exhibition of squalid misery and its concomitants, never witnessed by your Commissioners in any public receptacle, for even the most abandoned dregs of human society. Here, where the healing art had objects for its highest commiseration, was a scene of neglect, and filth, and putrefaction, and vermin. Of system or subordination, there was none. The same apparel and the same bedding, had been alternately used by the sick, the dying, the convalescent, and those in health, for a long period, as we were informed by inmates. The situation of one room was such, that it would have created contagion as the warm season came on; the air seeming to carry poison with every breath. It was a scene, the recollections of which are too sickening to describe." *Report of the Commissioners of the Alms House, Bridewell and Penitentiary,* New York City Board of Aldermen, *Document Number 32* (1837), 204.

Finally, let the State government be urged to make immediate and ample provision for *all* the indigent insane, cost what it may cost.[16]

Howe's sentiments were echoed by others, and their efforts met with considerable success. By the third quarter of the nineteenth century virtually every state had one (and in most cases several) mental hospitals supported by public funds and caring for all patients irrespective of their ability to pay.

IV

In spite of reforms, the transformation of the mental hospital was more apparent than real. Within a short period of time a number of factors converged to force the mental hospital into its older and more familiar role as an undifferentiated welfare and custodial institution. As a result, psychiatry, like innumerable other disciplines, continued to develop after 1850 within an institutional framework that placed a premium on extra-scientific and extramedical factors.

At precisely the same time that the state mental hospital was coming into existence, the United States was undergoing extraordinarily rapid growth. The rise of industry, the quickening pace of urbanization, and, above all, the increase in population combined to alter the character of American society. An increase in the number of mentally ill persons coincided with these changes. Mental illness was less likely to be tolerated in highly populated areas than in rural areas, and the number of institutionalized individuals rose rapidly. The success of the enlarged public mental hospitals was hampered by their multiple functions. They acted as homes for aged persons unable to care for themselves or to be cared for by their families, and as havens for unemployed and dependent individuals apparently incapable of surviving the vicissitudes of life without some type of aid. "The feeling is quite too common," complained the head of the New York City Lunatic Asylum in 1861, "that a lunatic asylum is a grand receptacle for all who are troublesome."[17] His feelings were echoed by other superintendents who recognized the ambiguous role of their institutions, but who were unable because of legal and practical difficulties to alter what at best was a distressing state of affairs.[18]

[16] Samuel Gridley Howe, "Insanity in Massachusetts," *North American Review*, 56 (January 1843), 191.

[17] New York City Lunatic Asylum, Blackwell's Island, *Annual Report* (1861), 18.

[18] See, for example, New Hampshire Asylum for the Insane, *Annual Report*, 23 (1864), 16; Longview Asylum, *Annual Report*, 12 (1871), 7–8; Insane Asylum of California, *Annual Report*, 11 (1863), 29.

The increase in patient populations at public mental hospitals usually included a disproportionate number from lower-class groups, including minorities and immigrants. At the New York City Lunatic Asylum, Blackwell's Island, 534 patients were immigrants (of whom virtually every one was destitute) and only 121 were native born in 1850—this despite the fact that the foreign born constituted slightly less than half of the city's total population.[19] While hospitals in the Northeast generally had the highest proportion of foreign-born patients, virtually all hospitals in the United States had a disproportionate number of lower-class immigrants.[20]

The high proportion of foreign born (especially the Irish) in public mental hospitals was by no means an isolated or unique phenomenon. At the New York City House of Refuge (an institution that cared for delinquent and neglected children), for example, a disproportionate number of inmates were Irish. Not only did the Irish—to take the most important immigrant group in the three decades prior to the Civil War—provide a far higher percentage of admissions to a variety of welfare institutions, but their death rate during cholera epidemics as well as during normal periods was significantly higher than that of native groups. The reasons are not difficult to understand. The Irish arrived in the United States in a state of almost total destitution. Their impoverished situation contributed to the disruption of the family unit. Fathers were often compelled to accept jobs as unskilled laborers away from their families on

[19] New York City Lunatic Asylum, Blackwell's Island, *Annual Report* (1858), 12.
[20] At Longview Asylum (Ohio) in 1861, 353 out of 521 patients were foreign born. At Taunton State Lunatic Hospital (Massachusetts) comparable figures for 1854 were 118 out of 330; at the Wisconsin State Hospital for the Insane the figures for 1872 were 221 out of 365. Longview Asylum, *Annual Report*, 2 (1861), 13; Taunton State Lunatic Hospital, *Annual Report*, 1 (1854), 32; Wisconsin State Board of Charities and Reform, *Annual Report*, 2 (1872), 291. An analysis of several public institutions in Massachusetts in the early 1880's revealed much the same picture. Out of 1,932 patients classified as to parentage, 1,132 were of foreign parentage (including 800 of Irish descent). Massachusetts State Board of Health, Lunacy, and Charity, *Annual Report*, 4 (1882), lxix. These figures were by no means unrepresentative of the situation throughout the United States.
Whether or not the incidence of mental illness was higher among lower-class groups is a question that cannot be answered with any degree of certainty on the basis of the surviving data. There is little doubt that poor persons had a shorter life expectancy and suffered from various diseases associated with an impoverished environment. It does not necessarily follow, however, that the mere struggle for survival among many lower-class and minority immigrant groups resulted in a higher incidence of mental disease. Furthermore, definitive knowledge about the epidemiology of mental illness, as Hollingshead and Redlich have observed, is at present lacking, making it very difficult to draw conclusions about the relationship between mental disease and socio-environmental factors. See August B. Hollingshead and Fredrick C. Redlich, *Social Class and Mental Illness: A Community Study* (New York: John Wiley & Sons, 1958), 370–371.

such projects as canal building, where the mortality from what officials called "canal fever" was abnormally high. The sub-marginal economic situation of most Irish families, moreover, encouraged mothers and children to seek employment in order to survive. Some immigrants turned to criminal activities, thereby helping to make the crime rate in Irish slums appreciably higher than that in other areas of the city. The result was a vicious cycle of poverty, disease, and delinquency among Irish immigrants, who then entered welfare and penal institutions at a significantly higher rate than their proportion in the general population.[21]

The growing heterogeneity of patients in public mental institutions was a factor of major importance, for it began to undermine the basis of moral therapy, which assumed a close and trusting relationship between doctor and patient. Most psychiatrists had come from a middle-class background and they shared its values. So long as they treated patients with similar values, no conflict ensued. But when these physicians began to deal with patients—especially impoverished immigrants—whose customs, culture, traditions, and values diverged sharply from their own, they found that they were unable to communicate in the easy manner to which they had grown accustomed. Even those psychiatrists who genuinely sympathized with the plight of less fortunate individuals found themselves in a difficult situation, for they recognized their inability to create the type of therapeutic relationship that was essential. "Our want of success in the treatment of their mental diseases," observed Isaac Ray with both chagrin and sympathy, "is in some degree to be attributed, I imagine, to our inability to approach them in a proper way . . . Modes of address like those used in our intercourse with our own people, generally fall upon their ears like an unknown tongue, or are comprehended just enough to render the whole misunderstood, and thereby excite feelings very different from such as were intended."[22]

[21] Robert S. Pickett, *House of Refuge: Origins of Juvenile Reform in New York State, 1815–1857* (Syracuse: Syracuse University Press, 1969), 1–20.

[22] Butler Hospital for the Insane, *Annual Report* (1849), 32. George Chandler, superintendent of the Worcester State Lunatic Hospital, had much the same comment. "Most of the foreigners are Irish," he reported in 1847. "The want of forethought in them to save their earnings for the day of sickness, the indulgence of their appetites for stimulating drinks, which are too easily obtained among us, and their strong love for their native land, which is characteristic with them, are the fruitful causes of insanity among them. As a class, we are not so successful in our treatment of them as with the native population of New England. It is difficult to obtain their confidence, for they seem to be jealous of our motives; and the embarrassment they are under, from not clearly comprehending our language, is another obstacle in the way of their recovery." Worcester State Lunatic Hospital, *Annual Report*, 15 (1847), 33.

As the patient populations at public institutions began to include a disproportionate number of lower-class groups, the feelings of optimism that mental illness could be conquered began to undergo a subtle transformation. While psychiatrists continued to affirm their belief that mental illness was curable, they also began to argue that lower-class and particularly immigrant lower-class groups had far less of a chance of recovering than other groups. "It is the experience of all, I believe, who have had the care of the insane Irish in this country," wrote the superintendent of the Maine Insane Hospital in 1852, "that they, from some cause or other, seldom recover."[23]

Most psychiatrists and public officials were aware of the complex relationships between lower-class immigrants and mental illness and the consequent implications for public welfare policy. Some advocated the adoption of a policy that would deal with the problem by limiting the immigration of socially undesirable groups; others advocated separate institutions for immigrants that would not drain the public treasury. But whatever the solutions advanced, it was evident that most individuals holding responsible positions had what could be described as an ambiguous attitude toward impoverished immigrants. Those who saw America as a land of equal opportunity and a haven for oppressed people sympathized with the newcomers and looked forward to the day when the immigrant would share in the benefits of American society. Others saw in such groups a threat to American institutions and a danger to the particular genius of the American people. "Never was a sovereign State so grievously burdened," observed the influential *Boston Medical and Surgical Journal* in speaking about the growing number of foreign paupers in public hospitals in the Bay State. "The people bear the growing evil without a murmur, and it is therefore taken for granted that taxation for the support of the cast-off humanity of Europe is an agreeable exercise of their charity."[24]

Such attitudes were by no means confined to the psychiatric or medical profession. A committee appointed by the Board of Guardians of the Poor in Philadelphia in 1827 to investigate how other northeastern urban areas handled indigency made virtually the same point as the *Boston Medical and Surgical Journal.*

[23] Maine Insane Hospital, *Annual Report,* 12 (1852), 19. For similar expressions of opinion see *American Journal of Insanity,* 7 (October 1850), 176; *ibid.,* 14 (July 1857), 79–80; *ibid.,* 27 (October 1870), 157–159; Taunton State Lunatic Hospital, *Annual Report,* 3 (1856), 18, 25–26.

[24] *Boston Medical and Surgical Journal,* 45 (January 28, 1852), 537. See also *ibid.,* 46 (February 25, 1852), 85; *New Orleans Medical and Surgical Journal,* 4 (July 1847), 133–135; *ibid.,* 6 (November 1849), 399–402; Conference of Charities, *Proceedings,* 3 (1876), 162–185.

"One of the greatest burthens that falls upon this corporation," it remarked,

> is the maintenance of the host of worthless foreigners, disgorged upon our shores. The proportion is so large, and so continually increasing, that we are imperatively called upon to take some steps to arrest its progress. It is neither reasonable nor just, nor politic, that we should incur so heavy an expense in the support of people, who never have, *nor never will* contribute one cent to the benefit of this community, and who have in many instances been public paupers in their own country. If ever the trite adage, "that charity begins at home," be adopted as a rule of conduct, either by individuals or communities, it is especially under circumstances like the present, that it should be admitted in its fullest extent; and that the people of this district, should unresistingly suffer it to become the reservoir into which Europe may pour her surplus of worthlessness, improvidence and crime, exhibits a degree of forbearance and recklessness altogether inexcusable.[25]

Hostility toward lower-class immigrant groups tended to be fairly widespread in the three decades prior to the Civil War, although this hostility was often tempered by a faith that America could somehow assimilate these groups. Nevertheless, such attitudes often played a part in shaping public welfare policies generally. Indeed, the twin problems of pauperism and mental illness seemed so serious that a number of state legislatures authorized lengthy investigations in the 1850's and 1860's in order to help them devise policies that would cope with the mounting social problems involved and also that would safeguard the financial interests of their constituents.[26]

[25] *Report of the Committee Appointed by the Board of Guardians of the Poor of the City and Districts of Philadelphia, to Visit the Cities of Baltimore, New-York, Providence, Boston, and Salem* (Philadelphia, 1827), 28.

[26] See the following: *Report on Insanity and Idiocy in Massachusetts, by the Commission on Lunacy, Under Resolve of the Legislature of 1854,* Massachusetts *House Document No. 144* (1855); Thomas R. Hazard, *Report on the Poor and Insane in Rhode Island; Made to the General Assembly at Its January Session, 1851* (Providence, 1851); *Report of Select Committee Appointed to Visit Charitable Institutions Supported by the State, and all City and County Poor and Work Houses and Jails,* New York *Senate Document No. 8* (January 9, 1857); Sylvester D. Willard, *Report on the Condition of the Insane Poor in the County Poor Houses of New York,* New York *Assembly Document No. 19* (January 13, 1865); *Report of the Commissioner to Visit Almshouses and Asylums, for the Insane Poor, Indigent Persons, or Paupers,* Rhode Island *Public Document No. 20, Appendix* (1865); *Report of the Special Joint Committee Appointed to Investigate the Whole System of the Public Charitable Institutions of the Commonwealth of Massachusetts, During the Recess of the Legislature in 1858,* Mass. *Senate Document No. 2* (January, 1859). These are only a few examples of the concern of legislatures with policy issues raised by the twins problems of poverty and mental illness. In other states investigations took a variety of forms, including the establishment of central boards to coordinate welfare policies.

By the third quarter of the nineteenth century it had become evident that the state mental hospital was an institution providing relatively inexpensive care for a patient population largely drawn from lower-class groups. The fact that a large percentage of patients came from poor and minority ethnic groups proved crucial in shaping public policy toward mental hospitals. Most Americans were ambivalent in their attitude toward the poor and indigent. Their sympathy and compassion often resulted in widespread charitable and philanthropic activities. "Foreigners who satirize that eagerness in the pursuit of wealth, which seems to them a prominent trait in the American character, either overlook or forget the great liberality with which this wealth is here expended for public objects," observed Francis Bowen, the conservative Harvard professor. "The sums which are contributed here by individuals for the support of schools, colleges, churches, missions, hospitals, and institutions of science and beneficence, put to shame the official liberality of the oldest and wealthiest governments in Europe."[27] On the other hand, many Americans attributed poverty to the improvident and evil behavior of the individual. A poor person was poor because of his own laziness and character defects and not because of any structural defects in society that prevented self-improvement and upward mobility. Society's obligation toward the poor, therefore, was minimal.[28]

The result of such polar attitudes (often held in conjunction with each other despite their outwardly contradictory nature) was a reinforcement of the image of the state mental hospital as both a medical and a welfare institution. In the former case

[27] Francis Bowen, *The Principles of Political Economy* (Boston, 1856), 545.

[28] One of the most perceptive analyses of poverty in the nineteenth century was made by Thomas R. Hazard in a report to the legislature of Rhode Island concerning the poor and insane in the state. Hazard pointed out that to most Americans poverty was a crime. "I believe," he wrote, "that it was a maxim of some ancient sage or philosopher—*that, that government was the best, which gave equal protection to its citizens, without distinction* of persons.

"If I understand the theory of our own republican institutions, they are sought to be based on this maxim. Our laws are not intended to be framed in reference to persons, but to things. It supposes the administrators of the law, to be deaf and blind to all but the facts relating to the subject before them. Under the same circumstances the same judgment is to be meted to the rich and the poor, the little and the great. It is a maxim of our laws that the *punishment shall not exceed the offence.* The Constitution of our country declares '*that cruel and unusual punishment shall not be inflicted.*'

"Now admitting the extremity of poverty to be a crime—in the name and in behalf of the pauper poor of the State, in all seriousness, I respectfully ask you as conservators of the people of Rhode-Island, to define what the punishment of that crime shall be." Thomas R. Hazard, *Report on the Poor and Insane in Rhode Island; Made to the General Assembly at its January Session, 1851* (Providence, 1851), 92.

the function of a hospital was to provide medical care for groups that could not afford the cost of treatment of an illness of such long duration. The hospital thus fulfilled the humanitarian obligation of society to care for its sick and needy. In the latter case, the hospital provided care for individuals whose diseased mind was a product of their own shortcomings (a view reflected in psychiatric etiological theories). In this sense the justification for its existence was the protection it afforded the community against socially disruptive and threatening behavior on the part of lower-class groups. Consequently, public mental hospitals were often classified, at least in part, in the same general category as welfare and penal institutions. As such, they tended to receive the same level of funding as these other institutions, thereby undermining their therapeutic and medical roles and reinforcing their custodial function.

A brief analysis of the municipal institutions that served the cities of New York and Boston provides convincing evidence of some of these generalizations. By the early nineteenth century New York City had the largest urban population in the United States, including a significant proportion of impoverished immigrant groups. Its citizens were forced to confront a variety of social problems at a relatively early date. Prior to 1839 New York had maintained a lunatic asylum as part of its almshouse and prison complex. Conditions at that time were so depressing that the commissioners charged with responsibility for the institution described it as

> a witness of the blind infatuation of prejudice and miscalculation; affording to a class more deserving commiseration than any other among the afflicted catalogue of humanity, a miserable refuge in their trials, undeserving the *name* of an "Asylum," in these enlightened days. These apartments, under the best superintendence cannot be made to afford proper accommodations for the inmates, much less can they be so, when (as your Commissioners first saw them,) the same neglect and want of cleanliness witnessed in other parts of the building, was visible here; and a portion of the rooms seemed more like those receptacles of *crime*, "to whose foul mouth no healthsome air breathes in," than tenements prepared for the recipients of an awful visitation of Divine Providence, justly considered the worst "of all the ills that flesh is heir to."[29]

In 1839 the New York City Lunatic Asylum was separated from the other municipal welfare and penal institutions and given autonomy as a mental hospital. The change in structure,

---

[29] *Report of the Commissioners of the Alms House, Bridewell and Penitentiary,* New York City Board of Aldermen, *Document No. 32* (September 11, 1837), 208.

however, proved more apparent than real. Conditions remained an open scandal for the next three or four decades. The number of patients increased from 278 in 1840 to about 1,300 in 1870, although the physical plant was incapable of caring for anywhere near that number. In order to save money, the city used convicts from the penitentiary of Blackwell's Island as attendants at the asylum. The diet of patients remained far below even the minimum standard for a hospital; epidemics were not infrequent; and political considerations often dictated hospital policy.[30] In general, the hospital was used as a dumping ground for impoverished mentally ill immigrants. In 1856, for example, 297 out of 366 patients admitted were foreign born, and little pretense was made to provide therapy.[31] Conditions at the New York City Lunatic Asylum, Ward's Island (opened 1871) and the Kings County Lunatic Asylum (which grew out of the poorhouse) were scarcely better.[32] Indeed, a committee appointed to investigate abuses at the Kings County institution reported in 1877 that the Lunatic Asylum was "a reproach and disgrace."[33]

In New York City the first municipal hospital had grown out of an undifferentiated welfare and penal institution. Boston, on the other hand, established an entirely new and independent hospital to deal with cases of mental illness. By 1837 the Worcester State Lunatic Hospital, which had been intended by the Legislature to care for all mentally ill persons within Massa-

[30] *Report of the Resident Physician of the Alms-House Establishment,* New York City Board of Aldermen, *Document No. 119* (May 8, 1843), 1403–1409; New York City Lunatic Asylum, Blackwell's Island, *Annual Report* (1848), in New York City Alms House Commissioner, *Annual Report* (1848), 119–120; New York City Lunatic Asylum, *Annual Report* (1851), in New York City Governors of the Alms House, *Annual Report,* 3 (1851), 98; New York City Lunatic Asylum, Blackwell's Island, *Annual Report* (1856), 5, 11–12; *ibid.* (1865), 3–15; New York State Commissioner in Lunacy, *Annual Report,* 2 (1874), 22–24; *ibid.,* 3 (1875), 10–16; James C. Hallock to Dorothea L. Dix, July 21, 1870, Dix Papers, Houghton Library, Harvard University.

[31] New York City Lunatic Asylum, Blackwell's Island, *Annual Report* (1856), 6; *ibid.* (1870), 6–8.

[32] James C. Hallock to Dorothea L. Dix, December 25, 1871, January 22, 1873, Dix Papers; New York Board of State Commissioners of Public Charities, *Annual Report,* 6 (1872), 64–71; New York City Asylum for the Insane, Ward's Island, *Annual Report,* 3 (1874), 13–19; *ibid.,* 4 (1875), 21–25; New York State Commissioner in Lunacy, *Annual Report,* 2 (1874), 28–44; *ibid.,* 3 (1875), 25–64.

[33] *Report of the Investigation of the Board of Supervisors of Kings County, in the Matter of Alleged Abuses at the Lunatic Asylum, Together with the Evidence Taken by the Committee. Presented April 19th, 1877* (New York, 1877), 6. The distinguished English psychiatrist John C. Bucknill, who was by no means an unfriendly critic (see Bucknill's letter to Henry I. Bowditch, January 23, 1877, Countway Medical Library, Harvard Medical School, Boston), thought that the public asylums in New York City were among the worst in the country. For his description of conditions in northern urban mental institutions, see his book, *Notes on Asylums for the Insane in America* (London, 1876), 40–53.

chusetts, had become so crowded that its officials began to return patients to their original place of residence. In order to deal with this difficult problem, the municipal authorities decided to establish their own institution, and in 1839 the Boston Lunatic Hospital received its first patients.[34]

Nevertheless, the history of the Boston institution was essentially the same as that of the New York asylum. The hospital rapidly filled up with indigent and immigrant patients, and all pretenses at providing therapy were soon abandoned. In 1846, 90 out of 169 patients were foreign born, and the hospital had in effect become an institution for lower-class groups.[35] "Our inmates," complained the superintendent in 1850, "are principally foreigners; and of this class a large majority are from Ireland . . . [The Irish] are generally found to be uneducated, superstitious, and jealous; and, being unused to the manners and customs of our countrymen, they are very suspicious of us; and therefore it is quite difficult to win their confidence, and of course, to treat them satisfactorily."[36] More than twenty years later the secretary of the Massachusetts Board of State Charities condemned the institution as completely unfit for either therapy or custody.[37] But despite a clear recognition by community leaders in Boston as early as the 1850's that drastic action was required, the hospital continued to serve as a custodial institution for lower-class groups.[38]

The transformation of the state mental hospital into a custodial lower-class institution was also accompanied by the rise of exclusive private institutions caring for middle- and upper-class patients. Although many of the early mental hospitals established prior to 1850 were private, they had always attempted to

[34] For the origins of the Boston Lunatic Hospital see the *Memorial of the Board of Directors for Public Institutions in Relation to the Lunatic Hospital. 1863,* Boston *City Document No. 11* (1863), 21–23.

[35] Boston Lunatic Hospital, *Annual Report,* 7 (1846), 11. See also *ibid.,* 4 (1843), 15–16; *ibid.,* 6 (1845), 16–17; *ibid.,* 9 (1848), 3–4.

[36] *Ibid.,* 11 (1850), 15.

[37] Massachusetts Board of State Charities, *Annual Report,* 10 (1873), 12.

[38] *Report of a Committee of the Board of Directors for Public Institutions in Relation to the Condition of the Lunatic Hospital, Made May 23, 1862* (Boston, 1862), 5–6; *Memorial of the Board of Directors for Public Institutions in Relation to the Lunatic Hospital. 1863,* Boston *City Document No. 11* (1863), 23–39. Massachusetts, in addition to establishing the first comprehensive system of public mental hospitals, also used its state almshouses to care for chronic indigent cases of mental illness. The State Almshouse at Tewksbury by 1874 had over 300 insane inmates, and conditions there were about as substandard as those at any of the other charitable and penal institutions in the state. See the *Annual Reports* of the Massachusetts State Almshouse at Tewksbury, 3 (1856), 5–6; 5 (1858), 4–5; 8 (1861), 14; 13 (1866), 6–7; 21 (1874), 9–13, 33–34; and the *Annual Reports* of the Massachusetts Board of State Charities, 1 (1864), 265–266; 2 (1865), 149–150; 3 (1866), 150–151; 10 (1873), liv; 12 (1875), lviii–lx.

make at least some provision for poorer and indigent patients.
The Friends' Asylum in Pennsylvania, the Bloomingdale Asylum in New York, the Butler Hospital in Rhode Island, McLean Asylum in Massachusetts, and the Hartford Retreat in Connecticut had all accepted indigent cases in their early days. But as various states and municipalities opened public mental institutions, these private hospitals began to limit their patient body to those groups willing and able to pay high charges for superior care. Such a policy was usually defended on the grounds that individuals were entitled to receive the type of care that they had been accustomed to in their private lives and also that they should not be forced to mix with groups with whom they had little in common.[39] As the superintendent of the Hartford Retreat remarked in 1867:

> It is evident that different classes will require different styles of accommodation. The State should provide for its indigent insane, liberally and abundantly, all the needful means of treatment, but in a plain and rigidly economical way. Other classes of more abundant means will require, with an increased expenditure, a corresponding increase of conveniences and comforts, it may be of luxuries, that use has made essential. This common sense rule is adopted in other arrangements of our social life—our hotels, watering places, private dwellings and various personal expenditures.
>
> In my opinion, it would be a very good general rule which should give to every case of insanity, when placed under treatment, all those essential, and not injurious or excessively costly indulgences which previous habits, tastes and even prejudices may require. Certainly it is evident that the more ignorant, unrefined and uncultivated do not require the same surroundings and appliances as the intelligent, cultivated and refined.[40]

By the Civil War, most, if not all, of the private mental hospitals had effectively excluded lower-class patients. This

[39] *Annual Reports* of the Connecticut Retreat for the Insane, 29 (1853), 23; 35 (1859), 21–25; 42 (1866), 20–21; 44 (1868), 22; 45–46 (1869–1870), 5–22; 50 (1874), 13; Butler Hospital for the Insane, *Annual Report*, 15 (1861), 3–6; *ibid.* (1870), 7–9, 11–12; McLean Asylum for the Insane, *Annual Report* (1833), in Massachusetts General Hospital, *Annual Report* (1833), 2–8. Also Massachusetts General Hospital, *Annual Reports* (1839), 10–18; (1841), 20–21; (1844), 12–13; (1846), 19; (1851), 15–22; (1853), 20; (1868), 34–37; Massachusetts Board of State Charities, *Annual Report*, 1 (1864), 85–86; New York Hospital and Bloomingdale Asylum, *Annual Reports* (1851), 15–16; (1852), 16–17; (1856), 19–20; (1862), 11; (1866), 17–25; Friends' Asylum for the Insane, *Annual Reports*, 24 (1841), 4–5; 32 (1849), 5–6; 48 (1865), 7–8; 51 (1868), 4–5.

[40] Connecticut Retreat for the Insane, *Annual Report*, 43 (1867), 33. The superintendent of the Butler Hospital thought that the policy of keeping paupers at public institutions rather than private hospitals was a beneficent one. "I think it will result in increased usefulness and a firmer hold upon the interest and good will of the people." John W. Sawyer to Dorothea L. Dix, September 16, 1870, Dix Papers.

development had an unforeseen consequence. As long as the mental hospital had not distinguished (at least in theory, if not in practice) between paying and nonpaying patients, the movement to upgrade conditions at public facilities had remained strong. When public institutions began to serve a predominantly lower-class population, on the other hand, there was a noticeable diminution in the pressure to improve conditions within these institutions. Samuel Gridley Howe, speaking for the trustees of the Worcester State Lunatic Hospital in 1854, warned of the dangers of a dual system of private and public hospitals. "The multiplication of these private establishments," he pointed out, "would be a great evil. It is one that may be prevented by making public hospitals unobjectionable residences for patients of any class; but it will be difficult of cure, if once it obtains footing."[41] Howe's warning, of course, went unheeded, and the state mental hospital became identified more and more in the public eye as a welfare-type institution caring for lower-class and minority groups.

The role of the state mental hospital as more of a welfare than a medical institution was given further legitimacy in the 1860's and afterwards by the growth of administrative structures established by most states and a few larger urban areas as part of a drive to develop a comprehensive public policy on indigency. During the first half of the nineteenth century local and state governments had become increasingly sensitive to the problems arising out of poverty. These problems were exacerbated not only by the general increase in population, but by the arrival in the United States of large numbers of impoverished immigrants, many of whom remained in the major urban areas. The concentration of indigent groups in localized geographical areas limited the possibility of maintaining an informal and voluntary approach to welfare. By the 1860's welfare had therefore grown sufficiently complex so as to induce a number of states to attempt to formulate a more rational and efficient means of administering their charitable institutions. The search for a new policy was often dominated by a sincere desire to create a situation where the need for welfare would no longer exist, for few Americans defended public charity as the solution to poverty.

The process of rationalization and centralization of welfare became evident in the larger urban areas, which were often among the first to confront complex social problems. The governing body of New York City as early as 1849, for example, passed an act that placed responsibility for its welfare institu-

---

[41] Worcester State Lunatic Hospital, *Annual Report*, 22 (1854), 12.

tions (including the mental hospital, penitentiary, almshouse, and other similar organizations) in the hands of a Board of Governors. Eleven years later, a new body—the Commissioners of Public Charities and Correction—replaced the older one. In both reorganizations it was clear that economy and efficiency were among the dominant motives in establishing a legal agency vested with full authority and responsibility for welfare and indigency. The goal was not to perpetuate but rather to eliminate state support of public welfare. How this objective would be reached, however, was not clear.[42]

In 1863 Massachusetts established the first Board of State Charities, an organization designed to centralize and rationalize the haphazard network of public welfare institutions. The new agency succeeded the Board of Alien Commissioners, which had been founded in 1851 to enforce all legislation pertaining to aliens and the support of state paupers (those individuals having no legal local residence). During its twelve years of life the Board of Alien Commissioners was instrumental in getting the Commonwealth to establish three state almshouses and a hospital for pauper and dependent sick as well as to deport non-resident and alien mentally-ill persons.[43] But as the social and

[42] See New York City Governors of the Almshouse, *Annual Report*, 1 (1849), *passim*, and New York City Commissioners of Public Charities and Correction, *Annual Report*, 1 (1860), *passim*.

[43] In answering charges that its policy was inhumane and unchristian, the Board of Alien Commissioners emphasized that many pauper lunatics were foreigners or natives of other states. "They are deserted upon our wharves," its members charged in 1859, "dropped in our streets, left in our depots; they are run in upon us from the Provinces, smuggled over in nearly every emigrant ship from Europe. They are ragged and filthy in person, as well as diseased in mind; and not a few of both sexes have been inmates of the lowest haunts of vice and crime on either continent." *Report of the Commissioners of Alien Passengers and Foreign Paupers* (1859), Massachusetts *Public Document No. 14* (1860), 10. And just prior to going out of existence in 1863, the Board, reflecting some fairly widely held views, summed up its own attitude toward certain pauper groups: "Shall we never learn the simple lesson that 'charity begins at home?' Shall we never realize that we are doing no good service in the holy cause of humanity, by relieving other communities of their rightful burdens, and thus encouraging them in their unchristian repudiation of their duties to God and their brethren? And all this to the discomfort, and perhaps irreparable injury of the sufferers from our own hearthstones, stricken of the Almighty, but dear to our hearts, and cherished, though absent, in our fondest memories! Will the people of Massachusetts ever awake to the shameful truth that their fathers and brothers, mothers and sisters, whether native or of alien birth, are compelled to eat, and lodge, and hold a daily intercourse with the convicts, drunkards, and strumpets, crazed by their crimes, poured in upon us from other States and other lands?— mainly because of the morbid sympathy of a class of would-be philanthropists, who ride their single hobby over the lacerated feelings and aching hearts of their hapless fellow-citizens? The wealthy can seclude their afflicted relatives, amid the luxuries of a private asylum, from all that can disgust their taste or shock their better instincts. Must the great middling interest of Massachusetts, the farmer,

economic costs of welfare continued to mount, the legislature moved toward further centralization in order to make the seemingly chaotic welfare system function more efficiently. The new Board of State Charities, though not possessing in its early days much substantive authority, nevertheless had the potential for growth—a potential that would be more than fulfilled during the next century. While its activities encompassed a variety of problems, the Board—precisely because mental hospitals came under its jurisdiction—tended to reinforce the growing identification of poverty, welfare, and mental illness. It linked from time to time illness and poverty with immoral behavior on the part of the individual. "There is a grain of truth," the Board wrote in 1868, "under the harsh expression that 'sick men are rascals'; for many are sick in body and sick in mind, not because nature makes them so, [but] because they make themselves sick or insane by persisting in courses which plainly lead to sickness and to insanity."[44]

Other states quickly followed the lead of Massachusetts in establishing central agencies vested with the responsibility of overseeing public welfare institutions and developing uniform policies to promote efficiency. Most of these agencies had authority over the operations of state mental hospitals as well as other institutions caring for various indigent groups. From the very beginning of the movement to rationalize welfare, then, the state mental hospital was considered to be as much an institution for poor and indigent groups as it was a medical facility. The relationship between pauperism and mental illness was further reinforced by the manner in which most state boards of charities approached the problems of indigency, illness, and welfare. In general, their members (who shared the traditional American ambivalence toward poverty and a feeling that the cure for poverty lay in the inculcation of proper attitudes on the part of the individual) often related crime, indolence, alcoholism, vagrancy, and poverty with mental illness. This is not to imply that the latter was considered to be a consequence of the former. Nevertheless, the general framework established by the words and deeds of state boards was such as to link in the mind of the public a relationship between poverty and mental

---

trader, and mechanic—must the larger class of the respectable and deserving poor be deprived of the privileges they are taxed to pay for, and subjected to associations and influences which necessity itself could hardly excuse, simply to gratify a sentiment?" *Ibid.*, 1863, Massachusetts *Public Document No. 15* (1863), 17–18.

[44] Massachusetts Board of State Charities, *Annual Report*, 5 (1868), lxxviii.

illness.[45] And since virtually no state or city government was ever able to develop effective policies and institutions to cope with the problems of the poor and indigent, the result was that few welfare institutions—including the mental hospital—ever lived up to the optimistic expectations of their supporters.

As the state mental hospital became an institution serving a predominantly lower-class population, its inner structure began to undergo important changes. The role of the psychiatrist, for example, began to alter slowly. When hospitals were small (less than two hundred patients in residence) and cared for a relatively homogeneous patient population, psychiatrists found their own ideology sufficiently broad to provide a rationale for treatment. But when they were confronted with large numbers of patients coming from socio-economic and ethnic backgrounds unfamiliar to their own experiences, they found themselves incapable of surmounting the barriers of class and ethnic differences. The result was a sharp decline in the effectiveness of moral therapy, which rested on the assumption that therapist and patient would have a trusting and harmonious relationship. As custodial considerations increased because of the influx of large numbers of lower-class patients, the tendency was for the demands of the mental hospital as a social system to outweigh the needs of therapy. More and more psychiatrists became hospital managers and administrators; their primary concern was with maintaining order and rationality in a large complex institution owing a greater allegiance to society than to the welfare of the individual patient.[46]

[45] In the third annual report of the Massachusetts Board of State Charities, to cite only one example, Franklin B. Sanborn (secretary of the Board and one of the most prominent figures in public welfare in the latter half of the nineteenth century) wrote as follows: "The four topics of this last division of this Report are so closely connected as to make any exact separation of them difficult. Pauperism and Crime; Pauperism and Disease; Crime and Disease; Insanity and Crime; Insanity and Pauperism,—how frequent are the permutations and combinations of these evils! Like Sin and Death, in Milton's allegory,—what are they indeed but forms of sin and death?—they breed from each other a mixed and woeful progeny." Massachusetts Board of State Charities, *Annual Report*, 3 (1866), 204.

For other examples of discussions by boards of charities see the *Annual Reports* of the Massachusetts Board of State Charities, 1 (1864), 409–410; 2 (1865), 213–220; 4 (1867), 129–144; 5 (1868), xix–xl; 9 (1872), xvii–l; Rhode Island Board of State Charities and Correction, *Annual Report*, 1 (1869), 23–34; North Carolina Board of Public Charities, *Annual Report*, 2 (1870), 2–44; Illinois Board of State Commissioners of Public Charities, *Biennial Report*, 4 (1875–1876), 195–209; Pennsylvania Board of Commissioners of Public Charities, *Annual Report*, 2 (1871), lxxxiv–lxxxviii.

For a contemporary statement of the need for central supervision of state charities see Franklin B. Sanborn, "The Supervision of Public Charities," *Journal of Social Science*, 1 (June 1869), 72–87.

[46] The dilemma facing a hospital superintendent was very well illustrated by the following statement of George Chandler, superintendent of the Worcester

Outside pressures further compounded the difficulties faced by institutional psychiatrists. The hospital, for example, played a dual role, one therapeutic, the other custodial. As long as it remained small, it was easy for the psychiatrist to combine both of these roles. The gradual growth in size of hospitals, however, made this more difficult. Increasingly, superintendents found themselves confronted with the responsibility of having to sacrifice one of these goals in order to achieve the other. Given a choice, therapeutic considerations might well have been dominant. But the superintendent could not only be concerned with the welfare of the patient; he had to take into account the demands of society for protection against those who ostensibly menaced the community. As more lower-class patients entered hospitals, such pressures tended to increase. Consequently, therapeutic considerations receded.

The growth of the hospital meant that responsibility for the daily routine and care of patients was shifted from the superintendent to the corps of attendants and nurses. In the mid-nineteenth century no formal training was available for non-professional personnel; as a result inexperienced persons were normally hired. Since salary and status were also very low, this occupation did not attract many competent individuals. It was not at all uncommon, therefore, for hospitals to have a turn-over rate among attendants and nurses of as high as 200 to 400 percent each year. This situation made difficult, if not impossible, an emphasis on therapy over custody.

Under these sets of circumstances psychiatry's immersion in administrative problems was hardly surprising. An intricate social institution like a mental hospital required formal mechanisms to ensure order and efficiency; formal mechanisms, in turn, often defeated the aim of moral treatment, which was based on the ability of the physician to manipulate the environment of the individual and group as the need arose. Custodial considerations merely reinforced administrative concerns, for

---

State Lunatic Hospital, in the late 1840's: "I confess my inability to do justice to my feeling in its management. I cannot sufficiently keep myself acquainted with the various departments to act understandingly. I cannot know the daily changes in the symptoms of 450 patients—the operations on the farm and in the workshops—the domestic operations—direct the moral treatment—conduct the correspondence with friends—wait upon such visitors as demand my personal attention and various other things which are daily pressing upon the attention of this Superintendent. Many of these matters in large Hospitals must be attended to, if attended to at all, by those who do not and cannot act so faithfully and understandingly as the Superintendent could and would." George Chandler, "On the proper number of patients for an institution . . ." undated manuscript (ca. late 1840's), Chandler Papers, American Antiquarian Society, Worcester, Massachusetts.

custody required a tight and efficiently run institution governed by rational and clearly defined procedures. In effect, the rise of what may be conveniently designated as administrative psychiatry reflected the dominance of an institution providing custodial care for poor and indigent groups.

V

The experiences of the Commonwealth of Massachusetts in caring and treating its mentally ill population during the first two thirds of the nineteenth century provides a case study of national developments. When the first public institution in the state opened its doors in 1833, Horace Mann—the individual responsible for its founding—expressed not only a sense of pride and satisfaction, but also a feeling of optimism for the future. "I have had great anxiety about it, and great care," he wrote. "I now feel great relief, as its commencement has been so auspicious, and I have every reason to believe that it is fast rising into favor with the intelligent and reflecting and humane part of the community."[47]

Despite Mann's hopes, the Worcester hospital, though enjoying some extraordinary successes in its early days, never fulfilled the hope that it would serve as a central repository for the state's insane population by curing and discharging patients, thereby providing room for new cases. In 1836 and 1843 the legislature had to provide expanded facilities at the hospital. Consequently, the average patient population rose from 107 in 1833 to 359 in 1846. Such rapid growth, however, had unforeseen consequences, with the result that the hospital's therapeutic role was more and more subordinated to its custodial function.[48]

So pressing were the hospital's difficulties that the legislature's Committee on Public Charitable Institutions in the spring of 1848 recommended the establishment of a joint committee to study the problem of mental illness in order to provide a sound basis for future policy.[49] Their suggestion coincided with the receipt of a number of petitions, several of which came from the western part of the state that lacked easy access to public facilities, indicating dissatisfaction with the existing state of affairs. Influenced by the committee's report and the petitions, the General Court on April 20, 1848, authorized the

[47] Horace Mann to Lydia B. Mann, January 6, 1833, Mann papers, Massachusetts Historical Society, Boston, Massachusetts.

[48] See Grob, *The State and the Mentally Ill*, Chaps. I–IV.

[49] *Report of the Committee on Public Charitable Institutions*, Mass. *House Document No. 139* (April 5, 1848).

formation of a joint committee "to consider the whole subject connected with Insanity within the Commonwealth." The new committee was directed to report back at the next session "upon the measure best to be adopted by the Commonwealth, in relation to an enlargement of the present Hospital, or the erection of a new one; and the different classification of its inmates—together with amendments of the present laws applying to Insanity; and if the Committee judge it needful, to erect a new Hospital, to examine the best location, and present a Plan, and an estimate of its cost of erection and equipment."[50]

From the beginning of their investigation the members of the committee elected to interpret the legislature's mandate broadly. They collected statistical data relating to the incidence of mental illness in their state, investigated conditions at all of the institutions (including jails) receiving mentally ill persons; and offered projections for facilities that would be required in the future. In many respects their comprehensive approach was a notable landmark in the evolution of public policy toward the insane. Previous discussions of mental illness had usually been narrow in scope and had often focused simply on the expansion of existing facilities. The investigation of 1848, however, was among the early attempts to consider the problem within its general societal context and with an awareness that the interplay of social, economic, medical, and humanitarian factors were involved.

Out of the joint committee's study came a recommendation that Massachusetts establish a second state hospital. In justifying the need for such an institution, the legislators emphasized three points. In the first place, there simply were not enough facilities —public or private—to care for the total insane population. Secondly, the therapeutic successes achieved by mental hospitals in curing this dreaded malady were so striking as to justify additional facilities. Finally, they firmly believed that the state had a moral responsibility to provide comfortable and decent accommodations for the chronic insane.[51]

At the end of its report the committee dealt specifically with the thorny problem of the Irish insane. Because of the strong anti-Catholic feelings then prevalent,[52] a number of prominent

[50] Boston *Daily Advertiser*, January 29, February 12, April 8, 21, 1848; *Report of the Joint Committee of the Legislature of Massachusetts, Appointed April 20, 1848, on the Subject of Insanity in the State, and Directed to Sit During the Recess of the Legislature, and to Report at the Early Part of the Session of 1849*, Mass. *Senate Document No. 9* (January 15, 1849), 3–4.

[51] *Report of the Joint Committee of the Legislature of Massachusetts, Appointed April 20, 1848, on the subject of Insanity*, 12–18.

[52] For this subject see Ray A. Billington, *The Protestant Crusade 1800–1860: A Study of the Origins of American Nativism* (New York: Macmillan Co., 1938). Also

individuals had suggested that Irish and native-born patients be classified separately. Similarly, curable patients were to be distinguished from incurable ones. Both proposals were closely related, for many believed that the Irish were less responsive to therapy and therefore provided a disproportionate number of incurable cases. To both of these suggestions the committee was unalterably opposed. The separation of Irish and native patients "would tend to an invidious distinction; a distinction not reconcilable with the humane and tolerant spirit of our country and age; and not in accordance with that lofty design of our institutions, to make all who occupy American soil American citizens." Likewise, distinguishing curable from incurable cases was equally ill-advised; how would one ascertain with any degree of certainty whether an individual was curable without first having tried some form of therapy? Even more compelling in the eyes of the committee was the odious impression that a hospital for incurables would make upon the public mind. Such a custodial institution could hardly attract competent physicians and would therefore be little better than jails or houses of correction.[53]

In mid-January 1849 the committee sent its report to the legislature. Thorough and dispassionate in its coverage, the report could hardly have been consigned to oblivion. Because of its far-reaching implications, however, it met with considerable opposition. By itself the recommendation for a second state hospital was not particularly revolutionary; others had made similar proposals in the past. What was novel was the assumption that the care of the insane was a state function, an assumption that implied not only a substantial broadening of the government's welfare functions, but increased expenditures as well. Consequently, the committee's recommendations were defeated in the legislature. Not until the spring of 1851 were supporters of a second hospital able to get the legislature to act favorably on their proposal. Three years later the Taunton State Lunatic Hospital opened its doors, and by the end of the year had accepted 330 patients.[54]

suggestive are John Higham, "Another Look at Nativism," *Catholic Historical Review*, 44 (July 1958), 147–158, and David Brion Davis, "Some Themes of Counter-Subversion: An Analysis of Anti-Masonic, Anti-Catholic, and Anti-Mormon Literature," *Mississippi Valley Historical Review*, 47 (September 1960), 205–224.

[53] *Report of the Joint Committee of the Legislature of Massachusetts, Appointed April 20, 1848, on the Subject of Insanity*, 26–27.

[54] Mass. *Senate Document No. 75* (March 19, 1849), 1–3,8; Mass. *Senate Document No. 2* (January 8, 1850), 8; *Report of the Committee on Public Charitable Institutions*, Mass. *House Document No. 118* (March 25, 1850), 1–4; *Massachusetts Spy*, June 18, 1851; Chap. 251, Act of May 24, 1851, in *Acts and Resolves Passed by the General*

The opening of a second state hospital, nevertheless, did not provide either an immediate or long-term solution to the problems of the mentally ill. The investigation of 1848 had estimated that facilities for about six hundred additional patients were required in the Bay State. Yet Taunton had provision for less than half of this number, and by the time it opened in 1854 the number of insane persons had increased with the general rise in population. Once again the state found that a supposed "solution" of a problem had been rendered obsolete by social and demographic changes.

In addition, the Worcester hospital had so deteriorated by the early 1850's that it was doubtful whether it could continue to function at all. In 1854 conditions had become so serious that the trustees, led by Samuel Gridley Howe and Linus Child, sent a lengthy memorial to the legislature. Speaking in blunt words, they sketched a dismal portrait of a once proud and great institution. When the hospital had opened in 1833, the city of Worcester had been a small and quiet agricultural village. Now, however, the city had a population of over twenty-four thousand and was rapidly becoming an industrial center because of its central location and excellent transportation facilities. Much of this urban growth had occurred in the vicinity of the hospital; consequently, patients had little privacy and often were forced to endure the jeers and taunts of passersby. Moreover, the sewerage system was defective and the heating plant imperfect and dangerous. Indeed, the physical plant, once considered a model worthy of emulation, had become completely obsolete. The hospital, the petitioners remarked, "was one of the first State hospitals built in this country. Since it was established, in 1832, many improvements have been made in the arrangements and structure of such institutions. Ours, however, remains, in these respects, as it was in the beginning. While the world has made progress, and other hospitals have been built on new and improved plans, ours has been obliged to stand still, and has, therefore, fallen behind the age; and that which we once proudly called the best, has become one of the poorest, if not the very poorest, in the country." Pointing out that immediate repairs would cost between $55,000 and $75,000, the trustees suggested that the legislature consider selling the land on which the hospital was situated (then valued between $150,000 and $225,000) and add the required sum necessary to construct a new modern hospital.[55]

Court of Massachusetts, in the Year 1851 (Boston, 1851), 748; Taunton State Lunatic Hospital, *Annual Report,* 1 (1854), 23.

[55] Mass. *Senate Document No. 60* (March 9, 1854), 1–8.

No doubt the memorial may have caused some consternation
among some legislators. Certainly few of them had anticipated
that even while the new hospital at Taunton was being built the
state would be faced with another crisis in its efforts to help the
insane. At any rate, the memorial of the Worcester trustees was
referred to the Committee on Public Charitable Institutions.
Within a few days the Committee reported its findings. It
concluded that the dark and somber picture portrayed in the
memorial was fully borne out by the facts. "Other States and
communities have taken advantage of experience, and built
their hospitals upon new plans, each avoiding the ascertained
faults of the preceding ones, and making new improvements,"
the committee pointed out. "Ours has necessarily remained a
fixture, and is now behind the other establishments of the
country." Most of the defects of the Worcester hospital de-
manded immediate relief, and the legislature was urged to
act.[56]

The committee took a significant step by avoiding any specific
judgment of the proposal to build a new hospital in Worcester.
Considering the difficulties that the hospital was experiencing,
the legislators realized that far more was at stake than merely
the future of a single institution. Condemning as illusory the
hope that the new hospital at Taunton (then nearing comple-
tion) would alleviate the general problem facing the Commonwealth, they argued that past studies of mental illness had not
dealt realistically with this problem. Earlier estimates of the
incidence of mental illness had been far too optimistic, and had
in fact underestimated the total. "Hospitals have been multiplied," they wrote, "but the applicants for admissions have multiplied yet faster. New wings have been added, and immediately
filled up; and the cry is still, 'they come.'" In fact there had been
a real as well as an apparent increase in the number of insane
persons. The real increase had grown out of the general rise
in population and the pressures upon individuals by a business-
oriented and competitive society; the apparent one had resulted
from the favorable publicity given to moral treatment, which
had made institutionalization more common. Finally, the total
had been augmented by the accumulation of incurable cases.[57]

While the committee felt that the new Taunton hospital would
not meet current needs, it did not, as its predecessors had done,
recommend the expansion of existing facilities or the construction of new ones. Instead it introduced into consideration the

---

[56] *Report of the Committee on Public Charitable Institutions,* Mass. *Senate Document
No. 83* (March 1854), 2.
[57] *Ibid.,* 2–3.

research of Dr. Edward Jarvis on population and hospitalization. In a study published several years earlier, Jarvis had attempted to demonstrate statistically that the proportion of mental patients to the whole population was always greatest in areas immediately adjacent to a hospital and decreased as the distance increased. Those persons living nearest a hospital derived the greatest advantage; those farthest off derived the least.[58] The implications of Jarvis's work were clear. He had demonstrated that earlier estimates relating to the incidence of insanity were in error because of two erroneous assumptions: namely, that all regions within the state benefited equally from public institutions; and that the number of insane persons could be predicted accurately without considering the influence of an existing or a proposed hospital within a given community.

In view of the complex issues raised by Jarvis's findings, the committee decided against offering any simple solutions. Instead, it suggested that an impartial three-member commission be appointed to conduct a broad study of all aspects of mental illness in the Commonwealth and to recommend the adoption of a "general and uniform system." The committee also proposed that the three commissioners consider the expediency of disposing of the Worcester hospital and constructing a new one. The legislature concurred, and on April 24, 1854, it passed a resolution establishing the commission.[59] The stage was now set for what probably was the single most significant and comprehensive investigation of mental illness and public policy in nineteenth-century America.

[58] *Ibid.,* 5. The committee had drawn specifically from Jarvis's article "The Influence of Distance From and Proximity to an Insane Hospital, on its Use by Any People," *Boston Medical and Surgical Journal,* 42 (April 17, 1850), 209–222. A summary of Jarvis's views appeared in his subsequent article "On the Supposed Increase of Insanity," *American Journal of Insanity,* 8 (April 1852), 333–364. Jarvis had also pointed out that the establishment of mental hospitals distinctly influenced the views of the surrounding community. "The opening of these establishments for the cure or the protection of lunatics, the spread of their reports, the extension of the knowledge of their character, power, and usefulness, by the means of the patients that they protect and cure, have created, and continue to create, more and more interest in the subject of insanity, and more confidence in its curability. Consequently, more and more persons and families, who, or such as who, formerly kept their insane friends and relations at home, or allowed them to stroll abroad about the streets or country, now believe, that they can be restored, or improved, or, at least made more comfortable in these public institutions, and, therefore, they send their patients to these asylums, and thus swell the lists of their inmates." Jarvis, "On the Supposed Increase of Insanity," 344.

[59] *Report of the Committee on Public Charitable Institutions,* Mass. *Senate Document No. 83* (March 1854), 5–8; Chap. 64, Resolve of April 24, 1854, in *Acts and Resolves Passed by the General Court of Massachusetts, in the Year 1854* (Boston, 1854), 438.

From the very beginning it was evident that the investigation
would differ from previous ones. The selection of the three
members of the commission, for example, was accomplished in
a unique manner. Between 1829 and 1849 the personnel for
committees charged with the responsibility of studying insanity
had come from within the legislature. Presumed experts, while
often called upon for advice, had never served directly on such
committees. Under the provisions of the resolve of 1854, however, the governor, with the consent of the Executive Council,
was to select three commissioners, and he chose Levi Lincoln,
Increase Sumner, and Edward Jarvis. The appointments of
Lincoln and Sumner were not surprising; both men had long
been prominent in public life. Lincoln, a native of Worcester,
had graduated from Harvard College in 1802. He then served
his fellow citizens in various capacities, including several terms
as governor between 1825 and 1834, during which time he had
given strong support to the movement to establish a public
mental hospital. Such was his success in the executive mansion
that he was re-elected with a degree of unanimity rarely found
in the turbulence of Massachusetts politics. After voluntarily
relinquishing the governorship, he was elected to Congress,
where he served for more than seven years. When appointed
to the commission on lunacy in 1854, Lincoln already had a
distinguished reputation as an able and informed public servant
and philanthropist. Increase Sumner, his fellow commissioner,
was not as well known, but he too was a highly respected figure.
Prominent in politics in the western part of the Commonwealth,
he had served in the state senate and had held various appoin-
tive offices. Both men brought dignity and experience to the
commission.[60]

The choice of Jarvis, on the other hand, was an indication that
the formulation of public policy regarding the mentally ill was
beginning to pass into the hands of professionals and that the
role of lay reformers was diminishing in importance. Indeed,
the modus operandi of the commission reflected this new trend.
From the very outset of the investigation the governor and the
two other commissioners agreed that Jarvis would collect all of

---

[60] "Levi Lincoln," in *Dictionary of American Biography*, eds. Allen Johnson *et al.*
(22 vols.; New York: Charles Scribner's Sons, 1928–1958), XI, 264–265; Pitts-
field *Sun*, February 16, 1871, in *Memorial Record. In Memory of Hon. Increase
Sumner, of Great Barrington, Mass.* (Bridgeport, 1871), 15–16.

the raw data, analyze its significance, and write the final report; his colleagues would simply serve as informal advisers.[61]

Unlike Lincoln and Sumner, Jarvis had never been active in politics. At the time of his appointment to the commission, he was just over fifty-one years of age. Born in Concord, Massachusetts, in 1803, he attended the local schools, and went to work in a textile mill at the age of sixteen. Though desiring to attend college, he was unwilling to impose an added burden on his father, who already was supporting an older brother in college. But when it became evident that his talents were clearly in a scholarly direction, his father withdrew him from the mill and arranged to have him continue his preparatory studies. Jarvis finally entered Harvard College in 1822 and received his degree four years later.[62]

Like many other young men from similar circumstances, Jarvis's original hope was to enter the ministry. Imbued with a strong sense of social consciousness characteristic of many nineteenth-century New Englanders, he saw in religion a means of fulfilling his desire to serve his fellow man and elevate society. Because he believed that his speech would impede his effectiveness in the ministry, he turned instead to medicine in the belief that it would provide him with the best opportunity for doing good. After completing his medical apprenticeship and earning his M.D., he opened an office in Northfield in 1830. Shortly thereafter he returned to his native town of Concord. His practice, however, was not particularly successful. When he failed in his attempt to be appointed to the superintendency of the McLean Asylum, he accepted an offer from a former classmate to set up a new practice in Louisville, Kentucky, in 1837, where he remained for nearly six years.

[61] Jarvis, Mss. Autobiography, Houghton Library, Harvard University, Cambridge, Massachusetts, 153. In the manuscript volume containing the raw data that served as the basis for the *Report on Insanity*, Jarvis made the same point. See his introductory statements in the "Report of the Physicians of Massachusetts. Superintendents of Hospital . . . and Others Describing the Insane and Idiotic Persons in the State of Massachusetts in 1855. Made to the Commissioners on Lunacy," Mss. volume in the Countway Library, Harvard Medical School, Boston, Massachusetts.

[62] Biographical material on Jarvis culled from the following sources: Jarvis, Mss. Autobiography; Robert W. Wood, *Memorial of Edward Jarvis, M. D.* (Boston, 1885); Andrew P. Peabody, "Memoir of Edward Jarvis, M. D.," *New England Historical and Genealogical Register*, 39 (July 1885), 217–224; "Edward Jarvis, M. D.," American Antiquarian Society, *Proceedings*, N. S. 3 (October 1883–April 1885), 484–487. The Jarvis manuscript collection at the Concord Free Public Library is rich on his personal life, while the Jarvis papers at the Countway Library at the Harvard Medical School in Boston, Massachusetts, are composed largely of letters to Jarvis by colleagues. There are a few items relating to Jarvis in the Houghton Library, Harvard University, and the Kirkbride Papers, Institute of the Pennsylvania Hospital, Philadelphia, Pennsylvania.

His stay in Kentucky, however, was not a happy one. He was dissatisfied with the frontier nature of the town and found that efforts to impose what to him were the more civilized standards and customs of Concord proved unavailing. The presence of slaves, Jarvis later recalled in his autobiography, was "hateful"; yet he found it impossible "to live there without, in some measure, using the services of bondsmen." In 1843, therefore, he returned to Massachusetts. After failing once again in his efforts to find a superintendency of a mental hospital, he settled permanently in Dorchester, where he specialized in treating milder cases of mental illness in his home. His real interests, however, lay elsewhere, and much of his time was devoted to research, writing, and public service. During his career he worked on the federal censuses of 1850, 1860, and 1870, was active in the public health movement, served as a trustee of the Massachusetts School for Idiotic and Feeble Minded Youth and the Worcester State Lunatic Hospital and as physician to the Perkins Institution and Massachusetts School for the Blind, and was also the dominant figure for more than thirty years in the American Statistical Association.

During his early years in Concord, Jarvis encountered several cases of mental disease. He became so intrigued with this subject that it became one of his major concerns. His interest in insanity, however, was not that of the practicing psychiatrist. On the contrary, his primary concern lay in unraveling a series of scientific questions about the nature and course of this malady and its relationship to a variety of other individual and social factors. That he became involved with mental illness as a subject for scientific inquiry was not entirely unexpected. While studying medicine he had become dissatisfied with much of the conventional knowledge of his day. Questions arose in his mind about the relationship between medical therapeutics and the course of a disease. Becoming distrustful of the efficacy of many of these so-called therapeutic agents, he came to the conclusion that the physician's greatest contribution was to act in a prophylactic capacity—to warn people of the dangers of violating the natural laws governing them and thus inviting the inevitable penalty of disease (including insanity). In effect, Jarvis married many of his religious and moral beliefs about the proper conduct of life to the speciality of medicine. "God," he wrote in 1843, "has put our lives, partially at least, into our own hands. Whether we shall live to the fulness of our years, and give to each day its fulness of strength and pleasure, or whether we shall be miserable invalids, ever moving toward the grave and cut off in the morn, noon, or eve of life; these depend upon our obedience to those laws which God has stamped upon our frames."[63] The physical and the moral order were simply parts of an organic whole and it was impossible to separate health and morality because of the indissoluble bond between them.

Convinced that disease was the consequence of ignorance and sin, Jarvis devoted a considerable amount of his time to educating the public about proper modes of conduct. "There is a general ignorance of the laws of vitality," he informed the members of the Massachusetts Medical Society in 1849. "Men do not understand the connection between their conduct and vital force; and they feel but little responsibility for the maintenance of health. They lay their plans and carry on their operations, without much regard to the conditions of their existence. Life and its interests are not always paramount considerations; but they are made subordinate to matters of inferior importance."[64] It followed that physicians had the difficult and grave responsibility for disseminating within all communities knowledge concerning the laws of health and illness. At the urging of Horace Mann, Jarvis published several books on physiology, the basic purpose of which was to provide the public with accurate information about proper behavior. And proper behavior meant more than the mere observance of the laws of physiology; it included the entire behavioral pattern of the individual. Jarvis not only advocated a proper diet, fresh air, and other prerequisites of physical development, but he also condemned the use of tobacco and alcohol, the overuse of the individual's intellectual capacities, and the overzealous pursuit of material gain, to cite only a few examples. His ideal, not surprisingly, corresponded to the ideal of many middle-class and Protestant New Englanders.[65]

Though the laws governing life were of diverse origin, Jarvis firmly believed that man, possessing as he did rational faculties, could formulate these laws in a fairly precise manner. God, after all, had not been capricious or arbitrary when he created the

[63] Jarvis, "Law of Physical Life," *Christian Examiner*, 35 (September 1843), 4.

[64] Jarvis, "The Production of Vital Force," in *Medical Communications of the Massachusetts Medical Society*, 2nd ser., vol. 4 (Boston, 1854), 23. Jarvis made much the same point in his review article of the *Report of the Sanitary Commission of Massachusetts . . . 1850* [Shattuck Report], which appeared in the *American Journal of the Medical Sciences*, 21 (April 1851), 391–409 (see especially 408–409).

[65] For Jarvis's views on the proper conduct of life see the following: "Law of Physical Life," 1–31; "The Production of Vital Force," 1–40; *Lecture on the Necessity of the Study of Physiology, Delivered Before the American Institute of Instruction, at Hartford, August 22, 1845* (Boston, 1845); *Practical Physiology: For the Use of Schools and Families* (Philadelphia, 1847); *Primary Physiology* (Philadelphia, 1848); *Practical Physiology: Or, Anatomy and Physiology Applied to Health* (rev. ed., New York, 1852).

universe; He had also promulgated a series of natural laws whose operations were regular and predictable. Because they were regular and predictable, these laws lent themselves to scientific inquiry. And the best way of deriving these laws, Jarvis maintained, was through a broad statistical analysis of a large body of empirical data. Consequently, much of his own research was concerned with quantitative data of various types. Moreover, Jarvis spent an extraordinarily large amount of time attempting to convince others of the value of such studies. When the Association of Medical Superintendents of American Institutions for the Insane was about to convene its first session in 1844, he wrote to Samuel B. Woodward in the hope of getting its members to recognize and discuss the importance of numerical studies. Individual experiences, he insisted, were not grounds for reaching scientific conclusions about mental disease. Only by collecting and analyzing a large body of facts could physicians "come to the true causes of insanity, and the real influences, that remove it."[66]

In emphasizing the importance of statistics, Jarvis was following the lead of many contemporary scientists and political economists. The application of a numerical method had been undertaken first in the seventeenth century by mercantilists who hoped that the quantitative data of natural life would result in knowledge that would enhance the authority and power of the nation-state. By the eighteenth century the possibilities inherent in the statistical analysis of disease were being increasingly recognized. Condorcet, the Enlightenment prophet of progress, for example, predicted that preventive medicine might ultimately lead to the eradication of communicable diseases. Shortly afterward, Philippe Pinel, considered by many the father of modern psychiatry, undertook to prove statistically the value of moral treatment, and he emphasized the importance of case histories containing quantifiable material. The philosophy of Ideology, with its empirical approach, markedly strengthened faith in analytic statistics.[67] Industrial and technological changes,

[66] Jarvis to Samuel B. Woodward, October 12, 1844, Woodward Papers.

[67] Based on the epistemological theory advanced by the Abbé Etienne de Condillac, the philosophy of Ideology was further developed by Destutt de Tracy, Helvétius, Condorcet, Cabanis, and others. According to Condillac, sensations were the primary data of cognition. All ideas and all the faculties of human understanding, furthermore, were simply compounds of sensations that could be resolved by an analytical method into their component parts. The basis of all ideas, in other words, was experience; nothing could be present in the mind except what entered it through the senses. To Condillac's disciples, this method of radical empiricism was crucial. Not only would it enable man to to learn and understand his nature, but he would be able to undertake a political, social, economic, and moral reconstruction in order to better his condition. See George Rosen, "The Philosophy of Ideology and the Emergence of Modern Medicine in France," *Bulletin of the History of Medicine*, 20 (July 1946), 328–331.

which gave rise to new social problems, also reinforced interest in the statistical analysis of the problems of health, and the numerical method of Pierre Louis and the Paris school of the early nineteenth century seemed to prove beyond a doubt the fruitfulness of a quantitative approach.[68]

Jarvis's first published work dealing with mental illness appeared during his stay in Louisville. Concerned over substandard conditions and inadequate facilities for the insane in Kentucky and the West, he published two lengthy articles designed to summarize existing knowledge about mental illness and to provide a rational basis for the expansion of public facilities.[69] Both contributions reflected the then current faith in the curability of insanity, provided that treatment was begun as early as possible in a mental hospital headed by a competent physician. The distinguishing feature of both articles was the author's detailed knowledge about conditions at every mental hospital in the United States. Also noteworthy were the lengthy statistical tables dealing with the incidence of insanity, etiology, treatment, and costs, to cite only a few examples.[70]

While active in the movement to provide adequate state facilities for the mentally ill in Kentucky, Jarvis became embroiled in a peculiar controversy arising out of the federal census of 1840. Published in 1841, the census had included a large amount of statistical data pertaining to the incidence of mental illness. There were, according to this compilation, over 17,000 insane and idiots in the nation. Of these, about 14,500 were white and nearly 3,000 black. In the North the ratio of insanity among whites was 1:995; the comparable figure for the South was 1:945. Of the 2.7 million blacks in the South, 1,734 were insane or idiotic, a ratio of 1:1,558. In the free states, however, nearly 1,200 blacks out of a total population of 171,894 were insane or idiotic, a ratio of 1:144. In other words, the

---

[68] Rosen, "Problems in the Application of Statistical Analysis to Questions of Health: 1700–1880," *Bulletin of the History of Medicine*, 29 (January–February 1955), 27–45; Richard H. Shryock, *The Development of Modern Medicine: An Interpretation of the Social and Scientific Factors Involved* (new ed.; New York: Alfred A. Knopf), 157–169.

[69] Jarvis first called attention to this subject in an article entitled "Insanity in Kentucky," *Boston Medical and Surgical Journal*, 24 (April 21, 1841), 165–171. His analysis was not fundamentally different from that of the superintendent of the Kentucky Eastern Lunatic Asylum a few years later. See Kentucky [Eastern] Lunatic Asylum, *Annual Report* (1844), 19–31.

[70] Jarvis, review article in the *Western Journal of Medicine and Surgery*, 4 (December 1841), 443–482 (also reprinted as a pamphlet entitled *Insanity and Insane Asylums* [Louisville, 1841]), and "What Shall We Do With Our Insane?," *Western Journal of Medicine and Surgery*, 5 (February 1842), 81–125 (also reprinted in pamphlet form with the title *What Shall We Do With the Insane of the Western Country?* [n.p., n.d.]).

census had revealed that the incidence of mental disease among free blacks exceeded that among slaves by nearly elevenfold and that among whites of about sixfold.[71]

The implications of these statistics, of course, were obvious—particularly to southerners seeking to defend the cherished institution of slavery. In his report for 1841, for example, Dr. Francis T. Stribling of the Virginia Western Lunatic Asylum not only reproduced all of the statistical data showing the differential incidence of mental disease among whites, slaves, and free blacks, but he also chided northern abolitionists for their activities in the light of such objective and scientific findings.[72] An article in the *Southern Literary Messenger* attributed the low rate of mental disease among southern blacks to the fact that he "cares not for the morrow, well knowing, that another will provide what he shall eat, what he shall drink, and wherewithal he shall be clothed; his simple mode of life secures him health, and in the winter of life, he crowns 'a youth of labor, with an age of ease.'"[73] And John C. Calhoun, while secretary of state, used the census of 1840 to rebuff attempts by the British government to further the abolition of slavery throughout the world. Pointing to the extraordinary high rates of insanity, pauperism, vice, and wretchedness among free blacks in the North, Calhoun emphasized the happiness and tranquility among southern slaves. "Experience has proved," concluded Calhoun, "that the existing relation, in which the one is subjected to the other, in the slaveholding States, is consistent with the peace and safety of both, with great improvement to the inferior."[74] Although the census did not create a racist ideology, adherents of slavery used its findings to confirm their own convictions that blacks represented an inferior racial typology.[75]

While incapacitated with a broken leg, Jarvis undertook a detailed analysis of the census of 1840, particularly those parts relating to insanity. Here, after all, was a vast body of raw

[71] The raw data on this subject can be found in the *Compendium of the Enumeration of the Inhabitants and Statistics of the United States, as Obtained at the Department of State, from the Returns of the Sixth Census* (Washington, D. C., 1841), 4–103. I have used the ratios computed by Edward Jarvis in "Insanity Among the Coloured Population of the Free States," *American Journal of the Medical Sciences*, N. S. 7 (January 1844), 72–73.

[72] Virginia Western Lunatic Asylum, *Annual Report*, 14 (1841), 38–43.

[73] C. B. Hayden, "On the Distribution of Insanity in the U. States," *Southern Literary Messenger*, 10 (March 1844), 180. See also "Reflections on the Census of 1840," *ibid.*, 9 (June 1843), 340–352.

[74] *The Works of John C. Calhoun*, ed. by Richard K. Crallé (6 vols., New York, 1870–1876), V, 333–339.

[75] For a discussion of antebellum racial theories see William Stanton, *The Leopard's Spots: Scientific Attitudes Toward Race in America 1815–59* (Chicago: University of Chicago Press, 1960).

statistical data. Might not a careful analysis confirm or deny many commonly held theories about the etiology, nature, and incidence of mental illness? Given Jarvis's faith in man's capacity to ascertain the laws governing his behavior, it was not surprising that he was attracted by such a detailed compilation.

Jarvis first turned his attention to the census in a paper published in September 1842. Much of the article was devoted to a demonstration of the inaccuracy of the census's findings about the total number of insane in the United States. Reports by local officials such as selectmen and overseers of the poor, he pointed out, generally revealed a far higher number of mentally ill persons within a given locality than did the federal census, and such local reports were usually the work of knowledgeable and informed men. The second half of the article was devoted to a discussion about the greater incidence of insanity among free blacks and its relatively low incidence among slaves. Jarvis was not particularly surprised at this state of affairs, since it seemed to confirm the popular belief that the lower the state of civilization, the smaller the incidence of mental illness. It was natural, therefore, that slaves—all of whom were insulated from excessive mental activity and the pressures of society—would show a very low frequency of insanity. Nevertheless, he felt that the subject was still unknown and the variables insufficiently accounted for as to merit further investigation.[76]

While compiling the figures for this article, Jarvis noted that the census volume had listed 133 colored insane paupers in the town of Worcester, Massachusetts. Assuming that an error had been made (he knew from personal observation that there were not 133 colored insane in the town), Jarvis transferred the figure to the columns of the white. Fearing that there would be other errors in the census, he examined the statistics for each town in the Bay State and carefully compared the total black population with the number of black insane. The results were astounding; localities that had no black inhabitants were listed as having black insane individuals. Twenty-one towns, for example, having twelve black inhabitants had, according to the census, no less than fifty-six black insane persons. Clearly, concluded Jarvis, the census was in error and should be corrected.[77] In a later and more detailed article that subjected the census to a very careful analysis, Jarvis ended by noting that the census

---

[76] Edward Jarvis, "Statistics of Insanity in the United States," *Boston Medical and Surgical Journal*, 27 (September 21, 1842), 116–121.

[77] Jarvis, "Statistics of Insanity in the United States," *Boston Medical and Surgical Journal*, 27 (November 30, 1842), 281–282.

has contributed nothing to the statistical nosology of the free blacks, and furnished us with no data whereon we may build any theory respecting the liability of humanity, in its different phases and in various outward circumstances, to loss of reason or of the senses. We confess, we are disappointed, we are mortified; nor are we alone in this feeling; our government had directed, that seventeen millions of people of various races and conditions, should be counted and their precise amount of derangement ascertained. Scientific men and philanthropists looked for the results of this investigation with confident hope; for henceforward the statistics of insanity, of deafness, and of blindness, were to be no more a mere matter of conjecture, but of positive and extensive demonstration. In due time the document came forth, under the sanction of Congress, and "corrected at the Department of State." Such a document as we have described, heavy with its errors and its misstatements, instead of being a messenger of truth to the world, to enlighten its knowledge and guide its opinions; it is, in respect to human ailment—a bearer of falsehood to confuse and mislead. So far from being an aid to the progress of medical science, as it was the intention of government in ordering these inquiries, it has thrown a stumbling-block in its way, which it will require years to remove . . . We commend this matter to the attention of the next Congress. We hope they will cause all the original papers respecting the sixth census to be revised, and all the errors which were made in copying them corrected, and a new and satisfactory edition sent forth, so that the correction of the mistakes and the refutation of the errors may follow them as early and as widely as possible. This is due to the honour of our country, to medical science, and to truth.[78]

So strong were his feelings about the census and the use (and misuse) to which its findings were being put that Jarvis began a campaign to convince Congress that it ought to recognize the errors of the census and to provide formally for their correction. He persuaded the American Statistical Association to prepare a memorial to Congress requesting remedial legislation, and he also worked with the Massachusetts Medical Society in helping to discredit the statistics of insanity pertaining to the Bay State.[79] For nearly a decade Jarvis labored in vain to have the census corrected. His antipathy toward slavery merely reinforced his hatred of improper and misleading statistics. When Calhoun

[78] Jarvis, "Insanity Among the Coloured Population of the Free States," *American Journal of the Medical Sciences*, N. S. 7 (January 1844), 83.

[79] "Memorial of the American Statistical Association, Praying the Adoption of Measures for the Correction of Errors in the Returns of the Sixth Census," 28 Cong., 2d Sess., *Senate Document No. 5* (December 11, 1844). The memorial was also reprinted in *Hunt's Merchants' Magazine*, 12 (February 1845), 131–139. The work of the Massachusetts Medical Society can be followed in the *Medical Communications of the Massachusetts Medical Society*, 7 (1845), 59, 67, 72, 83–84, 90–95.

used the census figures to defend slavery, Jarvis was indignant. "I little thought," he remarked, "when I wrote my pamphlet last fall, that so soon would the second officer of our nation make such use of the falsehoods of the census—and produce such an atrocious piece of sophistry as Mr. Calhoun has."[80] As late as 1852 Jarvis felt impelled to correct a writer who attemped to demonstrate that free blacks were more liable to insanity than slaves.[81]

During these years Jarvis worked on a variety of other problems that he felt lent themselves to statistical study. His paper in 1850 on the relationship between distance from a hospital and its use by people had shown that there was a direct correlation between these two factors. Those communities adjacent to a mental hospital took advantage of it the most; those farthest away the least. Indirectly he criticized past public policy and suggested that the state take demographical factors into greater consideration in the future. If the Commonwealth needed additional facilities for its insane, he wrote, then it would first have to determine which section had the greatest need. Then it would have to locate the center of population and communication. Only then could a rational and cohesive basis be found for state action.[82]

In addition to his work on the location of mental hospitals, Jarvis undertook several investigations dealing with the causes and incidence of mental illness. That he was concerned with this subject was not surprising. A clear understanding of the causes of insanity, after all, was more than simply a matter of scientific curiosity. On the contrary, it had immense practical value since

[80] Jarvis to Dorothea L. Dix, May 25, 1844, Dix Papers. See also Jarvis to John Gorham Palfrey, January 30, 1849, Jarvis Letters, Houghton Library, Harvard University, and the *Boston Medical and Surgical Journal*, 30 (June 5, 1844), 362–363.

[81] Jarvis, "Insanity Among the Coloured Population of the Free States," *American Journal of Insanity*, 8 (January 1852), 268–282. Jarvis was correcting an article that first appeared in the *New York Observer* and reprinted as an article entitled "Startling Facts From the Census" in the *American Journal of Insanity*, 8 (October 1851), 153–155.

For full treatments of the census controversy see Albert Deutsch, "The First U. S. Census of the Insane (1840) and Its Use as Pro-Slavery Propaganda," *Bulletin of the History of Medicine*, 15 (May 1944), 469–482, Leon Litwack, *North of Slavery: The Negro in the Free States, 1790–1860* (Chicago: University of Chicago Press, 1961), 40–46, and Stanton, *The Leopard's Spots*, 58–66.

[82] Jarvis, "The Influence of Distance From and Proximity to an Insane Hospital, on its Use by Any People," *Boston Medical and Surgical Journal*, 42 (April 17, 1850), 209–222. This article received a favorable notice in the *American Journal of Insanity*, 7 (January 1851), 281–285. The subject remained of interest to Jarvis for many years. See his paper "Influence of Distance From and Nearness to an Insane Hospital on Its Use by the People," *American Journal of Insanity*, 22 (January 1866), 361–406.

it could lead to effective preventive measures.[83] Jarvis's interest in this subject led to the publication in 1850 of a long paper that dealt with the comparative frequency of mental disease among men and women. The study was based on an analysis of the reports of about 250 American, British, Irish, Belgian, and French hospitals, some covering a period of many years. These reports, Jarvis noted, showed a higher incidence of insanity among males as compared with females despite the fact that the former did not appreciably outnumber the latter in the general population. Moreover, males had lower curability and higher mortality rates. What could account for these differences? The answer was not physiological, for neither clinical nor experimental evidence supported the view that brains differed by sex. The explanation, then, had to be found in terms of the causes of insanity, which operated in a differential manner since men and women played dissimilar roles in society. Men were more exposed to sensual temptation and the drive for materialistic rewards; women, having a more sympathetic and sensible personality, were more exposed to emotional factors. Generally, concluded Jarvis, "those causes of insanity which act upon males are more extensive and effective than those which act upon females, and therefore, within the periods covered by the reports which I have analyzed, and in those countries from which these reports come, males are somewhat more liable to insanity than females. But this must vary with different nations, different periods of the world, and different habits of the people."[84]

A year later Jarvis continued his statistical studies with a paper closely related to the one dealing with the disease in men and women. Much of the article was devoted to an exhaustive listing of the causes of insanity, which were divided into two broad categories, physical and moral. The former were the causes that produced "their primary effect on the physical structure of the brain or some other organs, and disturbing the cerebral actions, produce their secondary effect on the mental operations." The latter included behavior that reached "the brain through its functions and produce disturbance." Like many of his contemporaries, Jarvis firmly believed that there was a high correlation between the nature of American civilization and

[83] Jarvis, "Causes of Insanity," *Boston Medical and Surgical Journal*, 45 (November 12, 1851), 289.

[84] Jarvis, "On the Comparative Liability of Males and Females to Insanity, and Their Comparative Curability and Mortality When Insane," *American Journal of Insanity*, 7 (October 1850), 142–171. Jarvis retained his interest in this subject for many years. See Jarvis to Thomas S. Kirkbride, March 13, 1857, Kirkbride Papers, Institute of the Pennsylvania Hospital.

mental disease. "In this country," he wrote, "where no son is necessarily confined to the work or employment of his father, but all the fields of labor, of profit and of honor are open to whomsoever will put on the harness and enter therein, and all are invited to join the strife for that which may be gained in each, many are in a transition state, from the lower and less desirable to the higher and more desirable conditions. They are struggling for that which costs them mental labor and anxiety and pain. The mistake or the ambition of some leads them to aim at that which they cannot reach, to strive for more than they can grasp, and their mental powers are strained to their utmost tension; they labor in agitation; and they end in frequent disappointment . . . Insanity is, then, a part of the price which we pay for civilization."[85]

When Jarvis was appointed to the Commission on Lunacy in 1854, therefore, he already had a distinguished reputation not only as a scientist who had helped to unravel the circumstances

---

[85] Jarvis, "Causes of Insanity," 289–305. Jarvis had also given this paper in a slightly different form at the meetings of the Association of Medical Superintendents of American Institutions for the Insane in May, 1851. It was published under the title, "On the Supposed Increase of Insanity," *American Journal of Insanity*, 8 (April 1852), 333–364.

Jarvis's argument about the relationship between mental illness and social and economic conditions was not fundamentally dissimilar from the one advanced by contemporary scientists who have made the same point (generally using far more complex terminology and an imposing array of statistics). Yet it is difficult to avoid the conclusion that such a thesis oftentimes reflects strong personal and emotional convictions about society and is not a product of scientific study alone. Many nineteenth- and twentieth-century psychiatrists have accepted the romantic claim about the superiority of nature and natural man; consequently, they view the present as a degenerate retrogression from a supposedly golden past. Similarly, many individuals who were and are concerned about the social dislocations caused by technological and economic change have expressed their dislike of modern society by arguing that civilization, rather than bringing progress, has brought, among other things, an increase in the incidence of mental disease. For an excellent discussion of this theme see George Rosen, "Social Stress and Mental Disease From the Eighteenth Century to the Present: Some Origins of Social Psychiatry," *Millbank Memorial Fund Quarterly*, 37 (January 1959), 5–32. This article has been reprinted in Rosen's *Madness in Society*, 172–194.

The problem of evaluating the statistics (or estimates) of the incidence of mental illness over a long period of time is extraordinarily difficult, if not impossible. Many demographical studies of the incidence of insanity are of dubious reliability. Far more important, however, is the fact that the definition of mental illness has clearly changed over the years, thus making impossible any meaningful conclusions about changes in incidence. For an attempt to deal with this issue using hospital admissions to measure incidence see Herbert Goldhammer and Andrew W. Marshall, *Psychosis and Civilization: Two Studies in the Frequency of Mental Disease* (Glencoe, Ill.: The Free Press, 1953). They conclude that there was not a disproportionate increase in the incidence of mental illness in Massachusetts and New York in the nineteenth and twentieth centuries. Even this study, however, finds it difficult to take into account changing definitions of mental disease.

surrounding insanity, but also as a social-minded individual concerned with the welfare of society. The fact that his views reflected the moral outlook and values of the society into which he was born and the one in which he always felt most at ease no doubt facilitated his selection. Jarvis himself considered his appointment the most significant event of his career.

VII

From the very start Jarvis threw himself wholeheartedly into the project. For nearly eight months he devoted himself exclusively to the investigation, even to the point of abandoning temporarily his private practice and ignoring his health. Rising at 5 A.M., he often toiled until 10:00 in the evening. Such intensive work—for which he received only $5 per day from the Commonwealth—was by no means distasteful or unwelcome. On the contrary, such labor represented an opportunity to be of service to his fellow citizens while at the same time advancing the state of scientific knowledge. Later in life Jarvis judged this project to be "one of the most successful of his life" and one that "accomplished a very desirable purpose."[86]

Because of his conviction that the best way to uncover the laws governing human behavior was to analyze a large body of empirical data, Jarvis decided that a complete census of the insane in the state was an indispensable preliminary. Earlier enumerations of the insane—whether federal or state—had generally been marred by inaccuracies and inconsistencies. Consequently, public policy had often rested on an erroneous foundation. To remedy this deficiency, therefore, Jarvis undertook to identify every insane individual by name as well as to determine nativity, sex, means of support, place of residence or confinement, and prognosis for the future. This information was solicited by polling, insofar as it was feasible, every physician in the state. In localities without physicians an identical form was sent to the resident clergyman. In addition, the superintendents of all public and private hospitals and keepers of jails and houses of correction in Massachusetts were included in the survey, as were officers of hospitals in New England, the middle states, and some southern states, all of whom were asked to report any insane patients from Massachusetts. With the cooperation and support of the Massachusetts Medical Society and many local newspapers, this endeavor proved highly succcessful; in the end

[86] Jarvis, Mss. Autobiography, 165.

over 800 returns representing about 1,400 individuals were received.[87]

The responses to Jarvis's inquiry varied somewhat in nature. Most correspondents simply supplied the required data and offered neither their own analysis of the problems arising out of mental illness nor advice about alternative policies. A few, however, took up Jarvis's request for suggestions. One individual related the causes of insanity "to the mismanagement of schools —to the overtasking of pupils confined perhaps too long at a time in overheated and ill ventilated rooms." Another condemned the shortsighted and selfish policy of the towns, which preferred to retain chronic insane persons for their labor rather than paying for their support in a public hospital. A third attacked the relentless pursuit of money that characterized society —a chase that was "blunting the feelings of humanity and preparing us for a retrograde motion toward barbarism." One physician noted that the prevalence of certain diseases in his locality tended "rather to relieve insanity than to bring it forward; and to prevent idiocy than to produce it." Consequently, the area would be an ideal place for locating a new public facility. "Should such a hospital be founded," he added, "I should of course like for myself the appointment of physician-in-chief."[88]

In general, the returns—precisely because they were confined to the simple reporting of data—were not particularly enlightening about attitudes toward insanity and the insane. Occasionally a correspondent took the opportunity to express his feelings. "Very many of the foreign Irish population," one Boston physician wrote, "say one in ten, imported into this city for the last six years, are idiots, or at least no better. Three fourths of the remaining Irish importations, are *monomaniacs*, being the *dupes* of *Catholic Priests*. One half of the whole receive aid from charitable institutions, the City or State."[89] Such comments,

---

[87] All of the manuscript returns can be found in the "Report of the Physicians of Massachusetts. Superintendents of Hospitals . . . and Others Describing the Insane and Idiotic Persons in the State of Massachusetts in 1855. Made to the Commissioners on Lunacy." This collection, which was brought together in a large bound volume, is now in the Countway Medical Library of the Harvard Medical School. See also the *Report on Insanity and Idiocy in Massachusetts,* 11–16, and Walter L. Burrage, *A History of the Massachusetts Medical Society . . . 1781–1922* (n.p., 1923), 168.

[88] George Brill (Shelburne) to Jarvis, August 18, 1854; John Yale (Ware) to Jarvis, September 30, 1854; Silas Brown (Wilmington) to Jarvis, October 23, 1854; Charles M. Weeks (Lynn) to Jarvis, September 4, 1854, in "Report of the Physicians of Massachusetts. Superintendents of Hospitals . . . and Others Describing the Insane and Idiotic Persons in the State of Massachusetts in 1855. Made to the Commissioners on Lunacy."

[89] E. B. Moore to Jarvis, August 21, 1854, *ibid.*

however, were atypical; the overwhelming majority of the responses were confined to providing the information requested by Jarvis.

After receiving the questionnaires, Jarvis then checked the name of every mentally ill person to make certain that the final figures took into account any duplicate reporting by different correspondents. The result was undoubtedly the most reliable census of the insane ever taken in the United States. According to the final tabulations, there were 2,632 insane persons in Massachusetts in the autumn of 1854. Of this number, 1,522 were paupers (693 state, and 829 town, paupers), while 1,110 were supported by their own resources or by their friends. Only 625 were foreign born; 2,007 were natives. At the time 1,284 were either at home or in town or city poorhouses; 1,141 were in hospitals; and 207 were in receptacles for the insane, houses of correction, jails, and state almshouses. Perhaps the most revealing aspect of the survey was the fact that the overwhelming majority of those polled believed that most mentally ill persons were incurable. Out of the total of 2,632 insane persons, only 435 were regarded as curable, while 2,018 were listed as chronic cases (the prognosis of 179 was not reported) (pp. 17–18).*

That the statistics gathered by Jarvis represented by far the most careful and methodical survey of the incidence of insanity in Massachusetts was indisputable. His study, moreover, raised serious doubts about the past investigations that had been designed to provide information to serve as the basis of public policy. The legislative investigation of 1848, for example, had estimated that there were 1,512 mentally ill persons in the Bay State. Yet only six years later the new study revealed the existence of an additional eleven hundred insane persons. Jarvis argued that previous inquiries had been imperfect because of the improper techniques employed in compiling statistics. Massachusetts, he observed, was by no means alone in having underestimated the incidence of insanity; the situation was much the same in Britain and France (pp. 18–20).

After presenting a town-by-town breakdown of the number of insane persons (including their condition and pecuniary status), Jarvis moved on to an extended discussion of the relationship between pauperism and mental illness. His decision to devote attention to this problem was hardly surprising or novel. The state, after all, had originally become involved in caring for the insane largely because of the inability of individuals and

---

* Parenthetical page references are to the *Report on Insanity and Idiocy in Massachusetts,* reproduced as the second part of this volume.

private philanthropy to deal with the problem. If anything, the social implications of the disease were growing rather than diminishing. Furthermore, the increasing social, economic, and political tensions within Massachusetts—tensions that had grown out of ethnic, religious, and economic conflicts—had led to demands that the state reconsider its obligations toward the mentally ill, especially those coming from alien backgrounds. Here, then, was a golden opportunity to shed light upon an important question, and Jarvis chose to deal with the issues in a forthright and scientific manner.

His study, Jarvis wrote, had led to the inescapable conclusion that pauperism and insanity were intimately related. "There is manifestly a much larger ratio of the insane among the poor, and especially among those who are paupers," he pointed out, "than among the independent and more prosperous classes." What were the essential ingredients of poverty? In Jarvis's view poverty was much more than an external circumstance. Rather it was "an inward principle, enrooted deeply within the man, and running through all his elements . . . Hence we find that, among those whom the world calls poor, there is less vital force, a lower tone of life, more ill health, more weakness, more early death, a diminished longevity. There is also less self-respect, more idiocy and insanity, and more crime, than among the independent." Nor was the association between poverty and insanity a statistical accident. On the contrary, both were traceable to the same source, namely, an "imperfectly organized brain and feeble mental constitution" which carried with it "inherent elements of poverty and insanity." To put it another way, insanity and pauperism were not only accidents of a deficient environment but were partially dependent on an individual's innate characteristics (pp. 45, 52–56).

Having analyzed the relationship between poverty and mental illness, Jarvis then moved on to a discussion of what he called the "foreign element." He began by noting the greater incidence of insanity among foreigners (one case for every 368 persons) than among natives (one case for every 445 persons). Equally significant was the fact that 93 percent of foreign lunatics were paupers as compared with only 57 percent of the native born. There were two possible explanations for this state of affairs. Either foreigners (and by foreigners Jarvis meant the Irish) were more prone to insanity, or else they were ill-adapted to the physical and cultural conditions of American society. Jarvis implied that both possibilities were partly true. "There is good ground for supposing," he wrote that the habits and condition and character of the Irish poor in this country operate more unfavorably upon their mental health, and hence produce a larger number of the insane in ratio of their numbers than is found among the native poor. Being in a strange land and among strange men and things, meeting with customs and surrounded by circumstances widely different from all their previous experience, ignorant of the precise state of affairs here, and wanting education and flexibility by which they could adapt themselves to their new and unwonted position, they necessarily form many impracticable purposes, and endeavor to accomplish them by unfitting means. Of course disappointment frequently follows their plans. Their lives are filled with doubt, and harrowing anxiety troubles them, and they are involved in frequent mental, and probably physical, suffering.

The Irish laborers have less sensibility and fewer wants to be gratified than the Americans, and yet they more commonly fail to supply them. They have also a greater irritability; they are more readily disturbed when they find themselves at variance with the circumstances about them, and less easily reconciled to difficulties they cannot overcome.

Unquestionably much of their insanity is due to their intemperance, to which the Irish seem to be peculiarly prone, and much to that exaltation which comes from increased prosperity (pp. 61–62).

Although Jarvis seemed to establish a statistical correlation between insanity and pauperism, he had in reality made a far more fundamental point. What he had shown, at least to his own satisfaction, was that mental illness was greatest among the impoverished classes (which included a high proportion of the immigrant Irish). In turn, poverty was more dependent upon one's inherited character than upon external circumstances. If this analysis were accurate, then public policy since 1830 had been founded on an improper assumption: namely, that similar cases of insanity had equal chances for recovery irrespective of social and economic status. Thus the Worcester hospital had accepted patients on an undifferentiated basis and had disregarded—at least in theory—ethnic, religious, and economic factors.

Undoubtedly Jarvis was subtly influenced by the ethnic and economic conflicts that followed the increase in immigration. As tensions between groups grew sharper, many of the earlier optimistic attitudes that had accompanied the reform impulse of the 1830's and 1840's began to be transformed. By identifying mental illness with poverty, and then showing that recent ethnic groups had a higher percentage of both, Jarvis was implying that insanity was a function of inherited characteristics. An individual became insane because he was poor, and he was poor presumably because he came from inferior stock. If this were true, then mental hospitals would have to distinguish between mentally ill persons on the basis of class and ethnicity.

Like others coming from the same background, Jarvis saw the genteel New England society that he loved and valued being eroded by both unregulated immigration and the pursuit of crass materialistic objectives. In a very real sense, therefore, some of the points that he attempted to make in the *Report on Insanity* were a reflection of his own social ideology.[90] The more than eight hundred returns that he received, after all, contained little data (with some isolated exceptions) that would directly substantiate the way in which he related poverty and mental disease. What Jarvis did was to take a series of statistics and read them in the light of his own moral assumptions about the superiority of the traditional New England way of life.

To Jarvis the most tragic part of the situation was that aliens were enjoying the advantages of state hospitals to a much greater extent than natives. Virtually every foreign insane pauper, he noted, ended up in a public institution, while only 42.7 percent of native paupers were institutionalized. Such a state of affairs was not abnormal. The majority of the alien pauper insane, having no established residence, were wards of the state; hence they were usually sent to state-supported institutions. "Whatever may have been the design and the theory," Jarvis concluded, "the practical operation of our system is, to give up our hospital accommodations for permanent residence without measure to almost the whole of the lunatic strangers, while these blessings are offered with a sparing economy to a little more than a third of our own children who are in a similar situation" (pp. 65–68).

Complicating the problem still further was the accumulation of incurable cases of mental illness. In theory Jarvis believed insanity to be curable (although he did not apply this belief equally to all groups). At the same time he accepted the idea that neglected disorders of the brain causes permanent damage. The longer the disease remained untreated, therefore, the

[90] There is an excellent study of the changing ideology of the New England Brahmin intelligentsia in Barbara M. Solomon's *Ancestors and Immigrants: A Changing New England Tradition* (Cambridge, Mass.: Harvard University Press, 1956). Mrs. Solomon traces the declining democratic faith of this group of New Englanders as they faced the problems of an urban-industrial society. In the end they provided the intellectual rationale for the ending of immigration to the United States. In the 1850's, however, these men (like Jarvis) stood between two worlds; their attitudes toward lower-class Irish immigrants could only be described as ambivalent.

less were the chances of recovery. Over the years the number of chronic cases had been augmented by new ones, and the total continued to rise. Indeed, no less than 2,018 out of a total of 2,632 mentally ill persons were incurable and would represent a permanent burden upon society and the state (pp. 68–76).

Having dealt with both the extent of insanity and some of the social and economic factors involved, Jarvis moved on to a discussion of public policy. He began with the familiar proposition that the citizens of Massachusetts had a vested interest in preventing acute cases of mental illness from becoming chronic. In the long run it would be more economical to incur the higher costs of hospitalization in a therapeutic institution than it would be to support an insane person perpetually at a lower figure. It was in the public interest, he argued, to provide sufficient public facilities devoted to therapy rather than custody.

One of the major problems confronting the state, however, was the narrow and shortsighted attitude of many localities. In order to avoid paying the higher charges of hospitalization, local officials preferred to incarcerate insane paupers in jails or almshouses. But such a policy was actually more expensive, for many curable cases tended to become chronic and thereby remain a permanent welfare charge to the community. The only alternative, Jarvis maintained, was to have the state assume greater responsibility for care and treatment. Not only should the Commonwealth provide additional hospital space, but it should also compel localities to make use of it. Implicitly criticizing municipal welfare policies, Jarvis took the position that the role of the state in caring for the mentally ill should increase rather than decrease (pp. 104–110).

If the state were to meet its responsibilities toward the insane, new accommodations would be required. Of the 2,632 lunatics in Massachusetts, about nine hundred were mild and harmless; these could be kept at home or in public poorhouses. But there were over seventeen hundred who required institutionalization, either for therapeutic reasons or for the protection of the general public. During his investigation Jarvis had surveyed existing facilities, including public and private hospitals, county receptacles established under the legislation of 1836, jails, and poorhouses.[91] On the basis of his findings

[91] A few years after the Worcester hospital had opened its doors, the number of applicants sharply exceeded the available facilities. In 1835, therefore, the General Court passed a new law that permitted the trustees to return patients to jails or houses of correction in the county where they resided in the event of overcrowding. The following year the legislature passed another act requiring all houses of correction to have a suitable and convenient apartment or receptacle "for idiots and lunatic or insane persons not furiously mad." In effect,

Jarvis reached the conclusion that there were about seven hundred more patients than there were places for them. Although not all of these cases would be hospitalized even if space were available, it was still clear that existing facilities were inadequate (pp. 110–133).

After determining that an imperative need for new accommodations existed, Jarvis called upon a number of experienced alienists for advice; in this way the state could hopefully avoid the pitfalls inherent in hasty and precipitous action. He sent letters to superintendents of most successful American and English hospitals, questioning them on a wide variety of subjects: the best method of distributing and caring for the insane; separation of males and females, independents and paupers, foreigners and natives, curables and incurables, innocents and criminals; and the ideal size and best plan for a mental hospital. Included in the survey were such renowned alienists as Luther V. Bell, Isaac Ray, John S. Butler, John P. Gray, Horace A. Buttolph, and Daniel H. Tuke, to cite only a few. Taking under consideration their advice, Jarvis proceeded to present a long list of recommendations, some of which were of considerable importance.

Jarvis agreed with the recommendation of the Association of Medical Superintendents of American Institutions for the Insane that no hospital should have more than 250 patients.[92] If an institution contained more than this number, the principal physician could not know his patients, thus hampering medical and moral therapy. Jarvis also pointed out that the larger the hospital, the greater the area that it served. In such a situation the ratio of patients to the population sent to the hospital constantly diminished with the increase in distance. Thus a system of large hospitals widely scattered throughout the state was much inferior to a system of more numerous smaller hospitals, for any institution, regardless of size, tended to serve its adjacent area to a disproportionate degree. Jarvis's first major recommendation, therefore, involved the establishment of numerous small hospitals (250 patients or less) located in varying geographical areas (pp. 135–143).

---

localities were given authority to keep their pauper insane in custodial quarters without the benefit of any medical care or supervision. Such a policy represented a partial return to the state of affairs that existed prior to the establishment of the first state mental hospital. Chap. 129, Act of April 7, 1835, and Chap. 223, Act of April 13, 1836, in *Laws of the Commonwealth of Massachusetts . . . Beginning Jan., 1834 and Ending April, 1836* (Boston, 1836), 483–484, 917–918.

[92] The recommendations of the Association can be found in the *American Journal of Insanity*, 8 (July 1851), 79–81.

Next Jarvis considered the nature and characteristics of the patient population at an ideal hospital. Although admitting that most of his correspondents favored separate hospitals for male and female, he was inclined to disregard this suggestion. A hospital of 250 for a single sex, Jarvis emphasized, would have to draw its inmates from a wide geographical area, thus bringing into operation the generalization that areas distant from the hospital would use it the least. Similarly, he opposed different establishments for curable and incurable patients. Not only was it difficult to determine whether or not a patient was incurable, but the mixture of both types in a single institution was mutually beneficial. Quiet demented patients had a soothing influence on the violent ones, and curable patients imparted hope to those less fortunate than themselves (pp. 143–145).

On the other hand, Jarvis insisted that the hospital maintain the same social distinctions that existed in society at large. Indiscriminately mixing patients from all walks of life ran counter to human nature, and would also hinder the efficacy of therapy. While favoring retention of internal distinctions based on economic, social, and educational considerations, Jarvis opposed separate hospitals for native-born independent and pauper patients. Since there was an imperceptible graduation from the upper to the lower class, it would be difficult, if not impossible, to draw fine distinctions between individuals who shared a basically similar way of life, regardless of their economic status. Cognizant of the British practice of segregating pauper from paying patients in different institutions, he pointed out that the English poor were ignorant and uncultivated, and that a much wider gulf between classes existed there than in the United States. Under these circumstances the English authorities were justified in discriminating between patients on the basis of class (pp. 145–147).

Jarvis, however, included one significant exception to his recommendation that independent and pauper patients be treated at the same institution (though not necessarily equally). Specifically, he argued that state paupers (those who had no legal residence in Massachusetts)—most of whom were Irish aliens—could not be classified in the same category as native paupers. Coming from a different environment and holding dissimilar customs, attitudes, and religious beliefs, these aliens resembled the English poor rather than the native poor. The interests of all would best be served by keeping native and alien paupers apart. In this way, the latter could be kept in institutions that re-created a "style of life" not very different from the one to which they were normally accustomed. Such a policy had the added virtue of economy; institutions that cared for the alien pauper insane could be maintained at a lower cost than those caring for native patients. In addition, Jarvis suggested that institutions for the alien pauper insane provide discrete quarters for criminal lunatics, a group that should be separated from other categories of mentally ill persons (pp. 147–154).

After concluding that a general insane hospital that accepted all persons (except state paupers and criminal lunatics) was most desirable, Jarvis moved on to a consideration of the needs of old and incurable patients. Those fortunate enough to find their way into one of the state-supported institutions presented no great difficulty. The real trouble arose from the large proportion of this group who were confined in county receptacles (which had been made mandatory by the legislation of 1836), prisons, and almshouses, none of which was suitable for such inmates. The only proper policy was one that secured the transfer of all insane persons from poorhouses and jails to hospitals (pp. 154–174).

Before offering any specific proposals to the legislature, Jarvis felt constrained to discuss the Worcester hospital, which still cared for a substantial proportion of the state's mentally ill population. This institution, Jarvis wrote in regretful but clear words, represented "the past age, while the wants of the patients are measured by the means offered in the present." After listing the many deficiencies of the hospital, Jarvis recommended against investing any substantial sums in renovating the physical plant; instead he supported the suggestion that it be sold and the proceeds used to purchase a new site (pp. 174–182).[93]

[93] Several months before Jarvis completed his report, the trustees of the Worcester hospital had sent their annual report to the legislature. In this document they presented a detailed analysis of the problems facing the hospital. Led by Howe, the trustees pointed out that the proper function of a hospital was therapeutic; yet overcrowding was rapidly subverting the original ideal. Even more, the patients, "instead of being partly drawn according to the original purpose from an intelligent and educated yeomanry, are drawn mainly from a class which has no refinement, no culture, and not much civilization even [the alien Irish]—that hospital must certainly degenerate." Because the hospital contained large numbers of Irish and criminally insane patients, its public image was adversely affected. Consequently, many native citizens were reluctant to send their friends and relatives to Worcester, even though they had great difficulty paying the higher costs of a private institution. This situation, according to the trustees, was leading to greater pressure for additional private hospitals and asylums. The multiplication of private establishments, however, "would be a great evil," yet one that could be prevented only by making public hospitals unobjectionable residences for patients from all walks of life.

Unfortunately, the trustees continued, the Worcester hospital was considerably below the minimum standards that any institution ought to observe. The physical structure was obsolete, monotonous, and depressing, giving the hospital a melancholy appearance. Visitors were usually impressed "by the grave deportment, the serious countenances, the almost melancholy aspects of attendants and

Having discussed the problems of mental disease, Jarvis and his fellow commissioners then offered five distinct proposals to improve conditions and to establish a consistent policy for the Commonwealth. In the first place, they urged that a new hospital be built, preferably in the western part of the state. Second, the sale of the Worcester hospital should be postponed until the new one was ready for occupancy. Then, if the legislature gave its approval, it should be sold and the proceeds used for the erection of a new hospital in that city. Third, the legislature should consider establishing a separate hospital for state paupers. Fourth, the law of 1836, which had required counties to maintain receptacles for the nonviolent insane, should be repealed and the counties thereby relieved of the responsibility for these persons. Finally, the commissioners recommended that the laws relating to insanity and hospitals be revised and a more modern and systematic code be adopted (p. 184).

Early in March the final report was sent to the legislature. So thoroughly had Jarvis done his work that few critical or dissenting voices were heard. On the contrary, the initial reception of the report was highly laudatory. The Committee on Public Charitable Institutions, cognizant of the pioneering nature of the document, arranged for ten thousand copies to be printed (in place of the normal edition of sixteen hundred) and to be distributed nationally as well as locally; it also asked Jarvis to write its report to the legislature and draft the law providing for the establishment of a new state hospital. When the bill came up before the General Court it encountered no opposition; in less than three months a hospital for 250 patients and an appropriation of $200,000 had been authorized.[94]

---

patients . . . There is a leaden gravity which seems to defy relaxation; and a gloomy air about the establishment, which must be unfavorable to the cure of insane patients." Lack of facilities for occupational therapy further reinforced the unfavorable internal atmosphere; less than one quarter of the patients were able to find any sort of useful work.

The trustees were particularly vehement in their denunciation of seclusion and restraint. "Seclusion of an insane person," they remarked in revealing terms, "is a dainty word for expressing his imprisonment in a cell. Restraint is a dainty substitute for fettering his hands or feet, or both, the fetters being of leather instead of iron." Such techniques, they noted, resulted from crowded conditions. Restraint, in other words, was a means of maintaining order; therapeutic considerations were of secondary importance. The complete text of the discussion by the trustees can be found in the Worcester State Lunatic Hospital, *Annual Report*, 22 (1854), 8–36.

[94] Jarvis, Mss. Autobiography, 162–164; *Boston Medical and Surgical Journal*, 53 (December 20, 1855), 433; Chap. 454, Act of May 21, 1855, in *Acts and Resolves Passed by the General Court of Massachusetts, in the Year 1855* (Boston, 1855), 870.

I have not dealt with the brief discussion of idiocy that appeared in the *Report on Insanity*. Jarvis himself pointed out that the legislature's basic objective was to

The immediate result of Jarvis's work was the decision to erect a new state hospital. After a preliminary survey, the committee charged with the responsibility of selecting a site and supervising construction decided to locate the new hospital in Northampton, thereby giving the western part of the state access to a public facility. The legislature's favorable attitude, however, proved of short duration. Less than a year after giving its approval the House directed the Committee on Public Charitable Institutions to inquire into the expediency of suspending all further work and liquidating the project. The committee, in turn, reported back that a third hospital was not needed, that insanity was declining, and that the state did not lack adequate accommodations for the insane. Although the legislature eventually decided to continue work, further controversy developed when the Committee on Finance charged that the cost of the new hospital was exceeding the authorized limit. Finally, after many recriminations, the Northampton hospital was completed in 1858.[95]

If the sole result of the *Report on Insanity* was the erection of a single additional state hospital, it would hardly have merited Jarvis's own judgment that the project was "the most successful of his life." Far more significant were the long-range and intangible results of his study, which easily transcended the founding of one additional state hospital. Aside from the statistical data and the recommendations that the state assume greater responsibility for the mentally ill, Jarvis's most important contribution was his discussion of insanity in terms of social, ethnic, and class differences. More than any other person before him, Jarvis had explicitly related poverty to mental disease and offered hard evidence that seemed to prove his case. In the long run, therefore, he had supported a growing belief among many Americans that poverty and character were related and that mental (as well as other) diseases were associated with impoverished groups, particularly those coming from a minority ethnic background. His data, moreover, seemed to contradict the belief that insanity, given early treatment, was a largely curable malady. The result was a sharp reinforcement of the

---

amass knowledge of the insane and insanity rather than idiocy. Consequently, he had simply gathered some raw data on idiocy in the hope that it would serve in the future as a basis for developing a humane and comprehensive policy on idiocy. See the *Report on Insanity and Idiocy in Massachusetts,* 79.

[95] Mass. *House Document No. 18* (January 9, 1856), 2–3; *Report of the Committee on Public Charitable Institutions,* Mass. *House Document No. 138* (March 25, 1856), 1–4; Mass. *House Document No. 215* (April 22, 1856), 2–4; *Report of the Committee on Finance,* Mass. *House Document No. 146* (March 16, 1858), 1–8; *Boston Medical and Surgical Journal,* 54 (April 24, 1856), 246.

unfavorable image that state hospitals evoked in the minds of many citizens. For if state institutions received predominantly lower-class patients (as indeed they did) whose illness was related to moral deficiencies, did it not follow that they were undesirable (though necessary) places, especially if alternatives were available in the form of private asylums that accepted a more restricted clientele?

In other and more subtle ways Jarvis's report had an effect other than the one he had intended. He had begun with the assumption that a large number of small curative hospitals was superior to fewer but larger ones. Yet his one specific proposal was to have the state establish an additional hospital for 250 patients. While practical considerations may have prevented him from offering more fundamental suggestions, it was evident that he was still dealing with mental disease within the traditional individualistic framework. Could one more hospital, caring for 250 patients, meet the growing needs of the Commonwealth? Indeed, what would prevent the new hospital from becoming what the other two already were, namely, large custodial institutions? In other words, Jarvis's conception of the ideal mental hospital was phrased in the language and ideals of earlier decades. Not once in his long report did he discuss the hospital as a complex institution where the requirements of an individualisticly oriented therapy might clash with the necessities of social organization.

Why did Jarvis repeat themes that had been commonplace for several decades? Quite probably inertia played a part, for it was easier to restate accepted doctrine than to offer new approaches. By remaining within the prevailing intellectual and institutional framework, Jarvis avoided the controversy that might have easily followed more drastic or unorthodox recommendations. Perhaps most significant, however, was Jarvis's faith in individualized treatment in a small hospital where close personal relationships between doctors and patients were the rule rather than the exception. Like many Americans, his outlook and social philosophy had been conditioned by individualistic ideas and values. Implicitly rejecting the social, economic, and technological transformation of American society, Jarvis's values were characteristic of a rural and agrarian nation. So strong was the hold of his individualistic assumptions that his psychiatric ideas reflected his social ideology. In his view, the only proper hospital was one that remained small, emphasized close interpersonal relationships, cared for a homogeneous group of patients sharing a common cultural heritage and outlook and thereby preserved the identity of the individual. Responsibility for mental illness, he consistently averred, resided with the individual. And when moral therapy seemed ineffective, he chose to place the blame on the individual rather than the physician. Jarvis was never fully aware of the role that his own values and philosophy played in his analyses of the problems posed by mental disease. As a result, his investigation did little to impede the development of the public mental hospital as a broad welfare-type institution unable to fulfil its medical and therapeutic functions.

VIII

Had the *Report on Insanity* been merely another parochial document of concern and interest to only a few citizens in the Bay State, it would hardly merit a prominent position in the social history of nineteenth-century American psychiatry and welfare. Many state and local studies of mental illness, after all, have been consigned—with good reason—to the musty shelves of libraries. The *Report on Insanity*, however, occupies a somewhat unique place in the history of public policy toward mental illness. If only for its wealth of detail and the efforts that went into its preparation the report stands apart from other comparable investigations. But in addition, its analysis and conclusions anticipated the future evolution of mental hospitals, although in a way not clearly understood by Jarvis or his contemporaries. Having introduced social, class, and ethnic factors into his discussion of public policy, Jarvis never realized that these would far outweigh his prevailing optimism about the prognosis of mental illness. In the long run, therefore, his study reinforced a growing hostility toward mental hospitals, a hostility whose intensity increased as these institutions assumed a custodial function for poor and indigent groups.

The significance of the *Report on Insanity* was further enhanced by the influential role of the Commonwealth of Massachusetts during the nineteenth century. A center of learning and excellence, the Bay State was in many respect the cultural and intellectual leader of American society. At the same time, it was also the acknowledged architect and pioneer among states in developing institutions and structures relating to welfare and philanthropy, to say nothing of its activities in education. It was the first state to develop a comprehensive system of public mental hospitals; it pioneered in the area of public health; it also established the first Board of State Charities—the forerunner of the modern state welfare department.[96] Other states tended to follow its activities closely, and usually emulated its policies. As a result, the *Report on Insanity* received far greater notice than other state studies of social and medical problems.

A few months after its publication, the Jarvis report was the subject of an extended discussion at the tenth annual meeting of the Association of Medical Superintendents of American Institutions for the Insane. Virtually everyone attending the convention agreed that the report far surpassed in thoroughness and utility any previous study of mental illness. Luther Bell, for example, paid tribute to the "extraordinary care and accuracy with which the statistics of Massachusetts insanity had been reached." Thomas S. Kirkbride, echoing Bell's laudatory comments, expressed the hope that other states would follow the lead of the Commonwealth and undertake similar studies. Isaac Ray agreed that the *Report on Insanity* was worthy of "the highest commendation." Upon motion of Kirkbride, the Association unanimously adopted a resolution characterizing Jarvis's work "as the first successful attempt, in America, to secure entirely reliable statistics on this subject." It also expressed gratification at the special action of the legislature in approving a third state hospital.[97]

The laudatory comments made by the leaders of the young psychiatric profession were seconded by both the *Boston Medical and Surgical Journal* and the *American Journal of Insanity*. The former (a highly respected periodical with a national circulation) summarized the impressive response to the report in the Massachusetts legislature and then urged further involvement in social problems by the medical profession. The entire episode, it noted, "should furthermore encourage physicians to unite and exert themselves in any cause worthy of such an effort. How many such there are, and how much might be effected by the combined wisdom and strength of a profession, the vast majority of which is actuated by motives of the purest philanthropy!"[98] The *American Journal of Insanity* promptly reprinted much of the article appearing in the *Boston Medical and Surgical Journal* as well as the report by the Massachusetts legislature's Committee

[96] For an excellent study of the role of the state government in Massachusetts during the nineteenth century see Oscar and Mary F. Handlin, *Commonwealth: A Study of the Role of Government in the American Economy: Massachusetts, 1774–1861* (rev. ed.: Cambridge, Mass.: Harvard University Press, 1969). Richard M. Abrams, *Conservatism in a Progressive Era: Massachusetts Politics, 1900–1912* (Cambridge, Mass.: Harvard University Press, 1964), emphasizes the liberalism of nineteenth-century Massachusetts.

[97] The discussion at the convention can be found in the *American Journal of Insanity*, 12 (July 1855), 94–97.

[98] *Boston Medical and Surgical Journal*, 53 (December 20, 1855), 433.

on Public Charitable Institutions, both of which cast the *Report on Insanity* in a very favorable light.[99]

Within a year after its appearance, a number of nationally known journals also had published lengthy articles summarizing the findings of the Jarvis report. Pliny Earle, one of the most famous alienists of the nineteenth century, thought the document sufficiently significant to merit a detailed summary of its evidence and conclusions. After reviewing some of its major statistical contributions in a paper published in the *American Journal of the Medical Sciences*, Earle singled out those parts of the study relating to pauperism and mental illness in which Jarvis had discussed poverty in terms of an "inward principle." Although disagreeing slightly with Jarvis's calculations comparing the incidence of insanity among paupers with that of more affluent groups, Earle had only praise for the work. "The objects of this commission were of great import, regarded in the light of either medical science, humanity, or political economy," he concluded. "The pursuit of them involved a vast amount of labour; the results of which are embodied in a work which, in its kind, has never been equalled on this side of the Atlantic, never excelled beyond it. Its statistics are probably more accurate than any of a similar kind which have ever been collected. It is replete with suggestions which, although intended for specific and local application, will be of essential importance and assistance, in each and every other of the States of the Union where the same or similar objects may come before the attention of the legislature or its Commissioners."[100]

Earle's laudatory comments were echoed in an article in the *Journal of Prison Discipline and Philanthropy*, the organ of a group of Pennsylvania prison reformers. After summarizing Jarvis's impressive statistical contributions, the article went on to note that the most interesting feature of the document lay in its detailed information on the subject of pauperism. That the *Journal* emphasized this aspect of the Jarvis report was not surprising, since it had as one of its primary goals the extirpation of crime (which was related to poverty, indolence, and an imperfect welfare system). Quoting Jarvis's statement on poverty, the article went on to argue that his evidence clearly necessitated a greater emphasis on the prevention of poverty. "Very few paupers," it argued, "have enjoyed the advantages of a common, intellectual and industrial education . . . Whatever capacity

---

[99] "The Massachusetts Lunacy Commission," *American Journal of Insanity*, 12 (January 1856), 259–266.

[100] Earle's review of the *Report on Insanity and Idiocy in Massachusetts* appeared in the *American Journal of the Medical Sciences*, N. S. 31 (April 1856), 429–436.

they might have possessed has been buried, almost to extinction, under years of neglect; and habits of sloth and sheer animal indulgence have taken an iron grasp upon them." The moral was clear; society had a firm obligation to protect itself against the results of improper child rearing. "We cannot admit the right of any member of society to bring up his children as he lists. If a stranger is seen at midnight, approaching a haystack or a barn with a lighted torch in his hand, we are not bound to wait till he applies it before we arrest his arm. So neither are we to give the perverse or negligent head of a family the oppor- tunity to thrust upon society a troop of ignorant, ill-bred, and vicious (because idle) children, lest by timely interposition, we should seem to be trespassing on the liberty of the parent or citizen." Like many other contemporary reformers, the *Journal* saw no inherent contradiction between its individualistic values and its advocacy of the use of the power and authority of the state to achieve a desirable goal even at the expense of de- priving a socially undesirable group of certain rights. Fear of poverty and the poor outweighed moral principle. In effect, the thrust of the article demonstrated the peculiar relationship that some Americans of the 1850's drew between mental illness and pauperism—a relationship that played a crucial role in the evolution of the mental hospital in the United States.[101]

Undoubtedly the most detailed and perceptive analysis of the *Report on Insanity* was provided by Isaac Ray for the *North Ameri- can Review,* one of the most influential intellectual periodicals of the nineteenth century. Possessed of a keen, inquiring, and skeptical mind, Ray's pre-eminent position in American psy- chiatry had been confirmed in the late 1830's when he published a classic work on the medical jurisprudence of insanity.[102] Throughout his long career Ray subjected much of the accepted knowledge of mental disease to rigorous scrutiny and often found it wanting. His analysis of the Jarvis report, therefore, was that of an individual universally acknowledged as one of the foremost leaders of the young specialty of psychiatry.

Ray began his paper by pointing out that statistical evidence had hitherto been ambiguous in nature. It was possible, for

[101] *Journal of Prison Discipline and Philanthropy,* 11 (January 1856), 10–24. The remainder of the article was devoted to a discussion of the need for the early treatment of mental illness and the impropriety of incarcerating criminal lunatics in mental hospitals with guiltless and innocent individuals.

[102] Isaac Ray, *A Treatise on the Medical Jurisprudence of Insanity* (Boston, 1838). In addition to an English edition published a year after the American edition, the book went through four subsequent editions. By the fifth edition, which appeared in 1871, the work had been expanded from the original 480 pages to 658. The first edition has been recently reissued with an introduction by Win- fred Overholser (Cambridge, Mass.: Harvard University Press, 1962).

example, to ascertain the sex, age, and occupation of the insane. It was impossible, on the other hand, to determine precisely the causes of the disease or the chances for recovery. In this respect most reports of American mental hospitals were notably deficient; they had attempted, with little success, to present in a statistical form phenomena more or less doubtful and subjective. The major contribution of the Jarvis report was a hitherto unattained precision in collecting hard data and avoiding speculation. "Never, perhaps," Ray wrote, "has a statistical inquiry been pursued with such ample provisions against error and imperfection, or with results more worthy of reliance. In all those respects which render such a work of any value,—accuracy, completeness, and pertinence,—we doubt if it has ever been surpassed."[103]

Nevertheless, Ray was not convinced that the report was completely free from errors. He noted that it seemed clear that the incidence of insanity in Massachusetts was higher than in any other state. The explanation that this situation resulted from the fact that the foreign insane were more numerous than the native-born insane (as compared with the same population of their respective classes) did not necessarily follow. Ray particularly objected to the way in which idiots had been handled, since he was not at all certain that adult idiots (who according to the figures in the *Report on Insanity* outnumbered idiots under the age of sixteen by three to one) constituted a class distinct from the mentally ill. Moreover, if the idiot group (especially adults) were lumped together with the insane, the claim that the incidence of mental illness was highest among foreign born was invalid.[104]

If the high incidence of insanity in the Bay State could not be attributed to the accretion of immigrants in the population, what could account for it? The figures, Ray noted, did not lend themselves to the popular and widely held explanation that mental illness was more prevalent in manufacturing and mercantile communities than in farming areas. Some evidence existed, however, that older and more stable communities had the highest rates of insanity. Since at least one third of all cases of insanity had a hereditary origin, areas with an inbred population tended to perpetuate and increase the frequency of this malady. "In the old farming towns," Ray pointed out, "the

[103] Isaac Ray, "Statistics of Insanity in Massachusetts," *North American Review*, 82 (January 1856), 79–81. Like most articles published in this journal, Ray's was unsigned. Because of its approach and style, it is probable that most knowledgeable and informed individuals were able to identify its author.
[104] *Ibid.*, 82–84.

growth of which is chiefly limited by the natural increase of the inhabitants, the same families intermarry, year after year, and thus not only deteriorate the stock, but perpetuate any specific morbid tendencies they may have contracted." Nevertheless, Ray did not attempt to provide a definitive answer to the problem of the high incidence of mental illness in the Commonwealth.[105]

Ray then moved on to a discussion of the relationship between poverty and mental illness. In this respect it is worth noting that virtually every analysis of the report sooner or later focused on poverty as a significant element in the problem. Without doubt, argued Ray, insanity "may be traced, in many instances, more or less directly to poverty." After quoting Jarvis's statement that poverty was an "inward principle," he nevertheless questioned whether the kind of destitution implied in the report was particularly common in the United States. Yet in the next paragraph Ray expressed some doubt about the curability of insanity among foreigners as compared with native Americans. In New England hospitals Irish patients were "pre-eminently incurable, though promptly subjected to hospital treatment." Moreover, there was no doubt that the Irish occupied a disproportionately high percentage of places in hospitals and receptacles. In discussing this state of affairs, Ray strongly supported the recommendation that the state establish a separate institution for foreign insane patients. Such an arrangement, he maintained,

> would unquestionably obviate many of the evils which impair the usefulness of the present system, and is itself as free from objections as the case will ever permit. The native and the foreigner are no more disposed to mingle in the hospital than in the ordinary walks of life, and this repugnance of tastes, habits, and faith leads to mutual dislike and irritation. While the association of races is thus productive of many evils, it would be hard to find in it a single compensatory benefit. The management and attendance, being exclusively in the hands of natives, fail to inspire in the foreign patient that kind of regard and confidence which is necessary to the restorative process. Here something more is requisite than kindness and patience; for even though they secure his respect, they may utterly fail to gain his confidence. This result is the fruit of all those arts of management which require an intimate knowledge of the patient's ways and manners, his peculiar modes of thinking and expression, his local tastes and associations. Without this knowledge, the efforts of the attendant will make but little impression. His offers of service will be viewed with distrust, and the most innocent jest will be taken as an insult; while the utter want of any community of feeling in

[105] *Ibid.,* 84–85.

politics, religion, and historical associations, must prevent them from being anything but strangers to each other. If we would secure for the foreigner the highest amount of good from hospital treatment, we should place him in the charge of those whose sympathies are quickened by stronger ties than are generally produced by an abstract love of the race. On the native patient, the effect of the separation would be equally, if not more beneficial. Those whose disorder is not so grave as to deprive them of all sense of social propriety, or to destroy their susceptiblity to all moral impressions, must necessarily be annoyed and disquieted by persons whose looks and manifestations are of the most disagreeable kind. In passing through the public hospitals of this State, one is painfully struck by the large proportion of patients presenting the most degraded and hopeless phases of insanity. The stoutest heart might quail before this sad exhibition of humanity, and how can it be supposed that it can be contemplated without emotion by those whose sensibilities are all heightened by disease?[106]

Ray then followed up his proposal for a separate institution for foreign insane paupers with a suggestion that the Commonwealth consider the feasability of establishing two hospitals for state paupers. The first would care for curable patients; the other would provide custodial care for incurable cases. The former would by necessity remain small, since the requirements of therapy were complex and demanding. The latter, on the other hand, could accept more cases and subordinate staff could supervise much of the daily routine. "The State," concluded Ray, "has now another opportunity of establishing a hospital for the insane creditable to its intelligence and wealth, and if its authorites are governed by any regard to public sentiment, such must needs be their action. In the magnitude of its enterprises for advancing its material interests, Massachusetts stands without a rival. The higher distinction of outstripping its sister States in the unexceptionable excellence of its institutions for the relief of suffering, it has yet to achieve."[107]

Aside from the formal discussions of its findings, the *Report on Insanity* was often held up as a model for other states. The superintendent of the Maine Insane Hospital, for example, applied its statistical findings to his own state, thereby demonstrating the need for greater public support. Dr. Daniel H. Trezevant of the South Carolina Lunatic Asylum asked Jarvis to send him a copy of the report in order to induce the legislature of his state to provide greater financial support for its own mentally ill citizens. And as late as 1869 Isaac Ray could still applaud the Jarvis report as one of the few truly scientific

[106] *Ibid.*, 85–88, 94–96. The quoted extract is from pp. 95–96.
[107] *Ibid.*, 96–99.

documents in the history of American psychiatry. Critical or hostile evaluations of the *Report on Insanity* were virtually nonexistent.[108]

IX

Although written more than a century ago, the *Report on Insanity* still remains of considerable interest to our own generation. At the present time most Americans would probably favor concerted efforts to deal with the social and individual problems arising out of mental disease. Yet relatively few are aware of the dilemmas and complexities posed by this disturbing malady. For the fact of the matter is that mental illness, more so than other diseases, has involved differing and sometimes conflicting attitudes and values on the part of society, patients, and therapists. Nevertheless, those individuals and groups responsible for the formulation and implementation of public policy have rarely taken into account these attitudes and values, which have often played significant roles in determining the nature of care and therapy within mental hospitals.

In this respect the *Report on Insanity* is an excellent illustrative case study in the history of public policy toward mental illness. The highly favorable reception given to Jarvis's report was a clear indication that by 1855 the problems posed by mental illness were inextricably intertwined with the broader issues of indigency and welfare. Yet the belief that insanity was no different from other forms of disease was so pronounced that few individuals were able to recognize or understand that the report was also to a large extent related to a particular social ideology. Like many professionals, Jarvis had undertaken a study of a problem within the framework of his speciality. Consequently, he never grasped the full significance of what he had actually accomplished. Indeed, the importance of the *Report on Insanity* was that it accurately reflected many of the dominant characteristics of nineteenth-century American society. In the long run, therefore, the work of Jarvis was important not because of its specific recommendations, but because it defined the issue within a particular framework. In this sense it helped to legitimatize the emergence of the state mental hospital as a welfare-type institution.

[108] Maine Insane Hospital, *Annual Report*, 15 (1855), 19–20; Daniel H. Trezevant to Edward Jarvis, November 28, 1855, Jarvis Papers, Countway Medical Library, Harvard Medical School, Boston, Massachusetts; and Isaac Ray, *Address Delivered by Isaac Ray, M. D., of Philadelphia, on the Occasion of Laying the Corner Stone of the State Hospital for the Insane, at Danville, Pa. August 26, 1869* (Harrisburg, 1869), 17. The annual reports of American mental hospitals in the 1850's and 1860's abound with frequent references to the *Report on Insanity*.

REPORT

ON

INSANITY AND IDIOCY

IN

MASSACHUSETTS,

BY THE

COMMISSION ON LUNACY,

UNDER

RESOLVE OF THE LEGISLATURE OF 1854.

BOSTON:

WILLIAM WHITE, PRINTER TO THE STATE,

1855.

5028

BOSTON MEDICAL

MAR 10 1906

LIBRARY.

EXPLANATORY NOTE.

The facts contained in this Report were gathered, in accordance with the Resolve of the Legislature of 1854, during the autumn and December of that year. The returns of the number, condition and situation of the lunatics, which were received from the physicians, overseers of the poor, the superintending officers of hospitals and other public establishments, were digested, the tables were prepared, and the Report written, during the winter of 1854–5.

The Report shows these facts as they were when the returns were received; but since it was written, and while it was in press, several of the insane and idiotic State paupers were transferred from the receptacles, &c., to the State almshouses. This changed their location, but not their condition, nor their relation to the Commonwealth.

CONTENTS.

CONTENTS.

CONTENTS.

CONTENTS.

Commonwealth of Massachusetts.

In Senate, May 5, 1855.

ORDERED, That three thousand and five hundred copies of the Report of the Commissioners on Insanity and Idiocy, also the same number of the Report of the Committee on Public Charitable Institutions, (House Doc. 282,) be printed, and a copy of each bound together. Said copies to be in addition to any number which may have heretofore been ordered, and to be printed under the supervision of the said Commissioners ; and that a sufficient number of copies be placed in the hands of the Commissioners to enable them to send one copy to each Clergyman, Physician, Superintendent of Hospital, Sheriff, Town Officer, or other person in America or Great Britain, who aided the said Commissioners in preparing their Report, by furnishing facts, giving counsel, or otherwise ; and that the remainder be left with the Secretary for the use of the Commonwealth.

Sent down for concurrence.

P. L. COX, *Clerk.*

HOUSE OF REPRESENTATIVES, May 7, 1855.

Concurred.

H. A. MARSH, *Clerk.*

A true copy.

Attest :

P. L. COX, *Clerk of the Senate.*

●

Commonwealth of Massachusetts.

To His Excellency HENRY J. GARDNER, *Governor, and the Honorable the Council of the Commonwealth of Massachusetts :—*

The undersigned, the Commissioners appointed under the Resolve of the Legislature of 1854, " concerning the Insane in this Commonwealth, and the State Lunatic Hospital of Worcester," respectfully
●

REPORT.

The Resolves by which their commission was created required of them,—

1. " To ascertain the number and condition of the insane in the State, distinguishing as accurately as may be between the insane, properly so considered, and the idiotic or *non compos;* between the furious and the harmless, curable and incurable, and between the native and the foreigner, and the number of each who are State paupers."

2. " To examine into the present condition of the Hospitals of the State for the insane, and see what number of patients can properly, with due regard to their comfort and improvement, be accommodated in said Hospitals."

3. " To see what further accommodations, if any, are needed for the relief and care of the insane."

2

4. " And, generally, to examine and report the best and most approved plans for the management of the insane, so far as the size and character of Hospitals, and the number of patients proper to be under one supervision are concerned."

5. " To examine into the present condition of the State Lunatic Hospital at Worcester, and ascertain what kind and amount of repairs are needed, and at what probable cost, and consider the expediency of disposing of the said Hospital and the lands connected therewith, or any part thereof, and of recommending a site for the erection of a new Hospital or Hospitals."

6. " To report the estimated proceeds of the sale of the present Hospital and the grounds therewith connected at Worcester, if they deem such a sale desirable."

7. " To accompany their Report with plans, specifications and estimates of cost of any new Hospital which they may recommend."

As early as possible after receiving their appointment, the Commissioners addressed themselves to the work assigned them by the Legislature.

On careful consideration of the language and spirit of the Resolves and the purposes of the Legislature in reference to this matter, they thought that the number and condition of the insane in the State, their prospects and their wants, lay at the foundation of all further action, and that therefore this inquiry should be first made. They then determined to make the requisite enumeration of the insane and idiots, and ascertain all the facts concerning them specified in the law, as the first step in their work, before they should proceed to the others, except so far as they might be attended to incidentally, while in pursuit of the first object.

In order " to ascertain the number and condition of the insane and idiots in this Commonwealth," it was necessary either to visit every family, in person or by proper agents, to make the inquiry, or to obtain the facts of those who already knew them. The former, the personal inquiry from house to house, if done by the Commissioners, would probably require some years to accomplish the object; and if done by others, it would require the aid of so many as to make the work exceedingly expensive. And moreover, it is not probable that the facts could be thus ascertained by the inquiry of agents at the doors of the several families through the State; for most people, whose friends or relatives are disordered in mind or deficient in intellect, are unwilling to talk about it, and many would be still more unwilling to confess these painful and disagreeable facts and circumstances in their domestic relations, to a stranger. And if that inquiry were made by a public officer or agent of the government who had no personal claim upon their confidence, and who sought these facts apparently to be used in a public report, many of them would undoubtedly refuse to give the information required.

In 1850, the marshals, the agents of the National Government who were appointed to take the census, visited every family; and, among other items of information, they asked for the insane and idiots in the household.

By this personal and official inquiry, made of some responsible member of every family, the marshals obtained the account of only sixteen hundred and eighty insane persons and seven hundred and ninety-one idiots, which is but little more than two-thirds of the number ascertained by this Commission.

Making all due allowance for the increase of population, and consequently of the insane and idiots, these figures undoubtedly show far less than the real amount of insanity and idiocy at that time, and render it extremely probable, that many concealed the facts that the law required them to state to the marshals.

PLAN OF THE INQUIRY—PHYSICIANS EMPLOYED.

In view of these difficulties, of making the inquiry from each family, the Commissioners sought out other plans. They considered that there are very few families that are not within the personal knowledge of some practitioner of medicine, and that therefore the whole Commonwealth is, in detail, under the eye of the medical profession; and that they, knowing the domestic condition of the whole people, were of course acquainted with all those whose minds were disordered or defective.

Accordingly the Commission determined to address every

physician in the State, asking each one to give information relative to the persons and condition of all the lunatics and idiots within his own knowledge.   They sent a lithograph letter, stating the several objects of inquiry, and enclosed a printed schedule or form of return, which contained all the heads under which the answers were to be recorded.   They asked for the name, sex, color, age, country of birth, whether single, married or widowed, whether lunatic or idiot, present and usual condition, whether mild, manageable, troublesome excitable, furious or dangerous, whether subject for a hospital or not, length of disease, if periodical the number of attacks, whether curable or not, whether the remedial influences of any hospital had ever been tried for restoration, where resident if not in the town of the reporter, and whether State or town pauper, or independent.

It was supposed that these fifteen questions would elicit all the information which the Legislature required, all that science would desire, and all that could be conveniently obtained from those of whom the inquiry was made.

Although every family was presumed to come under the cognizance of some physician, as most families have one, who attends them in their sickness, yet there are some whose various members employ two or more physicians to heal them. Each of these might observe and return the same lunatic or idiot member of the family, who would thus be reported more than once.   Therefore the names were asked to enable the Commissioners to correct any mistake that might arise from this double or multiplied reporting.   In course of the inquiry this has happened in many instances.   With a view of this liability, the several reports from the same towns have always been compared, and the error of counting the same person more than once prevented.

To save the feelings of patients or friends who would be pained if their individual cases were told abroad, and to save the physicians from any violation of implied professional confidence, a pledge was given that none but the Commission should see the names of the persons reported.   And in fulfilment of this promise, after the reports were compared and corrections made for the duplications, the names were erased.

As in sixteen towns in the State there are no physicians, letters were sent to the clergymen, on the supposition that they were acquainted with the condition of all the families; and also the overseers of the poor were asked to return the paupers ; and besides these, the physicians of the neighboring towns who attended the sick in these places were especially asked to return any insane and idiots who might be in the families of the towns not their own.

Besides, similar letters and schedules were sent to the Superintendents of the Lunatic Hospitals in Worcester, Taunton, Somerville and Boston, to the officers of the county receptacles for the insane in Cambridge and Ipswich, and personal inquiry was made of the masters of all the Houses of Correction and Jails in the State, and of the proprietors of all the private houses or establishments devoted to the care of the insane, asking each to make a similar return of the lunatics and idiots under his care. And in order to complete this survey, letters were sent to officers of all the hospitals in the Northern and Middle, and some of the Southern States, asking them to make returns of all the insane patients belonging to Massachusetts who were intrusted to their charge.

By this means the Commissioners believed, that they should be able to reach nearly every insane and idiotic person who belonged to Massachusetts, and to reveal the sum of mental disorder or deficiency resting upon the children, citizens and wards of this Commonwealth, more completely than they could in any other way.

These letters were sent out in July and August, and were very kindly received. The physicians generally gave the work their ready sympathy and coöperation. The leading members of the medical profession encouraged and aided it. The Councillors of the Massachusetts Medical Society voted to approve the work and the plan of its operation, and advised all the members of the society to assist in the inquiry, and lend their influence to persuade all others to do the same. The County Societies which held their meetings within the period of this survey gave it their active assistance; and officers of every other society which did not meet gave their active and earnest help to this work within their respective spheres.

The Commissioners are also especially indebted to several physicians in the various parts of the State, who were indefatigable in their coöperation. They visited their neighboring towns; they wrote to, and used their personal influence with, the tardy brethren of their vicinity; and were ready to render any aid which the Commission, from time to time, might ask of them, to persuade the slow or the unwilling to answer the inquiry made of them.

Besides these, the Commission received assistance, from the hands of gentlemen out of the profession, in several towns where aid was wanted. And in all the towns, where their evidence seemed to be needed, the selectmen and the overseers of the poor rendered free and acceptable service in the work.

In the four western counties, and also in Worcester, Essex, Norfolk, Bristol, and in Barnstable County especially, the Commission received great aid from the newspapers, whose liberal editors urged upon the physicians and others to answer this call, and make complete returns of all the lunatics and idiots within their respective spheres of observation.

It was unfortunate for the immediate success of this inquiry that it was made in July, August and September, the most sickly season, when the physicians are the most intensely occupied and burdened with the greatest anxiety in the care of acute and dangerous diseases. Notwithstanding this, a great majority answered within the time prescribed; but yet there were many whose professional labors and cares prevented their doing so as early as was desired; and some thus overlooked and forgot the letter, and needed again to be reminded.

In order to create a further and more active interest in the work, one of the Commissioners visited the districts where new influence seemed to be needed, and had personal interviews with the physicians in sixty-four towns who had, thus far, failed to make the returns.

These circulars were sent to

Physicians within the State, ...	1,556
Clergymen, ...	20
Overseers of the Poor, ...	74
Selectmen, ...	4

Other gentlemen, ...   5
Superintendents of Hospitals and private establish-
    ments in the State, ...   6
Masters of County Receptacles, Houses of Correc-
    tion, Jails, and State Almshouses, . . .   11
Superintendents of Hospitals in other States, . .   14
Personal inquiry made of other Masters of Houses
    of Correction and Jailers, ...   12
                                                    ———
                                                    1,702

The names of the physicians were taken from the catalogues
of the County Societies, and from the list in Mr. Adams's
State Register, as furnished to him by the town clerks. But
it was ascertained that two hundred and thirty-seven of these
physicians were either dead, or not in practice, or had removed away, or were unreliable. From these, then, no answers
were expected, leaving thirteen hundred and nineteen who had
opportunities of observation, or whose testimony was reliable,
and from whom reports were therefore desired.

All of these thirteen hundred and nineteen physicians, except
four, made reports directly or indirectly to the Commission.
Most of them reported singly; but in many towns two or more
acted in concert, and sent their facts in one letter and through
one of their number.

Two regular physicians only refused to make any report,
and two irregular practitioners have neglected to make returns;
but the fields of observation of all these gentlemen were very
carefully examined by their more willing or more intelligent
neighbors, and extraordinary pains were taken to obtain collateral information from the overseers of the poor and other
municipal authorities; and thus their towns were thoroughly
examined, and every lunatic and idiot within their borders is
presumed to be returned.

Three or four of the clergymen had removed; but others of
their own profession or the town authorities answered for
them; the rest made the returns.

All the overseers of the poor answered except those in four

towns; in these the selectmen were addressed, and answers obtained.

In this survey the Commission placed their first and almost exclusive reliance on the physicians in the towns where they lived, and on the clergymen and overseers of the poor; but wherever there was any apparent deficiency, they sought information from other sources. After the medical returns had been made and the survey completed, the number of pauper idiots and lunatics thus received was compared with the State Report relating to the poor, published by the Secretary of State, and including the number of idiots and insane returned by the overseers of the poor, as relieved or supported within the year, and it was discovered that in forty-five towns the numbers in the overseers' report exceeded those in the medical returns. A new correspondence was then opened with these public functionaries, and resulted in the proof that, with the exception of four or five towns, the physicians had reported all the pauper insane and idiots that existed at the moment when they made their returns.

Notwithstanding the ready coöperation of a large part of the medical profession and the efficient aid rendered from others, yet it was necessary to write again and again to many, and to visit and confer with and persuade others, in various parts of the State, so that the returns were not all received until the end of December.

RELIABLENESS OF THE REPORTS.

The facts in respect to the number and condition of the insane and idiots in Massachusetts which have been received through these channels, and which are embodied in this report, derive an unquestionable authority from the number, character and position of the witnesses who have testified concerning them. These statements are not the estimates drawn from general observation, nor are they, either totally or in part, calculations founded on some facts; but they are the evidence of fourteen hundred and fifty-one witnesses, each of whom testified to that which he knew and spoke of that which he had seen. Where two or more reported the same cases independently of each other, there was such an agreement of statements as manifested that honest and intelligent men had observed and were speaking of the same facts.   Nearly all of these witnesses are the physicians who are living in every town and in almost every neighborhood.   They understand the nature of defective or diseased minds, and are competent to testify.   They are in the habit of frequent and familiar intercourse with the families, and have therefore the best possible opportunities of knowing the facts that are sought.

The testimony of these practitioners of medicine is aided and corroborated by the evidence of many others who had also opportunities of observation—clergymen, overseers of the poor, selectmen of some of the towns, and others whose position enabled them to know some cases of insanity and idiocy.

This Report of the lunacy and idiocy in Massachusetts may then be considered more complete than could be derived from any other sources and through any other channels.   It may be, however, that some families have moved into the State or the towns of their present residence with an insane or idiotic member, and have had no occasion to call any physician since their present settlement, and therefore none of our witnesses have had opportunity of learning their facts.   Yet these cases are very few, so few as not to vitiate the general accuracy of this Report.

It may then be confidently said that there are, at least, so many insane and idiots in the Commonwealth, and that our State and people have, at least, this amount of burden of insanity and idiocy resting upon them, and that herein is a safe basis of calculation of the amount of public and private responsibility for the restoration or protection of these unfortunate people among us.

NUMBER OF INSANE.

By these means, and with great correspondence, the Commission have ascertained that there were in the autumn of 1854, in the State of Massachusetts, two thousand six hundred and thirty-two lunatics, and ten hundred and eighty-seven idiots—making a total of three thousand seven hundred and nineteen of these persons who need the care and protection of their friends or of the public for their support, restoration or custody.

3

Of the Lunatics,

1,522 were paupers—693 State, and 829 Town, paupers.
1,110 were supported by their own property or by their friends.
—— 2,632

2,007 were natives.
  625 were foreigners.
——2,632

  435 were curable.
2,018 were incurable.
  179 not stated.
——2,632

1,284 were at their homes or in town or city poorhouses.
1,141 were in Hospitals.
  207 were in receptacles for the insane, in Houses of Correction, Jails and State Almshouses.
—— 2,632

Of the Idiots,

670 are supported by friends.
417 are supported by public treasury.
—— 1,087

1,043 are natives.
  44 are foreigners.
—— 1,087

COMPARISON WITH OTHER ENUMERATIONS.

These results differ from those obtained from other surveys made for a similar purpose on the same grounds in Massachusetts, and from the statements made of the number of the insane and idiots, and their ratio to the whole population, obtained from inquiry, estimate, calculation, conjecture, &c., in other countries.

In 1848, a committee of the Legislature, appointed to " consider the whole subject connected with insanity within the

Commonwealth," ascertained and reported the number of insane in this State to be fifteen hundred and twelve, of whom
two hundred and ninety-one were able to furnish the means
of their own support, and eleven hundred and fifty-six were
unable to do so, and the pecuniary condition of sixty-five was
not ascertained.[*]

In making that survey in 1848, the Commissioners addressed
their letters of inquiry " to the municipal authorities of every
city and town in the Commonwealth."

These public officers had direct means of knowing the number and condition of the pauper insane, and probably this part
of the report was complete ; but they had no other facilities of
knowing the condition of those lunatics who were in private
families, and supported by their own property or by their
friends, than other men not in office, and could only speak of
those who were within their circle of personal acquaintance.
Consequently the report included only a part of the independent insane who were then actually in, or belonged to, the
State.

The marshals engaged in taking the national census in 1850,
discovered and reported sixteen hundred and eighty lunatics
and seven hundred and ninety-one idiots—in all, two thousand
four hundred and seventy-one of both classes. It is probable
that many of the families refused or neglected to report to
these officers the insane and idiots who were within their
households.

The census of Great Britain for 1851 gives only the pauper
insane and idiots and those who are within the several public
and private licensed lunatic asylums, and omits all others ;
and the ratio of these to the whole population is given.

In 1844, the British Lunatic Commissioners, in a report of
great value on the state and progress of lunacy in England
and Wales, made an elaborate statement of the number of
lunatics within the kingdom; but this included only the paupers and the patients in all kinds of public and private establishments for them, and those others who were not paupers,

---

[*] Senate Document No. 9, 1849, pages 6, 7.

but under commission—that is, under the guardianship of the Lord Chancellor.

This report did not " include a considerable class of insane persons of all ranks of life under the care of guardians and relations ;" * and of course all those who were not paupers, and who were at their homes, or boarding with friends or in private families, were omitted.

An enumeration of the people of France was made within a few years. The facts were sought with great apparent care by the agents of the government, and the results published under its authority, aided by the counsel of men of science. Seventy pages of a folio volume are exclusively devoted to the statement of the number and condition of the insane in every department, in each of the seven years, from 1836 to 1841 inclusive. This would seem to be a perfectly reliable document ; yet a careful analysis suggests some doubt as to its accuracy.

Of the eighty-six departments into which the kingdom is divided, eleven return no lunatics through all of these seven years. Sixty-five return none at their homes or boarding in private families. Some report them in round numbers in even hundreds. Others report the same unvarying number through successive years. One reports two hundred for seven successive years, and another three hundred through six years, without variation. In one, the number increases, in two years, twenty-five hundred per cent., and diminishes as much in four years more. These and many similar statements, equally improbable and unnatural, lead to the inference that they were founded upon estimate, and even conjecture, rather than on personal inquiry and actual enumeration.

In some nations, the statement of the number of the insane includes only those in the public hospitals. A writer in the American Medical Journal assumes this ground to determine the number of insane in some parts of Italy, several of the large cities of Europe and Cairo, and calculates the proportion of lunacy to their several people on this basis.

A census of lunacy in Belgium, apparently taken from actual

* Report of Metropolitan Commission in Lunacy for 1844, page 182.

enumeration, is published in the report of the commissioners appointed to inquire into the means of ameliorating the condition of the insane. This report is complete, and perfectly reliable as a matter of fact and as a basis of calculation.

POPULATION OF MASSACHUSETTS IN 1854.

In order to show the ratio of lunatics and idiots to the existing population, the Commissioners caused the population of each town and county to be determined by logarithmic calculations, and this is included in some of the tables of this Report.*

NUMBER OF INSANE IN TOWNS.

The reports received from the physicians, overseers of the poor, and others, have been carefully analyzed, and their facts reduced to their appropriate heads and presented in the several tables which are incorporated into this Report.

The first table shows, in regard to each town, city and county in the State, the calculated population and the number of lunatics, distinguishing the independent from the pauper, the native from the foreigner, those at home from those in hospitals, receptacles, &c., and the curable from the incurable.

---

* The calculation is based on the census of 1840 and that of 1850. From these the rate of increase is determined, which is supposed to continue the same from 1850 to 1854.

Several new towns have been incorporated or divided subsequent to 1840. In these one of the primary facts was lost; and they are left blank, except that in a few an especial enumeration of the inhabitants was made, which was sufficient for this purpose.

TABLE I.—LUNATICS IN MASSACHUSETTS.

BERKSHIRE COUNTY.

TOWNS.	Population, 1854.	Pecuniary Condition.		Nativity.		Prospect.			Where.		
		Independent.	Pauper.	American.	Foreign.	Curable.	Incurable.	Not stated.	At home.	In hospital, &c.	Total.
Adams, . .	7,574	3	2	5	–	2	3	–	4	1	5
Alford, . .	510	–	1	1	–	–	–	1	1	–	1
Becket, . .	1,190	2	1	3	–	1	2	–	3	–	3
Cheshire, . .	1,450	2	1	3	–	–	3	–	2	1	3
Clarksburg, . .	390	–	1	1	–	–	1	–	–	1	1
Dalton, . .	948	–	–	–	–	–	–	–	–	–	–
Egremont, . .	1,003	–	–	–	–	–	–	–	–	–	–
Florida, . .	618	3	2	5	–	3	2	–	4	1	5
Gt. Barrington, .	3,519	3	4	6	1	2	5	–	5	2	7
Hancock, . .	741	1	–	1	–	–	1	–	1	–	1
Hinsdale, . .	1,397	1	2	3	–	–	3	–	3	–	3
Lanesboro', . .	1,267	3	–	3	–	1	1	1	3	–	3
Lee, . . .	3,604	9	–	9	–	5	4	–	9	–	9
Lenox, . . .	1,730	3	4	7	–	1	6	–	3	4	7
Monterey, . .	682	5	–	5	–	–	1	4	5	–	5
Mt. Washington, .	321	1	–	1	–	–	1	–	1	–	1
New Ashford, .	172	–	–	–	–	–	–	–	–	–	–
New Marlboro', .	1,918	5	5	9	1	3	7	–	8	2	10
Otis, . . .	1,243	–	1	1	–	–	1	–	–	1	1

BERKSHIRE—Continued.

| TOWNS. | Population, 1854. | Pecuniary Condition. | | Nativity. | | Prospect. | | | Where. | | Total. |
		Independent.	Pauper.	American.	Foreign.	Curable.	Incurable.	Not stated.	At home.	In hospital, &c.	
Peru, . . .	498	1	–	1	–	–	1	–	1	–	1
Pittsfield, . .	7,025	10	9	17	2	8	10	1	14	5	19
Richmond, . .	841	3	1	4	–	1	3	–	3	1	4
Sandisfield, . .	1,730	2	2	4	–	–	4	–	4	–	4
Savoy, . . .	971	–	2	2	–	–	2	–	1	1	2
Sheffield, . .	2,971	2	3	5	–	–	5	–	3	2	5
Stockbridge, .	1,920	1	1	2	–	–	–	2	1	1	2
Tyringham, . .	844	–	–	–	–	–	–	–	–	–	–
Washington, .	938	2	–	2	–	1	1	–	2	–	2
W. Stockbridge, .	1,833	1	1	2	–	–	–	2	2	–	2
Williamstown, .	2,847	6	4	8	2	–	10	–	6	4	10
Windsor, . .	897	2	1	3	–	–	3	–	3	–	3
Totals, . .	–	71	48	113	6	28	80	11	92	27	119

FRANKLIN COUNTY.

Ashfield, .	1,316	1	2	3	–	–	3	–	1	2	3
Bernardston, .	913	2	–	2	–	–	2	–	2	–	2
Buckland, .	1,045	1	3	4	–	–	4	–	4	–	4
Charlemont, .	1,182	1	4	4	1	–	5	–	3	2	5
Coleraine, .	1,701	1	1	2	–	1	1	–	2	–	2
Conway, .	2,031	1	–	1	–	–	1	–	1	–	1

FRANKLIN—Continued.

TOWNS.	Population, 1854.	Pecuniary Condition.		Nativity.		Prospect.			Where.		Total.
		Independent.	Pauper.	American.	Foreign.	Curable.	Incurable.	Not stated.	At home.	In hospital' &c.	
Deerfield, . .	2,635	5	5	10	–	3	7	–	7	3	10
Erving, . .	521	–	–	–	–	–	–	–	–	–	–
Gill, . . .	737	1	2	3	–	1	2	–	3	–	3
Greenfield, . .	3,009	–	2	2	–	–	2	–	–	2	2
Hawley, . .	845	–	3	3	–	–	3	–	2	1	3
Heath, . . .	769	–	2	2	–	1	1	–	2	–	2
Leverett, . .	980	1	4	5	–	1	4	–	5	–	5
Leyden, . .	753	2	2	4	–	–	3	1	4	–	4
Monroe, . .	244	1	–	1	–	1	–	–	1	–	1
Montague, . .	1,638	1	5	6	–	1	3	2	6	–	6
New Salem, . .	1,234	1	3	4	–	–	–	4	4	–	4
Northfield, . .	1,817	1	1	2	–	–	2	–	1	1	2
Orange, . .	1,790	3	–	3	–	–	3	–	3	–	3
Rowe, . . .	641	–	–	–	–	–	–	–	–	–	–
Shelburne, . .	1,336	1	3	4	–	–	4	–	2	2	4
Shutesbury, . .	876	4	2	6	–	–	5	1	6	–	6
Sunderland, . .	820	1	–	1	–	–	–	1	1	–	1
Warwick, . .	1,002	1	2	3	–	–	3	–	1	2	3
Wendell, . .	935	1	1	2	–	–	2	–	2	–	2
Whately, . .	1,113	6	–	5	1	1	5	–	5	1	6
Totals, . .	–	37	47	82	2	10	65	9	68	16	84

HAMPSHIRE COUNTY.

TOWNS.	Population, 1854.	Pecuniary Condition.		Nativity.		Prospect.			Where.		Total.
		Independent.	Pauper.	American.	Foreign.	Curable.	Incurable.	Not stated.	At home.	In hospital, &c.	
Amherst, . .	3,162	6	3	9	–	1	8	–	7	2	9
Belchertown, .	2,727	3	1	4	–	–	1	3	3	1	4
Chesterfield, . .	970	–	1	1	–	–	1	–	–	1	1
Cummington, .	1,147	–	3	3	–	–	3	–	2	1	3
Easthampton, .	1,723	1	1	2	–	1	–	1	2	–	2
Enfield, . .	1,060	2	1	3	–	–	3	–	3	–	3
Goshen, . .	495	1	1	2	–	–	2	–	2	–	2
Granby, . .	1,160	1	1	2	–	1	1	–	1	1	2
Greenwich, . .	844	1	4	5	–	–	3	2	5	–	5
Hadley, . .	2,061	–	3	2	1	–	3	–	1	2	3
Hatfield, . .	1,136	5	2	7	–	–	2	5	5	2	7
Middlefield, . .	526	–	2	2	–	–	2	–	2	–	2
Northampton, .	6,050	11	10	17	4	2	17	2	12	9	21
Norwich, . .	758	–	1	1	–	–	1	–	1	–	1
Pelham, . .	994	1	–	1	–	1	–	–	1	–	1
Plainfield, . .	779	4	2	6	–	1	5	–	6	–	6
Prescott, . .	720	1	1	2	–	–	2	–	1	1	2
Southampton, .	1,023	2	1	3	–	–	3	–	3	–	3
South Hadley, .	3,099	1	–	1	–	1	–	–	–	1	1
Ware, . . .	4,989	7	3	9	1	1	9	–	9	1	10
Westhampton, .	549	3	–	3	–	–	3	–	2	1	3
Williamsburg, .	1,639	–	2	2	–	–	2	–	2	–	2
Worthington, .	1,110	–	1	1	–	–	1	–	1	–	1
Totals, . .	–	50	44	88	6	9	72	13	71	23	94

4

HAMPDEN COUNTY.

TOWNS.	Population, 1854.	Pecuniary Condition.		Nativity.		Prospect.			Where.		
		Independent.	Pauper.	American.	Foreign.	Curable.	Incurable.	Not stated.	At home.	In hospital, &c.	Total.
Blandford, . .	1,414	1	–	1	–	–	–	1	1	–	1
Brimfield, . .	1,421	–	1	1	–	–	1	–	1	–	1
Chester, . .	1,479	1	5	6	–	1	5	–	4	2	6
Chicopee, . .	–	1	3	3	1	–	3	1	2	2	4
Granville, . .	1,264	10	2	12	–	2	9	1	11	1	12
Holland, . .	460	–	1	1	–	–	1	–	1	–	1
Holyoke, . .	–	3	3	4	2	1	4	1	4	2	6
Longmeadow, .	1,245	6	2	7	1	2	4	2	6	2	8
Ludlow, . .	1,155	–	–	–	–	–	–	–	–	–	–
Monson, . .	3,169	1	3	4	–	–	4	–	4	–	4
Montgomery, .	305	–	–	–	–	–	–	–	–	–	–
Palmer, . .	5,088	2	–	2	–	–	2	–	2	–	2
Russell, . .	409	–	–	–	–	–	–	–	–	–	–
Southwick, . .	1,084	3	2	5	–	1	4	–	4	1	5
Springfield, . .	–	16	15	23	8	9	21	1	15	16	31
Tolland, . .	581	–	1	1	–	–	1	–	1	–	1
Wales, . . .	721	–	2	2	–	–	1	1	2	–	2
Westfield, . .	4,475	8	4	10	2	1	8	3	9	3	12
W. Springfield, .	–	3	3	6	–	–	6	–	4	2	6
Wilbraham, . .	2,242	2	1	3	–	–	2	1	2	1	3
Totals, . .	–	57	48	91	14	17	76	12	73	32	105

WORCESTER COUNTY.

TOWNS.	Population, 1854.	Pecuniary Condition.		Nativity.		Prospect.			Where.		Total.
		Independent.	Pauper.	American.	Foreign.	Curable.	Incurable.	Not stated.	At home.	In hospital, &c.	
Ashburnham, .	1,972	–	3	3	–	–	3	–	3	–	3
Athol, . .	2,368	–	4	4	–	–	4	–	2	2	4
Auburn, . .	992	–	1	–	1	–	1	–	1	–	1
Barre, . .	3,071	–	3	3	–	–	3	–	3	–	3
Berlin, . .	920	2	1	3	–	–	3	–	1	2	3
Blackstone, .	5,945	5	9	7	7	3	11	–	6	8	14
Bolton, .	1,296	–	1	1	–	–	1	–	–	1	1
Boylston, .	971	1	1	2	–	–	2	–	1	1	2
Brookfield, .	–	5	3	8	–	–	8	–	6	2	8
Charlton, .	1,977	3	2	5	–	–	5	–	4	1	5
Clinton, .	–	–	3	–	3	–	3	–	1	2	3
Dana, . .	911	1	–	1	–	1	–	–	1	–	1
Douglas, .	1,991	6	6	11	1	–	6	6	12	–	12
Dudley, .	1,481	2	1	3	–	1	2	–	2	1	3
Fitchburg, .	6,712	4	7	10	1	3	8	–	7	4	11
Gardner, .	1,658	4	–	4	–	3	1	–	2	2	4
Grafton, .	4,373	5	4	9	–	2	7	–	2	7	9
Hardwick, .	1,572	–	4	4	–	2	1	1	4	–	4
Harvard, .	1,654	7	3	9	1	3	6	1	8	2	10
Holden, .	1,954	2	2	4	–	–	4	–	3	1	4
Hubbardston,	1,841	2	1	3	–	–	3	–	3	–	3
Lancaster, .	–	2	2	3	1	–	4	–	2	2	4
Leicester, .	2,543	1	7	7	1	–	7	1	6	2	8

WORCESTER—Continued.

TOWNS.	Population, 1854.	Pecuniary Condition.		Nativity.		Prospect.			Where.		Total.
		Independent.	Pauper.	American.	Foreign.	Curable.	Incurable.	Not stated.	At home.	In hospital, &c.	
Leominster, . .	3,679	17	1	18	–	2	16	–	18	–	18
Lunenburg, . .	1,240	–	8	8	–	–	8	–	8	–	8
Mendon, . .	1,420	3	2	4	1	–	5	–	3	2	5
Milford, . .	7,178	5	7	7	5	3	9	–	5	7	12
Millbury, . .	3,542	–	2	–	2	–	2	–	–	2	2
New Braintree, .	896	–	2	2	–	–	2	–	2	–	2
Northboro', . .	1,667	1	4	4	1	2	3	–	3	2	5
Northbridge, .	2,639	2	4	6	–	–	5	1	3	3	6
North Brookfield, .	2,158	1	3	4	–	–	4	–	2	2	4
Oakham, . .	1,180	3	–	3	–	–	1	2	3	–	3
Oxford, . .	2,695	2	6	8	–	–	8	–	7	1	8
Paxton, . .	928	1	–	1	–	–	1	–	–	1	1
Petersham, . .	1,373	5	2	7	–	–	5	2	7	–	7
Phillipston, . .	769	2	1	3	–	–	3	–	2	1	3
Princeton, . .	1,307	2	1	3	–	1	2	–	1	2	3
Royalston, . .	1,500	–	1	1	–	–	–	1	1	–	1
Rutland, . .	1,208	4	–	4	–	2	2	–	4	–	4
Shrewsbury, .	1,644	9	2	10	1	2	7	2	8	3	11
Southboro', . .	1,432	–	1	1	–	–	1	–	1	–	1
Southbridge, .	3,222	2	2	4	–	2	1	1	3	1	4
Spencer, . .	2,565	6	1	7	–	2	5	–	5	2	7
Sterling, . .	1,872	4	3	7	–	1	6	–	5	2	7
Sturbridge, . .	2,168	5	3	8	–	1	7	–	4	4	8

WORCESTER—Continued.

TOWNS.	Population, 1854.	Pecuniary Condition.		Nativity.		Prospect.			Where.		
		Independent.	Pauper.	American.	Foreign.	Curable.	Incurable.	Not stated.	At home.	In hospital, &c.	Total.
Sutton, . .	2,690	4	2	6	–	–	6	–	3	3	6
Templeton, . .	2,355	–	2	1	1	–	2	–	1	1	2
Upton, . .	2,302	3	4	7	–	–	3	4	6	1	7
Uxbridge, .	2,644	2	4	4	2	3	3	–	4	2	6
Warren, .	2,020	5	1	6	–	1	5	–	4	2	6
Webster, .	2,921	4	1	5	–	1	4	–	5	–	5
Westboro', .	2,736	7	2	9	–	–	7	2	6	3	9
W. Boylston,	2,042	3	3	5	1	–	6	–	3	3	6
W. Brookfield, .	–	1	1	2	–	–	2	–	1	1	2
Westminster, .	2,034	–	2	2	–	–	2	–	2	–	2
Winchendon, .	2,792	5	6	11	–	1	9	1	11	–	11
Worcester, .	23,694	13	26	19	20	7	30	2	4	35	39
Totals, . .	–	173	178	301	50	49	275	27	225	126	351

MIDDLESEX COUNTY.

Acton, . .	1,853	6	1	7	–	1	1	5	6	1	7
Ashby, .	1,193	1	1	2	–	–	2	–	1	1	2
Ashland, .	1,375	4	2	6	–	–	6	–	3	3	6
Bedford, .	994	1	–	1	–	–	1	–	–	1	1
Billerica, .	1,652	3	6	9	–	–	8	1	7	2	9
Boxboro', .	383	1	1	2	–	–	2	–	1	1	2

MIDDLESEX—Continued.

TOWNS.	Population, 1854.	Pecuniary Condition.		Nativity.		Prospect.			Where.		Total.
		Independent.	Pauper.	American.	Foreign.	Curable.	Incurable.	Not stated.	At home.	In hospital, &c.	
Brighton, . .	2,881	–	1	1	–	–	1	–	1	–	1
Burlington, . .	560	–	1	1	–	–	1	–	1	–	1
Cambridge, . .	19,286	11	8	12	7	2	17	–	2	17	19
Carlisle, . .	665	–	1	1	–	–	1	–	1	–	1
Charlestown, .	20238*	17	26	31	12	4	38	1	14	29	43
Chelmsford, . .	2,282	9	3	12	–	2	10	–	7	5	12
Concord, . .	2,468	4	2	6	–	1	5	–	4	2	6
Dracut, . .	4,228	3	3	6	–	2	3	1	3	3	6
Dunstable, . .	585	–	–	–	–	–	–	–	–	–	–
Framingham, .	5,079	2	5	7	–	1	6	–	5	2	7
Groton, . .	2,683	3	5	7	1	1	7	–	4	4	8
Holliston, . .	2,814	5	3	7	1	2	5	1	5	3	8
Hopkinton, . .	3,548	–	2	2	–	–	2	–	2	–	2
Lexington, . .	2,004	6	3	9	–	1	8	–	8	1	9
Lincoln, . .	733	–	3	3	–	–	1	2	3	–	3
Littleton, . .	1,012	2	1	3	–	1	2	–	2	1	3
Lowell, . .	40,349	17	6	16	7	8	14	1	12	11	23
Malden, . .	4,028†	7	1	8	–	1	4	3	7	1	8
Marlboro', . .	3,365	3	2	4	1	1	3	1	4	1	5
Medford, . .	4,424	10	1	11	–	1	10	–	4	7	11
Melrose, . .	–	1	–	–	1	1	–	–	1	–	1
Natick, . .	3,717	–	2	2	–	–	1	1	2	–	2
Newton, . .	6,296	4	3	4	3	3	3	1	3	4	7

*Including most of Somerville.   † Including Melrose.

MIDDLESEX—Continued.

TOWNS.	Population, 1854.	Pecuniary Condition.		Nativity.		Prospect.			Where.		Total.
		Indedendent.	Pauper.	American.	Foreign.	Curable.	Incurable.	Not stated.	At home.	In hospital, &c.	
North Reading, .	–	–	1	1	–	–	1	–	1	–	1
Pepperell, . .	1,833	3	3	6	–	2	4	–	6	–	6
Reading, . .	3,573*	3	4	7	–	2	5	–	6	1	7
Sherborn, . .	1,063	2	2	4	–	–	4	–	3	1	4
Shirley, . .	1,250	3	1	4	–	1	2	1	3	1	4
Somerville, . .	–	4	3	5	2	–	5	2	3	4	7
South Reading, .	2,895	1	–	1	–	–	1	–	–	1	1
Stoneham, . .	2,779	2	1	3	–	–	3	–	2	1	3
Stowe, . . .	1,556	3	1	4	–	2	1	1	3	1	4
Sudbury, . .	1,645	5	–	5	–	2	3	–	4	1	5
Tewksbury, . .	1,105	1	–	1	–	1	–	–	1	–	1
Townsend, . .	1,969	3	2	5	–	2	2	1	5	–	5
Tyngsboro', . .	772	1	1	2	–	–	2	–	1	1	2
Waltham, . .	5,625	2	3	3	2	2	3	–	1	4	5
Watertown, . .	3,396	–	6	2	4	3	3	–	4	2	6
Wayland, . .	1,166	1	2	3	–	–	3	–	3	–	3
W. Cambridge, .	2,668	4	5	8	1	–	9	–	5	4	9
Westford, . .	1,660	2	1	3	–	–	2	1	3	–	3
Weston, . .	1,123	–	–	–	–	–	–	–	–	–	–
Wilmington, .	880	1	–	1	–	1	–	–	1	–	1
Winchester, . .	–	2	–	2	–	1	1	–	–	2	2
Woburn, . .	4,423†	1	1	1	1	1	1	–	1	1	2
Totals, . .	–	164	128	249	43	53	215	24	169	123	292

* Including North Reading.   † Including a part of Winchester.

ESSEX COUNTY.

TOWNS.	Population, 1854.	Pecuniary Condition.		Nativity.		Prospect.			Where.		
		Independent.	Pauper.	American.	Foreign.	Curable.	Incurable.	Not stated.	At home.	In hospital, &c.	Total.
Amesbury, . .	3,461	1	6	7	–	–	6	1	3	4	7
Andover, . .	7,793	5	9	11	3	3	10	1	1C	4	14
Beverly, . .	5,678	9	15	24	–	–	16	8	18	6	24
Boxford, . .	999	1	4	5	–	–	3	2	5	–	5
Bradford, . .	2,798*	–	1	1	–	–	1	–	1	–	1
Danvers, . .	9,823	7	11	15	3	6	12	–	9	9	18
Essex, . . .	1,642	4	1	5	–	–	4	1	2	3	5
Georgetown,. .	2,301	2	3	4	1	–	2	3	3	2	5
Gloucester, . .	8,448	6	11	16	1	2	15	–	13	4	17
Groveland, . .	–	–	1	1	–	1	–	–	1	–	1
Hamilton, . .	919	8	–	8	–	–	8	–	5	3	8
Haverhill, . .	6,637	9	7	14	2	1	14	1	12	4	16
Ipswich, . .	3,500	2	11	7	6	2	11	–	3	10	13
Lawrence, . .	17,678	–	9	2	7	6	3	–	7	2	9
Lynn, . . .	16601†	6	16	17	5	2	19	1	8	14	22
Lynnfield, . .	2,461	–	1	1	–	–	1	–	–	1	1
Manchester,. .	1,767	4	3	6	1	1	6	–	5	2	7
Marblehead,. .	6,421	16	9	25	–	4	21	–	17	8	25
Methuen, . .	2,663	4	–	4	–	1	3	–	3	1	4
Middleton, . .	914	1	2	3	–	–	3	–	2	1	3
Nahant, . .	266	–	–	–	–	–	–	–	–	–	–
Newbury, . .	4,710‡	–	1	–	1	–	1	–	–	1	1
Newburyport, .	10750‡	18	6	20	4	5	18	1	13	11	24

* Including Groveland.   † Including Swampscott.

‡ A part of Newbury was set off to Newburyport, including, by estimate, about 2,200 people. These should be included in Newburyport.

ESSEX—Continued.

TOWNS.	Population, 1854.	Pecuniary Condition.		Nativity.		Prospect.			Where.		Total.
		Independent.	Pauper.	American.	Foreign.	Curable.	Incurable.	Not stated.	At home.	In hospital, &c.	
Rockport, . .	3,563	1	–	1	–	–	–	1	1	–	1
Rowley, . .	1,028	1	–	1	–	–	1	–	–	1	1
Salem, . . .	22,805	25	30	46	9	5	48	2	22	33	55
Salisbury, . .	3,257	3	1	4	–	–	4	–	2	2	4
Saugus, . .	1,782	5	4	7	2	–	8	1	4	5	9
Swampscott, .	–	–	–	–	–	–	–	–	–	–	–
Topsfield, . .	1,218	1	5	6	–	1	5	–	5	1	6
Wenham, . .	1,124	2	–	2	–	–	2	–	2	–	2
W. Newbury, .	1,827	1	–	1	–	–	1	–	–	1	1
Totals, . .	–	142	167	264	45	40	246	23	176	133	309

SUFFOLK COUNTY.

Boston, . .	167248	105	337	196	246	80	356	6	22	420	442
Chelsea, . .	12,151	5	7	10	2	5	4	3	5	7	12
Totals, . .	–	110	344	206	248	85	360	9	27	427	454

NORFOLK COUNTY.

Bellingham, . .	1,384	4	2	5	1	4	2	–	5	1	6
Braintree, . .	3,364	13	8	20	1	1	17	3	19	2	21
Brookline, . .	3,212	10	2	11	1	3	9	–	9	3	12

5

NORFOLK—Continued.

TOWNS.	Population, 1854.	Pecuniary Condition.		Nativity.		Prospect.			Where.		
		Independent.	Pauper.	American.	Foreign.	Curable.	Incurable.	Not stated.	At home.	In hospital, &c.	Total.
Canton, . .	2,287	6	3	8	1	1	5	3	7	2	9
Cohasset, . .	1,913	6	3	9	–	2	7	–	6	3	9
Dedham, . .	5,017	12	4	13	3	5	11	–	8	8	16
Dorchester, . .	9,700	12	12	19	5	4	18	2	11	13	24
Dover, . . .	682	1	–	1	–	–	1	–	–	1	1
Foxboro', . .	2,180	2	5	6	1	2	5	–	4	3	7
Franklin, . .	1,860	2	1	3	–	–	3	–	3	–	3
Medfield, . .	1,001	2	4	6	–	–	6	–	3	3	6
Medway, . .	3,142	2	1	3	–	–	3	–	3	–	3
Milton, . .	2,434	6	1	7	–	–	7	–	4	3	7
Needham, . .	2,163	3	2	4	1	1	4	–	2	3	5
Quincy, . .	5,803	5	8	9	4	3	10	–	3	10	13
Randolph, . .	5,544	5	2	6	1	–	7	–	4	3	7
Roxbury, . .	25478*	17	27	24	20	11	33	–	2	42	44
Sharon, . .	1,150	1	1	2	–	–	2	–	2	–	2
Stoughton, . .	4,249	3	5	5	3	–	7	1	3	5	8
Walpole, . .	2,168	4	–	4	–	2	2	–	4	–	4
West Roxbury, .	–	3	1	3	1	4	–	–	1	3	4
Weymouth, . .	6,206	9	8	16	1	5	11	1	9	8	17
Wrentham, . .	3,087	7	4	9	2	3	8	–	5	6	11
Totals, . .	–	131	104	193	46	51	178	10	117	122	239

* Including West Roxbury.

BRISTOL COUNTY.

| TOWNS. | Population, 1854. | Pecuniary Condition. | | Nativity. | | Prospect. | | | Where. | | Total. |
		Independent.	Pauper.	American.	Foreign.	Curable.	Incurable.	Not stated.	At home.	In hospital, &c.	
Attleboro', . .	4,475	1	5	5	1	2	1	3	3	3	6
Berkley, . .	917	2	2	4	–	2	2	–	2	2	4
Dartmouth, . .	3,766	2	2	4	–	–	4	–	2	2	4
Dighton, . .	1,760	–	2	2	–	–	1	1	2	–	2
Easton, . .	2,451	5	3	6	2	2	6	–	6	2	8
Fairhaven, . .	4,454	5	5	10	–	6	4	–	7	3	10
Fall River, . .	14,279	8	9	10	7	4	10	3	7	10	17
Freetown, . .	1,556	2	1	3	–	–	1	2	3	–	3
Mansfield, . .	1,984	3	3	5	1	2	4	–	5	1	6
New Bedford, .	18,597	13	14	25	2	4	19	4	16	11	27
Norton, . .	2,165	4	–	4	–	–	4	–	4	–	4
Pawtucket, . .	4,660	2	2	4	–	–	4	–	4	–	4
Raynham, . .	1,635	1	2	3	–	–	3	–	2	1	3
Rehoboth, . .	2,079	–	–	–	–	–	–	–	–	–	–
Seekonk, . .	2,350	2	2	4	–	2	2	–	3	1	4
Somerset, . .	1,237	2	1	3	–	1	2	–	–	3	3
Swanzey, . .	1,583	3	–	3	–	1	2	–	3	–	3
Taunton, . .	11,826	12	19	25	6	8	23	–	16	15	31
Westport, . .	2,785	5	7	12	–	4	8	–	10	2	12
Totals, . .	–	72	79	132	19	38	100	13	95	56	151

PLYMOUTH COUNTY.

TOWNS.	Population, 1854.	Pecuniary Condition.		Nativity.		Prospect.			Where.		Total.
		Independent.	Pauper.	American.	Foreign.	Curable.	Incurable.	Not stated.	At home.	In hospital, &c.	
Abington,	6,421	3	3	6	–	1	4	1	5	1	6
Bridgewater,	3,108	3	8	6	5	3	7	1	3	8	11
Carver,	1,272	3	2	5	–	1	4	–	5	–	5
Duxbury,	2,633	3	7	10	–	2	7	1	6	4	10
E. Bridgewater,	2,831	1	4	4	1	–	5	–	5	–	5
Halifax,	805	–	–	–	–	–	–	–	–	–	–
Hanover,	1,636	1	–	1	–	–	1	–	1	–	1
Hanson,	1,296	4	–	4	–	2	2	–	3	1	4
Hingham,	4,160	3	15	16	2	1	16	1	15	3	18
Hull,	262	–	–	–	–	–	–	–	–	–	–
Kingston,	1,656	2	3	5	–	–	5	–	1	4	5
Lakeville,	1,105	1	2	3	–	–	2	1	3	–	3
Marion,	–	1	–	1	–	1	–	–	1	–	1
Marshfield,	1,868	3	2	5	–	1	4	–	3	2	5
Middleboro',	4,335	7	5	12	–	4	8	–	11	1	12
N. Bridgewater,	4,640	1	–	1	–	–	–	1	1	–	1
Pembroke,	1,443	–	3	3	–	–	3	–	3	–	3
Plymouth,	6,350	6	15	21	–	2	18	1	5	16	21
Plympton,	967	2	1	3	–	–	–	3	3	–	3
Rochester,	3,786*	5	5	10	–	–	10	–	6	4	10
Scituate,	2,156	3	–	3	–	2	1	–	3	–	3
South Scituate,	1,776	–	3	3	–	–	3	–	3	–	3

* Including Marion.

PLYMOUTH—Continued.

TOWNS.	Population, 1854.	Pecuniary Condition.		Nativity.		Prospect.			Where.		Total.
		Independent.	Pauper.	American.	Foreign.	Curable.	Incurable.	Not stated.	At home.	In hospital, &c.	
Wareham, . .	3,837	3	–	3	–	–	3	–	3	–	3
W. Bridgewater, .	1,559	2	4	6	–	1	3	2	5	1	6
Totals, . .	–	57	82	131	8	21	106	12	94	45	139

BARNSTABLE COUNTY.

TOWNS.	Population, 1854.	Independent.	Pauper.	American.	Foreign.	Curable.	Incurable.	Not stated.	At home.	In hospital, &c.	Total.
Barnstable, . .	5,164	8	9	17	–	6	9	2	12	5	17
Brewster, . .	1,526	1	–	1	–	1	–	–	1	–	1
Chatham, . .	2,482	1	2	3	–	–	3	–	1	2	3
Dennis, . .	3,392	1	3	4	–	1	3	–	3	1	4
Eastham, . .	805	1	–	1	–	–	1	–	1	–	1
Falmouth, . .	2,634	2	3	5	–	–	5	–	4	1	5
Harwich, . .	3,399	5	4	9	–	5	1	3	8	1	9
Orleans, . .	1,800	2	5	7	–	–	6	1	7	–	7
Provincetown, .	3,701	2	–	2	–	1	1	–	1	1	2
Sandwich, . .	4,658	2	6	6	2	–	5	3	3	5	8
Truro, . . .	2,106	1	1	2	–	–	2	–	1	1	2
Wellfleet, . .	2,425	4	3	7	–	2	3	2	6	1	7
Yarmouth, . .	2,611	1	10	11	–	2	9	–	11	–	11
Totals, . .	–	31	46	75	2	18	48	11	59	18	77

NANTUCKET COUNTY.

TOWNS.	Population, 1854.	Pecuniary Condition.		Nativity.		Prospect.			Where.		
		Independent.	Pauper.	American.	Foreign.	Curable.	Incurable.	Not stated.	At home.	In hospital, &c.	Total.
Nantucket, . .	8,238	3	9	10	2	1	10	1	3	9	12

DUKES COUNTY.

Chilmark, . .	766	1	–	1	–	–	1	–	1	–	1
Edgartown, . .	2,102	3	8	11	–	3	8	–	8	3	11
Tisbury, . .	1,930	4	3	6	1	2	5	–	6	1	7
Totals, . .	–	8	11	18	1	5	14	–	15	4	19

This table shows the number and distribution of the insane in the towns of Massachusetts, and that some are to be found almost everywhere, as only nineteen small towns are exempt from them.

This table does not include many in Receptacles, Prisons, &c., who are referred to, and belong to no town.

The condition and prospect of the lunatics may be found from the following table.

TABLE II.—LUNATICS.

COUNTIES.	SEX.		CONDITION.*				PROSPECT.				
	Male.	Female.	Mild—manageable.	Troublesome—excitable.	Furious—dangerous.	Not stated.	Curable.	Incurable.	Not stated.	Total.	Subject for hospital.
Berkshire,	63	56	52	51	11	5	28	80	11	119	69
Franklin,	42	42	52	23	8	1	10	65	9	84	44
Hampshire,	46	48	49	33	6	6	9	72	13	94	41
Hampden,	42	63	50	45	7	3	17	76	12	105	59
Worcester,	168	183	152	143	39	17	50	275	26	351	216
Middlesex,	184	173	174	125	46	12	56	277	24	357	214
Essex,	191	186	141	187	45	4	43	311	23	377	167
Suffolk,	182	276	186	237	28	7	87	362	9	458	446
Norfolk,	122	119	147	73	18	3	52	178	11	241	183
Bristol,	82	76	88	50	20	–	35	108	15	158	105
Plymouth,	69	70	78	53	7	1	21	106	12	139	82
Barnstable,	31	47	42	18	14	4	18	49	11	78	42
Nantucket,	4	8	6	5	1	–	1	10	1	12	11
Dukes,	10	9	7	8	4	–	5	14	–	19	16
Not stated,	18	22	14	16	9	1	3	35	2	40	17
Totals,	1254	1378	1238	1067	263	64	435	2018	179	2632	1713

* The physicians and other reporters were requested to state, in respect to each patient, whether he was mild, manageable, excitable, troublesome, furious or dangerous. These are condensed, in this table, into three classes, which will sufficiently show their condition and liability.

This table exhibits the precise amount and condition of the burden of insanity, and shows where it lies. This includes all that live in, or belong to, the several counties—both those at home and those who are in the hospitals, receptacles, houses of correction, jails, and towns or State Almshouses. It includes both the independent and the pauper—the native and the foreign insane. Several in the hospitals, State Almshouses, and State Prisons have no home in any county. These are in a separate column under the head—*not stated.*

The third column includes those who are quiet and harmless, who can ordinarily be kept at their homes and be watched and guided by their friends. If their disorders are not recent, or if they have had a fair trial of remedial measures, they need not be removed from their homes or the poorhouse.

The fourth column includes those who, perhaps, are usually quiet and harmless, but are uncertain and variable, and may be excited by many of the common events of life, and become troublesome and unmanageable. When managed with due discretion many of them are peaceable and create no trouble ; but, wanting power of self-control, they are easily thrown off their balance, and then cause disturbance. In hospitals they are quiet and comfortable, and while there, they seem to those who are not familiar with the nature of their disease to hardly need the confinement and discipline of such an institution. Some lunatics of this class are subjected to many and variable plans of treatment. Their friends and families, finding that they cannot manage them at all times at home, and becoming weary of their ineffectual attempts to control them in their waywardness and excitability, send them to some hospital for their own relief as well as for the good of the patients. Under the judicious discipline and soothing influences of the institution, where every thing is adapted to meet their peculiarities, and from the even tenor of life they lead there, they become calm, and seem to have regained the power of self-control, and to be sufficiently well to enjoy the comforts and bear the trials of home. They are taken away, again become excited, and again returned to the hospital, to be soothed and calmed, and again carried home, with the same result and the same alternation of experiments.

The fifth column includes those who were returned by the

physicians as violent, unmanageable, furious or dangerous. Most of them are confined in some way or other, in hospitals, or in prisons, or in cages, and are "manifestly dangerous to the peace and safety of the community to be at large."

The seventh and eighth columns show the prospects of the insane.

The eleventh column shows the number of those who, in the opinion of the reporters, were subjects for a hospital—those who, either on account of their dangerous or troublesome condition, or liability to uncontrollable excitement, should be confined for the good of their friends or of the public, or who, on account of the recency of their malady and their probable curability, should be submitted to the remedial influences of a hospital for their restoration.

The facts in this column are in almost all cases given exactly as found in the original records; but as, in a few instances, those who made the returns seem to understand the purpose of a hospital to be merely custodial, and reported some mild cases, which were of recent origin, and perhaps curable, certainly not incurable, as not fit subjects for such an institution and as a few others, probably thinking the objects of the hospital were curative merely, returned some old and incurable cases, which were furious or dangerous, as not fit subjects for hospital treatment, the record of all these is changed, and they are included under this head in the tables presented.

Of course, then, this column includes all the third class, and most of the second, and should contain all those of the first, whose diseases are recent, and susceptible of improvement or removal by the curative measures to be found in a hospital.

PECUNIARY CONDITION OF LUNATICS.

As a matter of political economy, and in an investigation made by order of the State, it is of the first consequence to determine the amount of this burden that is borne by the property of the families and friends of the sufferers, and of that which falls upon the public. This inquiry, therefore, was made, and the returns distinguished the independent from the pauper lunatics, and among the latter those who were supported by the State from those who were supported by the cities and towns.

Of the two thousand six hundred and thirty-two lunatics, eleven hundred and ten are independent, or supported by their own property, or by that of their friends; and fifteen hundred and twenty-two are paupers, of whom eight hundred and twenty-nine are supported by the cities and towns, and six hundred and ninety-three are supported by the State. Of the independent lunatics, three hundred and eighty-seven are in hospitals, seven in prisons or in receptacles connected with them, and seven hundred and sixteen at home.

Of the pauper lunatics, nine hundred and fifty-four are in hospitals or places for healing or custody, and five hundred and sixty-eight at home or in almshouses.

INDEPENDENT LUNATICS.

The independent lunatics are mostly natives, very few are foreigners, and a majority are at their homes, as is shown in the following tables :—

TABLE III.—INDEPENDENT LUNATICS.

| COUNTIES. | AT HOME. | | | | | | IN HOSPITAL, &c. | | | | | |
| | CONDITION. | | | | | | CONDITION. | | | | | |
	Mild—manageable.	Excitable—troublesome	Furious—dangerous.	Not stated.	Total.	Subject for hospital.	Mild—manageable.	Excitable—troublesome	Furious—dangerous.	Not stated.	Total.	Subject for hospital.
Berkshire, .	38	18	1	5	62	30	3	5	1	–	9	8
Franklin, .	26	9	–	1	36	14	1	–	–	–	1	1
Hampshire, .	31	8	–	1	40	8	4	5	1	–	10	10
Hampden, .	30	12	–	3	45	21	1	10	1	–	12	11
Worcester, .	76	42	1	7	126	57	5	29	12	1	47	47
Middlesex, .	54	25	4	7	90	52	27	36	11	–	74	73
Essex, . .	47	27	5	2	81	27	15	34	11	1	61	61
Suffolk, . .	9	4	3	3	19	9	35	50	3	3	91	90
Norfolk, .	59	23	4	1	87	40	22	22	4	1	49	49
Bristol, . .	34	16	4	–	54	25	9	9	–	–	18	18
Plymouth, .	27	15	–	1	43	23	4	8	1	–	13	13
Barnstable, .	12	6	2	3	23	11	1	3	4	–	8	8
Nantucket, .	2	–	–	–	2	1	–	1	–	–	1	1
Dukes, . .	2	4	2	–	8	5	–	–	–	–	–	–
Totals, .	447	209	26	34	716	323	127	212	49	6	394	390

TABLE IV.—INDEPENDENT LUNATICS.

COUNTIES.	Mild—manageable.	Excitable—troublesome	Furious—dangerous.	Not stated.	Total.	Subject for hospital.
		CONDITION.				
Berkshire, . . .	41	23	2	5	71	38
Franklin, . . .	27	9	–	1	37	15
Hampshire, . . .	35	13	1	1	50	18
Hampden, . . .	31	22	1	3	57	32
Worcester, . . .	81	71	13	8	173	104
Middlesex, . . .	81	61	15	7	164	125
Essex, ...	62	61	16	3	142	88
Suffolk, . . .	44	54	6	6	110	99
Norfolk, . . .	81	45	8	2	136	89
Bristol, . . .	43	25	4	–	72	43
Plymouth, . . .	31	23	1	1	56	36
Barnstable, . . .	13	9	6	3	31	19
Nantucket, . . .	2	1	–	–	3	2
Dukes, . . .	2	4	2	–	8	5
Totals, . . .	574	421	75	40	1,110	713

These tables show that, of the independent lunatics, twenty-six who were furious, and two hundred and nine excitable and troublesome, and three hundred and twenty-three who should be in hospital, were kept at their homes, and that all of the three hundred and ninety-four but four, who were in hospitals, were proper subjects for their care.

PAUPERS.

Pauperism has extensive and intimate connection with lunacy; and herein this disease offers the most important point of interest to the State and to the political economist; for the greater part of the burden of supporting it falls upon the public treasury.

There were one thousand one hundred and ten independent lunatics, and one thousand five hundred and twenty-two pauper lunatics, who were maintained by the town or the State. The condition and distribution of the latter are shown in Tables V., VI., VII. and VIII.

In these, as in the subsequent tables, the same, or some of the same, patients are included, to show various facts and illustrate various principles.

TABLE V.—PAUPER LUNATICS AT HOME.

COUNTIES.	AMERICAN.						FOREIGN.							
	CONDITION.						NATION.		CONDITION.					
	Mild—manageable.	Excitable—troublesome	Furious—dangerous.	Not stated.	Total.	Subject for hospital.	Irish.	Others.	Mild—manageable.	Excitable—troublesome	Furious—dangerous.	Not stated.	Total.	Subject for hospital.
Berkshire, . .	9	16	4	–	29	14	1	–	1	–	–	–	1	–
Franklin, . .	21	6	5	–	32	14	–	–	–	–	–	–	–	–
Hampshire, .	12	13	1	5	31	10	–	–	–	–	–	–	–	–
Hampden, . .	15	8	2	–	25	6	2	1	1	2	–	–	3	1
Worcester, . .	59	23	5	9	96	30	2	1	2	1	–	–	3	3
Middlesex, . .	42	17	11	3	73	37	4	2	2	3	1	–	6	4
Essex, . . .	48	32	6	–	86	19	6	3	3	4	1	1	9	7
Suffolk, . . .	4	1	–	–	5	4	3	–	1	2	–	–	3	3
Norfolk, . . .	16	7	6	1	30	20	–	–	–	–	–	–	–	–
Bristol, . . .	20	9	10	–	39	16	2	–	–	1	1	–	2	2
Plymouth, . .	32	15	2	–	49	15	1	1	1	1	–	–	2	–
Barnstable, . .	22	7	6	1	36	13	–	–	–	–	–	–	–	–
Nantucket, . .	–	–	1	–	1	1	–	–					–	–
Dukes, . . .	3	2	2	–	7	7	–	–	–	–	–	–	–	–
Totals, . .	303	156	61	19	539	206	21	8	11	14	3	1	29	20

TABLE VI.—PAUPER LUNATICS IN HOSPITAL, &c.

| COUNTIES. | AMERICAN. | | | | | | FOREIGN. | | | | | | | |
| | CONDITION. | | | | | | NATION. | | CONDITION. | | | | | |
	Mild—manageable.	Excitable—troublesome	Furious—dangerous.	Not stated.	Total.	Subject for hospital.	Irish.	Others.	Mild—manageable.	Excitable—troublesome	Furious—dangerous.	Not stated.	Total.	Subject for hospital.
Berkshire,	1	9	3	–	13	12	3	2	–	3	2	–	5	5
Franklin,	3	8	3	–	14	14	1	–	1	–	–	–	1	1
Hampshire,	1	4	3	–	8	8	2	3	1	3	1	–	5	5
Hampden,	2	7	1	–	10	10	9	1	1	6	3	–	10	10
Worcester,	5	22	10	–	37	37	39	3	5	26	11	–	42	42
Middlesex,	14	17	5	–	36	21	71	7	35	27	14	2	78	27
Essex,	18	39	5	–	62	20	48	30	11	50	17	–	78	33
Suffolk,	51	45	7	–	103	103	213	24	86	135	15	1	237	237
Norfolk,	22	9	3	–	34	33	32	9	28	12	1	–	41	41
Bristol,	20	8	2	–	30	29	15	–	5	7	3	–	15	15
Plymouth,	12	11	4	–	27	27	5	–	2	3	–	–	5	5
Barnstable,	5	2	2	–	9	8	2	–	2	–	–	–	2	2
Nantucket,	2	4	–	–	6	6	1	1	2	–	–	–	2	2
Dukes,	2	2	–	–	4	4	–	–	–	–	–	–	–	–
State Almshouses,	3	3	3	–	9	3	19	12	11	14	5	1	31	14
Totals,	161	190	51	–	402	335	460	92	190	286	72	4	552	439

TABLE VII.—PAUPER LUNATICS

At Home, and in Hospitals, Receptacles, &c.

| COUNTIES. | AMERICAN. | | | | | | FOREIGN. | | | | | | | |
| | CONDITION. | | | | | | NATION. | | CONDITION. | | | | | |
	Mild—manageable.	Excitable—troublesome.	Furious—dangerous.	Not stated.	Total.	Subject for hospital.	Irish.	Others.	Mild—manageable.	Excitable—troublesome.	Furious—dangerous.	Not stated.	Total.	Subject for hospital.
Berkshire,	10	25	7	–	42	26	4	2	1	3	2	–	6	5
Franklin,	24	14	8	–	46	28	1	–	1	–	–	–	1	1
Hampshire,	13	17	4	5	39	18	2	3	1	3	1	–	5	5
Hampden,	17	15	3	–	35	16	11	2	2	8	3	–	13	11
Worcester,	64	45	15	9	133	67	41	4	7	27	11	–	45	45
Middlesex,	56	34	16	3	109	58	75	9	37	30	15	2	84	31
Essex,	66	71	11	–	148	39	54	33	14	54	18	1	87	40
Suffolk,	55	46	7	–	108	107	216	24	87	137	15	1	240	240
Norfolk,	38	16	9	1	64	53	32	9	28	12	1	–	41	41
Bristol,	40	17	12	–	69	45	17	–	5	8	4	–	17	17
Plymouth,	44	26	6	–	76	42	6	1	3	4	–	–	7	5
Barnstable,	27	9	8	1	45	21	2	–	2	–	–	–	2	2
Nantucket,	2	4	1	–	7	7	1	1	2	–	–	–	2	2
Dukes,	5	4	2	–	11	11	–	–	–	–	–	–	–	–
State Almshouses,	3	3	3	–	9	3	19	12	11	14	5	1	31	14
Totals,	464	346	112	19	941	541	481	100	201	300	75	5	581	459

Table VIII.—PAUPER LUNATICS

Of all Nations, at Home and in Hospitals, &c.

COUNTIES.	CONDITION.				Total.	Subject for hospital.
	Mild—manageable.	Excitable—troublesome	Furious—dangerous.	Not stated.		
Berkshire, ...	11	28	9	–	48	31
Franklin, ...	25	14	8	–	47	29
Hampshire, ...	14	20	5	5	44	23
Hampden, ...	19	23	6	–	48	27
Worcester, ...	71	72	26	9	178	112
Middlesex, ...	93	64	31	5	193	89
Essex, ...	80	125	29	1	235	79
Suffolk, ...	142	183	22	1	348	347
Norfolk, ...	66	28	10	1	105	94
Bristol, ...	45	25	16	–	86	62
Plymouth, ...	47	30	6	–	83	47
Barnstable, ...	29	9	8	1	47	23
Nantucket, ...	4	4	1	–	9	9
Dukes, ...	5	4	2	–	11	11
State Almshouses, . . .	14	17	8	1	40	17
Totals, ...	665	646	187	24	1,522	1,000

7

These are all the pauper lunatics in, or belonging to, Massachusetts.   Those who, by owning property, paying taxes, and
by sufficient inhabitancy or heirship, have gained or inherited
a local residence, are supported by the towns and cities.   The
others are supported by the State.

STATE PAUPERS.

The state paupers include most of the foreigners who are
strangers in this land, and some from other States.

The returns from the house of correction in New Bedford
state that the eight lunatics and idiots in that prison were supported by the county.   All other paupers are stated to be supported by the Commonwealth or the towns.   The printed report
of the Secretary of State concerning the jails and houses of correction states that the lunatic in Barnstable jail was also supported by the county.   Nevertheless, all of these nine are included among the State paupers in the tables of this Report.

Table IX. shows the number, and condition, and prospect
of the State paupers, lunatics and idiots.   The last are included
here, though not elsewhere, for the convenience of presenting
these classes of facts together.

TABLE IX.—STATE PAUPERS.

COUNTIES.	Lunatics.	Idiots.	CONDITION.			PROSPECT.		Native.	Foreign.
			Mild—manageable.	Excitable—troublesome	Furious—dangerous.	Curable.	Incurable.		
Berkshire, . .	9	2	2	6	3	1	10	6	5
Franklin, . .	4	3	6	–	1	–	7	6	1
Hampshire, . .	6	–	1	4	1	1	5	5	1
Hampden, . .	15	4	6	10	3	3	16	6	13
Worcester, . .	51	1	8	29	15	6	46	8	44
Middlesex, . .	98	7	52	35	18	9	96	20	85
Essex, . . .	116	1	22	74	21	16	101	31	86
Suffolk, . . .	268	–	98	144	26	35	233	35	233
Norfolk, . . .	49	–	32	14	3	16	33	9	40
Bristol, . . .	18	–	6	7	5	8	10	5	13
Plymouth, . .	11	1	3	8	1	4	8	5	7
Barnstable, . .	4	–	3	–	1	–	4	2	2
Nantucket, . .	3	–	2	1	–	–	3	1	2
Dukes, . . .	1	–	–	1	–	–	1	1	–
State Almshouses, .	40	25	27	29	9	3	62	24	41
Totals, . .	693	44	268	362	107	102	635	164	573

Of the whole seven hundred and thirty-seven State paupers, almost four-fifths, or five hundred and seventy-three, are foreigners, and only one hundred and sixty-four natives. Out of the whole five hundred and eighty-one foreign pauper lunatics, about one-fifteenth gained a residence in some town or city so as to become town paupers.

There is manifestly a much larger ratio of the insane among the poor, and especially among those who are paupers, than among the independent and more prosperous classes.

NATURE OF POVERTY.

In this connection it is worth while to look somewhat at the nature of poverty, its origin, and its relation to man and to society. It is usually considered as a single outward circumstance—the absence of worldly goods; but this want is a mere incident in this condition—only one of its manifestations. Poverty is an inward principle, enrooted deeply within the man, and running through all his elements; it reaches his body, his health, his intellect, and his moral powers, as well as his estate. In one or other of these elements it may predominate, and in that alone he may seem to be poor; but it usually involves more than one of the elements, often the whole. Hence we find that, among those whom the world calls poor, there is less vital force, a lower tone of life, more ill health, more weakness, more early death, a diminished longevity. There are also less self-respect, ambition and hope, more idocy and insanity, and more crime, than among the independent.

The preponderance of mental defect and disease among the poor is unquestionably shown by the comparison of the number of lunatics and idiots in the two classes. None could for a moment suppose that the total of these classes, the independent and the pauper, are in this ratio.

The whole number of permanent and temporary paupers who were relieved or supported from the public treasury in Massachusetts, during the last year, was 23,125. At the same time the calculated population of the State was 1,124,676, of whom 1,102,551 were independent and self-supporting. These are in the ratio of one to forty-seven, whereas the lunatics are in the ratio of 72.9 independent to 100 paupers. Comparing these ratios, we find that the pauper class furnishes, in ratio of its numbers, sixty-four times as many cases of insanity as the independent class.

A similar law of distribution prevails in England and Wales. The pauper lunatics are stated to be 16,821, and those of the independent classes amount to somewhat over 8,000,* making the ratio of the pauper to the independent insane about two to one. The ratio of the pauper to the independent classes in the whole population of the kingdom was about as one to twenty, showing the proportion of lunacy among the poor to be about forty times as great as that among those who were not supported by public charity. Whatever reasonable allowance may be made for the defect in the report of the independent lunatics, it is very plain that the ratio of insanity among the paupers is very much larger than that among the self-sustaining class.

This is not only a demonstrable fact in Massachusetts and Great Britain, and probably elsewhere, but it proceeds out of a principle which is fixed in the law of our being—that poverty is not a single fact of an empty purse, but involves in various degrees the whole man, and presents as many facts as there are elements of our nature that can be depreciated or perverted. Insanity is, then, a part and parcel of poverty; and wherever that involves any considerable number of persons, this disease is manifested.

It needs no philosophy to show that some, perhaps many, lunatics, by their disease lose their power of self-sustenance, and are thereby removed from the independent to the pauper class. The laboring but self-supporting poor, whose daily and monthly toil yields barely sufficient for their nourishment, gather no store and gain no capital to rest upon when production is suspended. Of course, when they cease to be producers, they become dependent on others for their support; and this is the more inevitable when that cause is sickness, which cuts off the supply, and creates the necessity of a greater expenditure. In these families the income of the day is only sufficient for its ordinary support, and will bear no more burden. Any increase, then, of expense, must diminish the comfort or the sustenance which was before deemed necessary, or make a demand upon their friends or the public for support.

* Report of Commissioners in Lunacy, 1844, p. 7.

When the poor become thus sick and dependent, although friends may, in some instances, be able and willing to step in and meet this expense, yet unfortunately they, too, are generally poor, and the public treasury is the only and the necessary resort for help ; and especially when any one becomes insane, the town or the State necessarily assumes the burden. Moreover, as this disease, more than others, is lasting, it would more certainly exhaust any little gathered store of the poor and the power and the patience of friends ; and then, if the lunatic is not at once thrown upon the public, he must ultimately reach that end.

Besides all this, the difficulty of keeping a lunatic in the dwellings and families of the poor is great and insurmountable. They have no spare room to keep him, and no surplus strength or help to attend upon him, for all of these are appropriated to the irresistible wants of the household from day to day. For this and the preceding reason, any subordinate member of a poor family becoming insane must be sent to the poorhouse or the hospital, to be supported and cared for by the public treasury, and thus become a pauper, at least through the period of the insanity, while yet the rest of the family support themselves. It necessarily follows, that some lunatics are paupers while their families are yet independent. Therefore, in determining the ratio of lunatics to their respective constituent classes, it is not a safe method to divide the whole number of the paupers, sane and insane, by the number of lunatics among them, because all these who have just been described as coming from self-supporting, although poor families, must be assumed to represent those who are not paupers and are not included in the pauper class.*

Nevertheless, even if all the self-sustaining poor were included with the paupers in the calculation, there will unquestionably be found a much greater ratio of lunatics among them than among the classes more favored in respect to outward estate.

A careful examination of the causes of poverty and lunacy, and of the character and condition and health of the poor,

---

* The Report of the Paupers of Massachusetts for the year ending November 1, 1854, published by the Secretary of State, shows that nine hundred and twenty-five of those relieved or supported became paupers by reason of insanity or idiocy.

would lead to the inference that there would be an excess of lunacy among them.

CONNECTION OF PAUPERISM WITH INSANITY.

It may be supposed, from what has been already said, that much of poverty has a common origin with insanity—both of them grow out of and represent internal mental character, or physical condition, as well as external circumstances.

Men of unbalanced mind and uncertain judgment do not see the true nature and relation of things, and they manifest this in the management of their common affairs. They do not adapt the means which they possess or use to the ends which they desire to produce. Hence they are unsuccessful in life; their plans of obtaining subsistence for themselves or their families, or of accumulating property, often fail; and they are consequently poor, and often paupers.

This unbalanced and ill-regulated mind, and these wayward or loose habits of thought, are among the common causes of insanity.

The weak mind cannot grasp any complicated design in affairs, nor combine means to produce ends, nor lay and carry out plans of business; the unstable mind changes it purposes, and does not carry out its plans, however well laid. Both of these fail of securing worldly prosperity, and often bring on poverty and pauperism, and they also often produce insanity. People of this class falter beneath the struggles and trials of life, and disappointments bear them down. Their minds become more and more unbalanced and irregular, and at length disordered.

Likewise some physical causes have their doubly destructive influence upon both the estate and the mind.

Intemperance in stimulating drinks and all sorts of dissipation disturb and exhaust the brain, and affect its power of correct and ready action ; and hence the mind becomes wayward, its operations uncertain and unfitted for the business of life. Hence follow derangements in the affairs of the world, and ill success and poverty. Hence, too, follow disorders of the nervous system and insanity, which, according to hospital records, find their most common origin in the exciting and exhausting effects of alcohol, especially among the poor.

Whatever depreciates the vital energies lowers the tone of the muscles, and diminishes the physical force, and lessens thereby the power of labor and of production; it also lowers the tone of the brain and the capacity of self-management. In this state the cerebral organ struggles, and may be deranged; consequently we find in the hospital records that ill health is one of the most commonly assigned causes of insanity. It has its first depressing effect on the energy of physical action and the soundness of the judgment in worldly affairs, and next on the power and discipline of the mental faculties.

PAUPER AND INDEPENDENT—PROSPECT.

Among the paupers, eighty-six per cent. are shown to be incurable; while among those of the independent class, a smaller proportion, seventy-five per cent., are returned as beyond hope of restoration. It is not to be supposed that pecuniary pauperism is in itself more destructive to the vital forces which would overcome disease and restore the balance of mental action when the brain is disordered—but the cause of the incurableness and permanence of their mental derangement lies behind, and is anterior to, their outward poverty. The permanence of the disease is often the cause of destitution. They are both frequently traceable to the same source; for an imperfectly organized brain and feeble mental constitution not only carry with them the inherent elements of poverty and insanity, but they have insufficient recuperative power to regain even their original health when deranged, and therefore their disorder remains.

In some cases, the family of an insane patient, although independent, are unable to pay for the expenses of his support at a hospital. They have a becoming self-respect which will not permit them to ask for aid from the public, and yet they are too poor to furnish the means of restoration themselves; consequently the lunatic is neglected, and his malady suffered to become chronic and hopeless. His family maintain him at home until both their means and his chance of recovery are exhausted; and then he is sent to the poorhouse, and at once swells the list of incurable paupers.

In other cases, the families of the poor and those of small estates make extraordinary exertions, and support an insane member at the hospital as long as the disorder seems to be curable; but when it becomes fixed and past remedy their strength gives out and their courage fails, their pride is overcome, and then they allow their relative to become a public charge. In these cases, the incurability alone is the cause of the pauperism.

FOREIGN ELEMENT.

The results of this lunatic inquiry reveal the great number of foreigners among our insane; and this is the more remarkably seen in the public institutions appropriated to the guardianship and the care of those afflicted with this malady.

The following table shows the numbers of the native and the foreign lunatics of the different classes, and in different situations, in the several counties and in the State :—

8

TABLE X.—LUNATICS IN MASSACHUSETTS.

Native and Foreign.

COUNTIES.	Independent		Pauper.		Both Classes		At Home.		In Hospital, &c.	
	Native.	Foreign.	Native.	Foreign.	Native.	Foreign.	Native.	Foreign.	Native.	Foreign.
Berkshire, . . .	71	–	42	6	113	6	91	1	22	5
Franklin, . . .	36	1	46	1	82	2	68	–	14	2
Hampshire, . . .	49	1	39	5	88	6	70	1	18	5
Hampden, . . .	56	1	35	13	91	14	70	3	21	11
Worcester, . . .	168	5	133	45	301	50	219	6	82	44
Middlesex, . . .	155	9	109	84	264	93	157	12	107	81
Essex, ...	139	3	148	87	287	90	165	11	122	79
Suffolk, ...	98	12	108	240	206	252	17	10	189	242
Norfolk, . . .	130	6	64	41	194	47	113	4	81	43
Bristol, . · . .	67	5	69	17	136	22	89	6	47	16
Plymouth, . . .	56	–	76	7	132	7	92	2	40	5
Barnstable, . . .	31	–	45	2	76	2	59	–	17	2
Nantucket, . . .	3	–	7	2	10	2	3	–	7	2
Dukes, ...	7	1	11	–	18	1	14	1	4	–
State Almshouses, . .	–	–	9	31	9	31	–	–	9	31
Totals, . . .	1066	44	941	581	2007	625	1227	57	780	568

Here is a large number of foreign lunatics within the State, and in the hospitals and places of public custody ; and these, unquestionably, bear a larger ratio to the sane population of their own class than the native lunatics.

There are not the means of calculating the approximate number of the foreigners in Massachusetts as is obtained for the whole population of the State.   If the same data, the census of 1840 and that of 1850, are assumed, 34,818 foreigners at the former and 164,448 at the latter period, and the calculations made, founded on the increase between these two periods, the result will indicate a number of people at the present time that will be extremely improbable and unworthy of belief.

But, taking the number of the foreigners ascertained to be here in 1850, adding to these the arrivals in the four subsequent years, according to the registers of the Commissioner of Alien Passengers, and making a deduction for those who passed beyond the State and who have died between 1850 and 1854, we have then the probable foreign population in Massachusetts of 230,000 in 1854.   Subtracting these from the calculated number of the total population of Massachusetts in 1854, we have the native population of 894,676.   Dividing these respectively by the ascertained numbers of the insane shows that the native insane were one in four hundred and forty-five of the total native population, and the foreign insane were one in three hundred and sixty-eight of the whole number of aliens in the State.   There is, then, a larger proportion of the foreigners than of the natives who are lunatics.

It would seem from this, either that our foreign population are more prone to insanity, or their habits and trials, their experiences and privations, and the circumstances which surround them, and the climate of this country, are more unfavorable to their mental health than to that of the natives.

It is worth while to analyze this state of things, and see how far this excess of lunacy among the foreigners is due to any peculiarities in them, and how far any circumstances and conditions which are common both to them and to those who were born in the United States.

FOREIGN POVERTY.

The most observable fact among the foreign lunatics is, that they have a very great preponderance of paupers.

The following table shows this distribution of the alien lunatics, independent and pauper, in the several counties, and also their sanitary condition, prospect and situation :—

TABLE XI.—FOREIGN LUNATICS.

COUNTIES.	Pecun'y Condit'n			CONDITION.				PROSPECT.			SITUATION.			
	Independent.	Pauper.	Total.	Mild—manageable.	Excitable—troublesome.	Furious—dangerous.	Not stated.	Curable.	Incurable.	Not stated.	At home.	In hospital.	In receptacles and prisons.	In state almshouses.
Berkshire,	–	6	6	1	3	2	–	1	5	–	1	5	–	–
Franklin,	1	1	2	2	–	–	–	–	2	–	–	2	–	–
Hampshire,	1	5	6	2	3	1	–	2	4	–	1	5	–	–
Hampden,	1	13	14	2	9	3	–	2	12	–	3	11	–	–
Worcester,	5	45	50	10	28	12	–	8	41	1	6	44	–	–
Middlesex,	9	84	93	41	35	15	2	14	78	1	12	31	50	–
Essex,	3	87	90	16	55	18	1	16	73	1	11	34	45	–
Suffolk,	12	240	252	93	141	17	1	39	213	–	10	238	4	–
Norfolk,	6	41	47	31	13	3	–	16	29	2	4	42	1	–
Bristol,	5	17	22	8	10	4	–	11	11	–	6	13	3	–
Plymouth,	–	7	7	3	4	–	–	1	6	–	2	5	–	–
Barnstable,	–	2	2	2	–	–	–	–	2	–	–	2	–	–
Nantucket,	–	2	2	2	–	–	–	–	2	–	–	2	–	–
Dukes,	1	–	1	–	1	–	–	–	1	–	1	–	–	–
State Almshouses,	–	31	31	11	13	6	1	2	27	2	–	–	–	31
Totals,	44	581	625	224	315	81	5	112	506	7	57	434	103	31

It is a noticeable fact, that most of the foreign lunatics, viz., 93 per cent., are paupers. It is also noticeable that only 6 per cent. of these foreign pauper lunatics are supported by the towns and cities; while 94 per cent. are State paupers. The State treasury, then, supports 87 per cent. of all the foreign lunatics who are in Massachusetts.

The proportion of native insane who are dependent is much smaller, being fifty-seven per cent. of all.

Among all the paupers, the natives, 13,454, who were relieved and supported in 1854, were as one in sixty-six of the whole native population; the foreign, 9,671, were as one in twenty-five of the whole foreign population.

These show that a much larger proportion of the aliens are dependent, or below the level of self-sustenance; and it is extremely probable that the proportion of those who barely support themselves when in health—that is, the poor—is much greater than even this. This is corroborated by the universal observation, that in most of the towns many, and in the eastern part of the State most, of the day laborers are Irish; and on the other hand, very few of the foreigners belong to the prosperous classes. Few of them have any capital, most are struggling with poverty and find some difficulty, and many find great difficulty in supplying their wants. It may be safely said, then, that most of the foreigners in Massachusetts are poor.

The greater liability of the poor and the struggling classes to become insane seems to be especially manifested among these strangers dwelling with us; and as a larger proportion of them are poor, they must, therefore, have a larger proportion of lunatics to their whole number than the Americans.

Besides these principles, which apply to the poor as a general law, there is good ground for supposing that the habits and condition and character of the Irish poor in this country operate more unfavorably upon their mental health, and hence produce a larger number of the insane in ratio of their numbers than is found among the native poor. Being in a strange land and among strange men and things, meeting with customs and surrounded by circumstances widely different from all their previous experience, ignorant of the precise state of affairs here, and wanting education and flexibility by which they could adapt themselves to their new and unwonted position, they necessarily form many impracticable purposes, and endeavor to accomplish them by unfitting means. Of course disappointment frequently follows their plans. Their lives are filled with doubt, and harrowing anxiety troubles them, and they are involved in frequent mental, and probably physical, suffering.

The Irish laborers have less sensibility and fewer wants to be gratified than the Americans, and yet they more commonly fail to supply them. They have also a greater irritability; they are more readily disturbed when they find themselves at variance with the circumstances about them, and less easily reconciled to difficulties they cannot overcome.

Unquestionably much of their insanity is due to their intemperance, to which the Irish seem to be peculiarly prone, and much to that exaltation which comes from increased prosperity.

Mr. Chadwick, the Secretary of the Poor Law Commission and of the Board of Health of England, in explanation of the apparent excess of lunacy among the Irish in the United States, attributes it to the sudden prosperity and means of indulgence which they find here beyond that which they left at home. He says: " If we were to take the poorest and the worst paid and the worst educated English, bred up in single-roomed hovels, with the pig for a companion, and suddenly give them three or four times the wages they had ever seen or dreamed of getting, and at the same time reduce the price of gin or whiskey and all stimulants to one-third the price which had formerly kept such physical excitements out of their reach, I should be very confident of finding a disproportionately large class of cases of lunacy amongst them." *

There is no evidence that insanity is more prevalent in Ireland than in England or Scotland, or even in the United States among the natives. We are informed, by the best authority on these subjects in Great Britain, that they have a large Irish population in that island, who go there as they come here, to seek for labor in the lowest capacity. They congregate in the cities, and live in the most unhealthy districts,

* Letter to the Commission.

in narrow lanes and dense courts, in small and unventilated apartments, and even in the many cellars of Liverpool, Manchester, Glasgow, &c. They undergo great privations and suffering, and are much subject to fevers, dysentery, and other diseases incident to bad air and meagre sustenance; but there is no ground for suspicion that in that country they have more lunacy than the natives.

Among the natives, three hundred and twenty-three are stated to be curable, and one thousand five hundred and twelve to be incurable; and among the foreigners, there were one hundred and twelve whose cases presented a hope of restoration, while five hundred and six seemed to be destined to incurable lunacy. This might lead to the inference that insanity in the alien and in the native American was equally remediable. But it must be remembered that our incurable lunatics are, in large proportion, old and long-established cases, many of whom have been deranged five, ten, thirty, and even fifty years. Those of more than ten years' standing constitute no small part.

The foreign population are of comparatively recent introduction into this country; there were only 9,620 in 1830; 34,-818 in 1840; and 164,448 in 1850; and probably 230,000 in 1854. Unless, therefore, there were some lunatics brought over from Europe, who, at most, were so extremely few that they can hardly be assumed as a part of the elements of this calculation, they would naturally have fewer of the old cases, and of course fewer of the incurables, than the natives.

Moreover, it is an undeniable fact that the foreigners, as a whole, have the best and the first advantage of our public institutions for the cure or custody of the insane.

TABLE XII.—SITUATION AND NATIVITY OF FOREIGN LUNATICS.

PRESENT SITUATION.	WHERE BORN.													
	Ireland.	British Provinces.	Great Britain.	Germany.	France.	Spain.	Holland.	Italy.	Sweden.	Austria.	Greece.	Egypt.	Unknown.	Total.
Worcester Hospital,	110	3	13	4	–	–	–	2	1	–	–	–	–	133
Taunton " .	93	–	5	8	1	–	–	–	–	–	–	–	–	107
Boston, " .	164	7	7	3	–	–	–	–	–	1	–	–	2	184
McLean " .	3	1	3	1	–	–	–	–	–	–	–	–	–	8
Ipswich Receptacle,	26	2	6	3	4	–	2	–	1	–	–	1	–	45
Cambridge, " .	42	1	3	–	–	–	–	–	–	–	1	–	–	47
Concord Jail, . .	–	–	–	–	–	–	–	–	1	–	–	–	–	1
Boston " . .	1	–	–	–	–	–	–	–	–	–	–	–	–	1
Boston House of Cor.	3	–	–	–	–	–	–	–	–	–	–	–	–	3
Dedham " .	1	–	–	–	–	–	–	–	–	–	–	–	–	1
N. Bedford, " .	3	–	–	–	–	–	–	–	–	–	–	–	–	3
Bridgewater State Almshouse, .	8	–	–	1	–	–	–	–	–	–	–	–	5	14
Monson State Almshouse, .	–	–	1	1	–	1	–	–	–	–	–	–	–	3
Tewksbury State Almshouse, .	11	–	2	1	–	–	–	–	–	–	–	–	–	14
At home—Pauper, .	21	2	5	1	–	–	–	–	–	–	–	–	–	29
At home—Independ't	23	1	3	–	1	–	–	–	–	–	–	–	–	28
State Prison, . .	2	–	–	–	–	–	–	–	–	–	–	–	–	2
Brattleboro' Hospital,	1	–	1	–	–	–	–	–	–	–	–	–	–	2
Totals, . .	512	17	49	23	6	1	2	2	3	1	1	1	7	625

FOREIGN LUNATICS IN HOSPITALS OF MASSACHUSETTS.

Among the foreign lunatics, a little more than a third of the independent class are in any hospital ; but almost the whole of the foreign paupers are in some public establishment for their restoration or protection.   71.9 per cent. are in the cura-tive hospitals, 17.7 per cent. in the custodial receptacles and prisons, and 5.3 per cent. in the State Almshouses, and most of those who are in the custodial institutions and State Alms-houses have had a fair trial of the remedial measures of the public hospitals before they were sent to their present abodes.

Among the American lunatics, only 35.4 per cent. of the in-dependent class, and 42.7 per cent. of the paupers, and 38.8 per cent. of all were in these establishments, and only 35 per cent. of the whole were in the curative hospitals.   Of all the insane, eight hundred and twenty-four of the natives and only sixteen of the foreigners have never had the benefit of such an institu-tion for the cure of their malady.

It is manifest, then, that the foreigners have enjoyed and are now enjoying the blessings of our hospitals to a greater degree than has been allowed to our own children in proportion to their numbers.

This might be expected from the relation of the alien to the State, which is the provider of these institutions.   Nearly the whole of the foreign lunatics, that is, 93 per cent. are paupers ; and as but few of these have gained any local residence, they are mostly wards of the State.   And if they are not originally paupers, but independent, or members of independent families, while in health, yet, as their friends cannot or will not provide for them when deranged, they are thrown at once upon the public treasury for support, and sent to the hospital as early as possible.   In doing this, the friends incur no responsibility of further burden.   On the other hand, they are relieved of that which is already on them, for they are thereby saved from the expense of supporting the patient, and consequently expend less when he is in the hospital than when he is at home.

The Commonwealth owns the hospitals, and, of course, takes its wards at once to those houses which it has in possession ; and if they cannot be restored, it still retains a part in these

9

institutions, and provides for the transfer of the rest to the
County Receptacles and the Houses of Correction, and recently
to the State Almshouses, and in one or other of these places it
still maintains them.   There is, then, no hesitation, no room
for doubt, on the part of the friends of a foreign pauper lunatic,
in regard to removing him from home to the hospital, and no
difficulty in his being received.

But the native lunatic is not so unhesitatingly and readily
removed from his home to the public institution.

If he belongs to the independent class, there are the objections of both affection and economy.   Many friends hesitate
and doubt whether they will send a beloved relative away in
the time of his sickness, when he seems to need their sympathy
and care more than ever.   Many of them cling to him, and are
willing to make any sacrifice and try every domestic means
and experiment before they can consent to part with him and
consign him to the care of strangers.

Beside these, there are the motives of economy, which influence the friends in the choice of means of providing for those
under their charge whose minds are diseased.   The payment
of the expenses of a patient in the hospital, in money, is a
burden not easily borne by a large portion of our farmers,
mechanics and professional men, although they may have
sufficient income for sustenance and for the enjoyment of every
comfort at their homes.   These families, therefore, are induced to wait before they consent to assume this burden of
boarding their lunatic member abroad, until the necessity of
removal becomes too great to be resisted.   But too often, as
the returns show, these motives of affection or economy prevail
effectually, and the patient is kept at home so long that his
disease is suffered to become permanent and incurable.

The same motives of economy weigh with the municipal
authorities in regard to the pauper lunatics under their charge.
As they can keep them at their poorhouses at a less cost than
at the hospitals, some are fearful of incurring the additional
expense, and retain their patients, as long as possible, at their
homes; some others never send them to a hospital; and in
either case the disease becomes incurable.

Thus, while those who have the charge of the native lunatics, the friends and the overseers of the poor, are generally required to meet and overcome the obstacle of increase of expense in sending their patients to a proper place for cure or custody, and therefore find strong motives for delay or entire neglect of this measure, the friends of the foreigner find a relief of a burden and a diminution of expense by adopting this measure and sending their patients to be cured.

The same economical reason that induces the friends and guardians of a foreign lunatic to provide the best means for the healing of his disease, or for his protection and comfort in the State hospitals, operates on the contrary to close them against the American, who is suffering from the same malady and has the same wants. So the State, while it offers a bounty to the foreign population and families for sending their lunatics to its hospitals, levies a tax upon the native population and families for doing the same.

We consequently find that, while 36 per cent. of the American lunatics were sent to the Worcester Hospital within three months after their supposed attack, 70 per cent. of the foreign lunatics were sent within the same period; and while 43 per cent. of the natives were not sent until their disease had been established a year or more, only 11 per cent. of the aliens were kept away as long.

In those protracted cases, where the best hospital measures are tried for the native patient and fail, and the disease becomes permanent, the resources or the courage of his friends and guardians are often exhausted; and, being unable or unwilling to bear the burden of maintaining him away from home or from the town poorhouse merely for the sake of custody, they take him back to their private dwellings or to the almshouses, where he remains, if possible, through the remainder of his days.

But the alien has no such home to fall back upon. His relations cannot receive him. Or if he be a pauper, he is not subject to the charge of the town, but to that of the State. He has, therefore, no poorhouse to return to, and must remain in the only places which the Commonwealth has provided for its wards—that is, the State hospitals, receptacles, &c.

Seeing, then, that the State necessarily makes the first use of its own dwellings, the public hospitals and receptacles, for its own wards, who are mostly foreign, and retains the incurables there permanently because it has no other home for them—seeing, also, that the independent and town pauper lunatic can be admitted only on condition of paying the cost, which keeps many out, and takes others away if they are not restored,—the natural tendency is to fill the hospitals at Worcester, Taunton and Boston, and the receptacles of Middlesex and Essex, with a great disproportion of foreign inmates, while their advantages are enjoyed in a comparatively small degree by the natives.

Thus, while our bountiful Commonwealth apparently provides hospitals liberally for its own people, and has, in terms, offered them to all within its borders who need them, the law and the custom, and the irresistible force of circumstances, have given these first to the children of another land. Whatever may have been the design and the theory, the practical operation of our system is, to give up our hospital accommodations for permanent residence without measure to almost the whole of the lunatic strangers, while these blessings are offered with a sparing economy to a little more than a third of our own children who are in a similar situation.

The propriety and expediency of this generous provision for the alien lunatics will not be questioned here, for not one of these thus provided for should be neglected. Indeed, it is the great honor of our Commonwealth that it has built—not monuments of glory—but these institutions for the relief of the suffering of even the humblest of the strangers that come among us. That which we have done in this way is well done; but then there is another duty superadded to this—many think it should take precedence—of providing for the cure and the protection of our own sons and daughters when bereft of reason, and of placing the means within the reach and the motives of those who stand to them as guardians in their illness, so that these may be practically enjoyed by them in as great a degree as they are by the aliens; for surely "these ought we to have done, and not to leave the others undone."

PROSPECT OF THE INSANE—INCURABILITY AND CURABILITY.

The evidence that comes from our own and many other hospitals shows that there are manifold disorders of the brain, producing perversion of mental and moral action in numberless forms, classed under the general term of insanity. These are usually grave diseases; and yet they are among the most curable of maladies of their severity, provided they are taken in season and the proper remedies applied and continued. In recent cases, the recoveries amount to the proportion of 75 to 90 per cent. of all that are submitted to the restorative process. Yet it is an equally well-established fact that these disorders of the brain tend to fix themselves permanently in the organization, and that they become more and more difficult to be removed with the lapse of time. Although three-fourths to nine-tenths may be healed if taken within a year after the first manifestation of the disorder, yet if this measure be delayed another year, and the diseases are from one to two years' standing, the cures would probably be less than half of that proportion, even with the same restorative means. Another and a third year added to the disease diminishes the prospect of cure, and in a still greater ratio than the second; and a fourth still more. The fifth reduces it so low as to seem to be nothing. Then hope has no visible ground to rest upon; and if it still remain, it is rather founded on desire and affection than on any established principles of pathological science. After this period, insanity is usually deemed to be incurable; nevertheless there are few and occasional recoveries; but these are so rare and uncertain, and have such a doubtful connection with the means and appliances used for such cases, that they seem to be rather the offspring of chance than the results of rational calculation and treatment.

Notwithstanding the very great probability of recovery in the early stages of insanity, approaching nearer to a certainty than the cure of fevers, dysenteries, pneumonia, or other severe diseases, which are never neglected, and notwithstanding the almost certain incurability of the malady if allowed to pass over several years, there are found in the State eight hundred and forty lunatics who have never been in any hospital, and probably have never enjoyed the recognized means of recovery.

Some of these have been deranged more than thirty years, some forty, and some fifty years, and of course their diseases began and were probably fixed beyond power or even hope of removal before they had a chance of obtaining relief in the hospital. Yet a great proportion of these old cases date no farther back than 1833, when that institution was opened and offered to all. These, as well as the other chronic cases, have mostly passed beyond the power of man to restore them. They are deemed to be incurable, and remain standing and abiding monuments of the neglect of the State to provide the means of health, and place them within the reach or the comprehension of the friends and guardians who had immediate charge of them, or of the neglect of those friends and guardians to avail themselves of these opportunities of restoration when they were offered to them.

The physicians were asked to state whether the patients were supposed to be curable or incurable. This is done in a large part of the cases; and the following tables show how these were distributed in the several counties :—

TABLE XIII.—PROSPECT OF LUNATICS AT HOME.

COUNTIES.	NATIVE.				FOREIGN.				ALL NATIONS.			
	PROSPECT.				PROSPECT.				PROSPECT.			
	Curable.	Incurable.	Not stated.	Total.	Curable.	Incurable.	Not stated.	Total.	Curable.	Incurable.	Not stated.	Total.
Berkshire, . . .	26	55	10	91	–	1	–	1	26	56	10	92
Franklin, ...	9	50	9	68	–	–	–	–	9	50	9	68
Hampshire, . . .	6	51	13	70	–	1	–	1	6	52	13	71
Hampden, . . .	10	48	12	70	1	2	–	3	11	50	12	73
Worcester, . . .	28	169	22	219	–	6	–	6	28	175	22	225
Middlesex, . . .	23	113	21	157	6	5	1	12	29	118	22	169
Essex, ...	12	132	21	165	7	3	1	11	19	135	22	176
Suffolk, ...	5	6	6	17	7	3	–	10	12	9	6	27
Norfolk, ...	21	84	8	113	1	1	2	4	22	85	10	117
Bristol, ...	10	64	15	89	2	4	–	6	12	68	15	95
Plymouth, . . .	12	68	12	92	–	2	–	2	12	70	12	94
Barnstable, . . .	14	34	11	59	–	–	–	–	14	34	11	59
Nantucket, . . .	–	2	1	3	–	–	–	–	–	2	1	3
Dukes, ...	5	9	–	14	–	1	–	1	5	10	–	15
Totals, . . .	181	885	161	1227	24	29	4	57	205	914	165	1284

TABLE XIV.—PROSPECT OF LUNATICS

In Hospitals, Receptacles, Prisons and State Almshouses.

| COUNTIES. | AMERICAN. | | | | FOREIGN. | | | | ALL NATIONS. | | | |
| | PROSPECT. | | | | PROSPECT. | | | | PROSPECT. | | | |
	Curable.	Incurable.	Not stated.	Total.	Curable.	Incurable.	Not stated.	Total.	Curable.	Incurable.	Not stated.	Total.
Berkshire, . . .	1	20	1	22	1	4	–	5	2	24	1	27
Franklin, ...	1	13	–	14	–	2	–	2	1	15	–	16
Hampshire, . . .	1	17	–	18	2	3	–	5	3	20	–	23
Hampden, . . .	5	16	–	21	1	10	–	11	6	26	–	32
Worcester, . . .	14	65	3	82	8	35	1	44	22	100	4	126
Middlesex, . . .	19	86	2	107	8	73	–	81	27	159	2	188
Essex, ...	15	106	1	122	9	70	–	79	24	176	1	201
Suffolk, ...	43	143	3	189	32	210	–	242	75	353	3	431
Norfolk, ...	15	65	1	81	15	28	–	43	30	93	1	124
Bristol, ...	14	33	–	47	9	7	–	16	23	40	–	63
Plymouth, . . .	8	32	–	40	1	4	–	5	9	36	–	45
Barnstable, . . .	4	13	–	17	–	2	–	2	4	15	–	19
Nantucket, . . .	1	6	–	7	–	2	–	2	1	8	–	9
Dukes, ...	–	4	–	4	–	–	–	–	–	4	–	4
State Almshouses, . .	1	8	–	9	2	27	2	31	3	35	2	40
Totals, ...	142	627	11	780	88	477	3	568	230	1104	14	1348

Table XV.—PROSPECT OF ALL THE LUNATICS IN MASSACHUSETTS.

COUNTIES.	NATIVE.				FOREIGN.				ALL NATIONS.			
	PROSPECT.				PROSPECT.				PROSPECT.			
	Curable.	Incurable.	Not stated.	Total.	Curable.	Incurable.	Not stated.	Total.	Curable.	Incurable.	Not stated.	Total.
Berkshire, . . .	27	75	11	113	1	5	–	6	28	80	11	119
Franklin, . . .	10	63	9	82	–	2	–	2	10	65	9	84
Hampshire, . . .	7	68	13	88	2	4	–	6	9	72	13	94
Hampden, . . .	15	64	12	91	2	12	–	14	17	76	12	105
Worcester, . .	42	234	25	301	8	41	1	50	50	275	26	351
Middlesex, . .	42	199	23	264	14	78	1	93	56	277	24	357
Essex, ...	27	238	22	287	16	73	1	90	43	311	23	377
Suffolk, . . .	48	149	9	206	39	213	–	252	87	362	9	458
Norfolk, . . .	36	149	9	194	16	29	2	47	52	178	11	241
Bristol, . . .	24	97	15	136	11	11	–	22	35	108	15	158
Plymouth, . .	20	100	12	132	1	6	–	7	21	106	12	139
Barnstable, . .	18	47	11	76	–	2	–	2	18	49	11	78
Nantucket, . .	1	8	1	10	–	2	–	2	1	10	1	12
Dukes, ...	5	13	–	18	–	1	–	1	5	14	–	19
State Almshouses, .	1	8	–	9	2	27	2	31	3	35	2	40
Totals, . . .	323	1512	172	2007	112	506	7	625	435	2018	179	2632

10

TABLE XVI—PROSPECTS OF LUNATICS IN CLASSES.

		CURABLE.				INCURABLE.				
		At home.	In hospital.	In receptacles, jails, &c.	Total.	At home.	In hospital.	In receptacles, jails, &c.	Total.	Ratio of all.
Independ't	Native, . . .	137	84	2	223	454	274	6	734	76
	Foreign, . . .	13	4	–	17	12	10	–	22	56
	Totals, . . .	150	88	2	240	466	284	6	756	75
Pauper.	Native, . . .	44	50	6	100	431	288	59	778	88
	Foreign, . . .	11	76	8	95	17	344	123	484	83
	Totals, . . .	55	126	14	195	448	632	182	1,262	86
Both Classes.	Native, . . .	181	134	8	323	885	562	65	1,152	82
	Foreign, . . .	24	80	8	112	29	354	123	506	82
	Totals, . . .	205	214	16	435	914	916	188	2,018	82

There is a greater proportion of the incurable in the hospitals, receptacles and prisons, than at home, being in the ratio of 81.89 per cent. to 71.18 per cent. among the whole. But in the lunatic hospitals this ratio is only 70 per cent.; while in the receptacles, prisons and State almshouses, it was 91.8 per cent.

SOME CASES OF INSANITY PRIMARILY INCURABLE.

It is not to be assumed that all of those now at their homes, who are stated to be incurable, could have been restored if they had been allowed to enjoy the remedial measures and influences offered in a hospital or elsewhere, nor that the incurables now in hospitals would have been cured if they had been sent there in the early stages of their disease; because the opposing fact is also known, that some of the former have been in such institutions, and some of the latter were submitted to their treatment within a few weeks or months after their disorder came upon them.

There is a diversity in those diseases of the brain by which insanity is produced; they differ in their origin and in their manifestation, in the effect they have upon, or the changes they produce in, the physical organ of the mind, and consequently in their permanence. Some, in their very beginning, produce such changes in the brain as to destroy all power of returning to its healthy condition. Of course these never recover; and any one becoming insane from these causes is primarily and forever incurable.

The experience of hospitals testifies to this doctrine: Wherever they have discriminated and classified their cases according to their origin, and determined the result of the treatment of each class, they show that there is a difference in the curability of the diseases that arise from various causes. Including all of these classes of cases submitted to its care, the printed reports of the Hospital in Worcester show that 72 per cent. of those which were supposed to be produced by religious excitement and emotions, 70 per cent. of those from ill health, 15 per cent. of those from epilepsy, and only 11 per cent. of those which were caused by the lowest sensuality, were restored. These results are corroborated by the experience of the Ohio Hospital at Columbus. Thus, notwithstanding their best remedial influences were applied to all of them with equal faithfulness and energy and with equal promptness, while nearly three-fourths of one class were restored, nearly nine-tenths of another class permanently resisted all these efforts, and remained uncured and incurable.

Besides the incurability of some cases of lunacy inherent in their very origin, there are also other and subsidiary influences that afterwards intervene to prevent the possibility of restoration, however judiciously and perseveringly it may be sought.

Even supposing, then, that every case of lunacy was, in its beginning, submitted to the best remedial measures that human skill has yet devised, there would still be some that baffle all effort and remain unhealed, and there must be a surplus of cases to be supported in their disease during their earthly lives.

As every year adds to the number of the insane, and will do so until we lead more perfect lives, and learn, by a better self-administration, to avoid the causes of this disease, and as, in the present state of science a portion of them will fail of being restored, there will be an annual surplus to be added to the list of incurables. This process has been going on in Massachusetts for years, until there are two thousand and eighteen of those who cannot enjoy the light of reason again on earth. But with all this unavoidable addition to their numbers, they need not amount to the great proportion—more than three-fourths of the whole—that we now have among us.

A part of the two thousand and eighteen incurables necessarily become so from the nature of their malady. But another, and perhaps a larger, part become so from the want of early means of restoration.

MALES AND FEMALES.

There were twelve hundred and fifty-nine males and thirteen hundred and seventy-three females among the insane of this State. These were in proportion to the whole calculated population of their respective sexes—one male lunatic in four hundred and forty-two, and one female lunatic in four hundred and thirteen, being a small excess of the latter. Among the natives, this ratio to the population is nearly the same, being one in every four hundred and forty-four males, and one in every four hundred and forty-three females.

There is, however, a marked difference in the sexes among the foreigners, there being two hundred and seventy-eight males, or one in four hundred and thirty-five, and three hundred and forty-seven females, or one in three hundred and twenty-six of their sexes respectively.

A larger proportion of the males are supported by the towns; but a considerably larger proportion of the females are State paupers, which is due to the excess of foreign female lunatics. A larger proportion of the females than of the males are in the curative hospitals; but a much larger proportion of the males are in the receptacles and prisons.

The present condition of both sexes is nearly the same, and the prospects are shown to be exactly alike, there being the same proportion of each who are curable and who are incurable, as is shown in the last line of table XVII.

The excess of females among the lunatics of Massachusetts is owing to accidental circumstances, and in a great measure to the number of foreigners. But insanity is not universally, nor even generally, distributed in this proportion among the sexes. The reports of two hundred and fifty hospitals in America and Europe show that, during the various periods of their existence, they received sixty-four thousand seven hundred and eighty-six male, and sixty thousand two hundred and forty-two female, patients.

The following table shows the distribution of various classes of the insane among the sexes in Massachusetts:—

TABLE XVII.—SEXES.

	MALES.						FEMALES.					
		CONDITION.			PROSPECT.			CONDITION.			PROSPECT.	
	Total.	Mild—manageable.	Excitable—troublesome	Furious—dangerous.	Curable.	Incurable.	Total.	Mild—manageable.	Excitable—troublesome	Furious—dangerous.	Curable.	Incurable.
Native, . .	981	503	331	94	147	777	1026	511	362	73	178	752
Irish, . .	201	77	92	21	28	167	311	105	157	43	43	228
British, . .	40	15	12	6	4	28	26	9	11	3	1	15
German, . .	20	7	12	1	1	19	3	2	–	–	1	–
Other Foreign,	17	3	10	–	1	14	7	3	1	1	2	4
Total Foreign,	278	102	126	28	34	228	347	119	169	47	47	247
Independent, .	525	295	186	26	107	362	585	278	221	36	128	391
Town Paupers,	420	229	136	52	46	359	409	201	162	33	36	285
State Paupers,	314	114	149	43	45	268	379	120	192	58	55	319
Total Paupers,	734	343	285	95	91	627	788	321	354	91	91	604
At Home, .	602	383	161	53	102	437	682	415	226	42	106	508
In Hospitals, .	522	220	241	56	85	434	619	200	305	82	109	413
In Receptacles,	92	32	58	2	2	90	54	19	31	4	3	51
In Prisons, .	16	8	3	5	7	9	5	2	2	1	1	4
State Almsh'ses	18	7	8	3	–	18	22	8	9	5	3	19
Ratio, . .	1000	530	371	99	152	848	1000	512	391	95	152	848

IDIOTS.

The main object of the Legislature in ordering this inquiry was, to ascertain the number and condition of the insane, in order to determine the amount and kind of the responsibility which rests upon the State or the people for their restoration or protection, or for the safety of the community. The preliminary Memorial of the Trustees of the Worcester Hospital and the Report of the Committee of Charitable Institutions, to whom the matter was referred, and who proposed this Resolve, seem to have this object exclusively in view.

Nevertheless, as the Resolve specified idiots among the subjects of inquiry, the Commission included them in their circulars, and answers were obtained to these questions through the same channels—the physicians and others who reported the insane.

And although in this connection all information in regard to idiots will have no other importance than to supply statistical information in respect to one of the most humiliating infirmities of the human race, and may lead to no immediate measures for their relief or the relief of the State, yet, as it shows the extent and kind of one of the burdens resting upon the people, and as a matter of future reference, the facts respecting idiocy are presented here in detail.

DISTINCTION BETWEEN DEMENTED AND IDIOT.

In making this inquiry, the witnesses were especially requested to regard the scientific and recognized distinction between lunatics and idiots, and cautioned against the commonly received idea, that the term *idiocy* should be applied to all who are deprived of mental power. An idiot is one who was originally destitute of mind, or in whom the mental faculties have not been developed. Those who have once had the use of their mental faculties, but have lost them through the process of disease, are not idiots, but demented, deprived of mind, which has once been enjoyed. This is a very common result of insanity; and a large portion of lunatics whose disease is protracted, and some in the earlier stages of their malady, fall into this condition; then they present similar manifestations of those of idiots, and by many are classed among them.

Nevertheless, these demented patients are sometimes called lunatics, and sometimes idiots, by those who look exclusively at their present condition, and not at their history. From this looseness of interpretation, there is a great variety in the classification of those who report these facts, some including more, and some less, of the demented among the insane or the idiots.

In taking the census of the United States in 1850, the marshals differed very widely in their interpretation of this matter; and hence the tables of the insane and idiots show a corresponding difference in the proportion of these two classes in the several States. There are stated to be in Rhode Island forty-two idiots, in Massachusetts forty-six, in New York sixty-three, in Virginia one hundred and fifty-seven, in Tennessee one hundred and seventy-eight, and in Alabama two hundred and six, for every one hundred lunatics within these States respectively. And there are all degrees of difference between these extremes in the other States. In some of the newer States the difference is much greater than this, which may be owing, in part at least, to the fact that the immigrants did not carry their idiots with them, while their lunatics may have become diseased since their removal.

Idiots, if they belong to independent families, are usually kept at home; and if paupers, in the almshouses. Sixty-one of these are violent and dangerous, and need the confinement and guardianship of a hospital for the public security at least.

From the report of the physicians the following table is prepared, showing the distribution, sex, nativity, pecuniary condition and age of the idiots in the State:—

TABLE XVIII.—IDIOTS IN TOWNS.

Pecuniary Condition and Age.

BERKSHIRE COUNTY.

TOWNS.	SEX.		INDEPENDENT.			PAUPER.		
	Male.	Female.	Under Sixteen.	Sixteen and over.	Subject for hospital.	Under Sixteen.	Sixteen and over.	Subject for hospital.
Adams, ...	6	2	2	3	–	1	2	3
Alford, ...	–	2	–	2	–	–	–	–
Becket, ...	2	1	–	–	–	–	3	–
Cheshire, . . .	2	3	–	1	–	–	4	–
Clarksburg, . . .	–	–	–	–	–	–	–	–
Dalton, ...	–	–	–	–	–	–	–	–
Egremont, . . .	1	–	–	1	–	–	–	–
Florida, ...	–	–	–	–	–	–	–	–
Great Barrington, . .	1	3	1	1	–	–	2	1
Hancock, . . .	–	–	–	–	–	–	–	–
Hinsdale, . . .	–	2	–	2	–	–	–	–
Lanesboro', . . .	2	–	–	2	–	–	–	–
Lee, ...	–	2	–	2	–	–	–	–
Lenox, ...	1	–	–	–	–	–	1	1
Monterey, . . .	2	–	–	2	–	–	–	–
Mount Washington, .	4	–	1	3	–	–	–	–
New Ashford, . .	–	–	–	–	–	–	–	–

BERKSHIRE—Continued.

TOWNS.	SEX.		INDEPENDENT.			PAUPER.		
	Male.	Female.	Under Sixteen.	Sixteen and over.	Subject for hospital.	Under Sixteen.	Sixteen and over.	Subject for hospital.
New Marlboro', . .	–	1	1	–	–	–	–	–
Otis, ...	–	–	–	–	–	–	–	–
Peru, ...	–	–	–	–	–	–	–	–
Pittsfield, . . .	3	4	–	4	–	1	2	1
Richmond, . . .	–	1	1	–	–	–	–	–
Sandisfield, . . .	5	2	4	1	–	1	1	–
Savoy, ...	–	–	–	–	–	–	–	–
Sheffield, . . .	3	3	1	2	–	–	3	–
Stockbridge, . .	4	1	1	–	1	1	3	1
Tyringham, . . .	–	2	–	–	–	1	1	–
Washington, . . .	–	–	–	–	–	–	–	–
West Stockbridge, .	3	–	–	2	–	1	–	–
Williamstown, . .	4	1	–	5	2	–	–	–
Windsor, . . .	–	1	–	–	–	–	1	–

FRANKLIN COUNTY.

TOWNS.	SEX.		INDEPENDENT.			PAUPER.		
Ashfield, . . .	1	–	–	–	–	–	1	–
Bernardston, . . .	2	1	–	2	–	–	1	–
Buckland, . . .	–	–	–	–	–	–	–	–
Charlemont, . . .	–	–	–	–	–	–	–	–
Coleraine, . . .	2	–	–	1	–	–	1	–

FRANKLIN—Continued.

TOWNS.	SEX.		INDEPENDENT.			PAUPER.		
	Male.	Female.	Under Sixteen.	Sixteen and over.	Subject for hospital.	Under Sixteen.	Sixteen and over.	Subject for hospital.
Conway,	1	2	2	1	–	–	–	–
Deerfield,	1	6	2	4	1	–	1	–
Erving,	–	–	–	–	–	–	–	–
Gill,	–	3	1	1	–	–	1	–
Greenfield,	–	–	–	–	–	–	–	–
Hawley,	2	1	–	2	–	–	1	–
Heath,	2	2	–	–	–	–	4	–
Leverett,	1	–	–	1	–	–	–	–
Leyden,	2	1	–	–	–	1	2	–
Monson,	–	–	–	–	–	–	–	–
Montague,	2	1	1	2	–	–	–	–
New Salem,	1	4	1	2	–	–	1	–
Northfield,	4	1	2	2	–	1	–	–
Orange,	5	2	–	7	–	–	–	–
Rowe,	–	–	–	–	–	–	–	–
Shelburne,	–	–	–	–	–	–	–	–
Shutesbury,	1	1	–	–	–	1	1	1
Sunderland,	–	–	–	–	–	–	–	–
Warwick,	–	2	–	1	–	–	1	–
Wendell,	–	–	–	–	–	–	–	–
Whately,	–	–	–	–	–	–	–	–

HAMPSHIRE COUNTY.

TOWNS.	SEX.		INDEPENDENT.			PAUPER.		
	Male.	Female.	Under Sixteen.	Sixteen and over.	Subject for hospital.	Under Sixteen.	Sixteen and over.	Subject for hospital.
Amherst, . . .	1	2	–	–	–	–	3	–
Belchertown, . .	2	2	1	3	–	–	–	–
Chesterfield, . . .	2	–	–	–	–	–	2	–
Cummington, . .		–	–	–	–	–	–	–
Easthampton, . .	2	1	–	2	–	–	1	–
Enfield, ...	5	1	–	2	1	–	2	–
Goshen, . . .	–	–	–	–	–	–	–	–
Granby, . . .	–	–	–	–	–	–	–	–
Greenwich, . . .	3	2	–	4	–	–	1	–
Hadley, ...	3	4	–	7	–	–	–	–
Hatfield, . . .	–	1	–	1	–	–	–	–
Middlefield, . . .	–	–	–	–	–	–	–	–
Northampton, . .	2	2	1	3	1	–	–	–
Norwich, . . .	–	–	–	–	–	–	–	–
Pelham, . . .	1	–	–	–	–	1	–	1
Plainfield, . . .	1	2	–	3	–	–	–	–
Prescott, . . .	–	–	–	–	–	–	–	–
Southampton, . .	1	1	–	1	–	–	1	–
South Hadley, . .	2	1	2	1	–	–	–	–
Ware, ...	2	–	–	1	–	–	1	1
Westhampton, . .	–	–	–	–	–	–	–	–
Williamsburg, . .	–	–	–	–	–	–	–	–
Worthington, . .	1	–	–	–	–	–	1	–

HAMPDEN COUNTY.

TOWNS.	SEX.		INDEPENDENT.			PAUPER.		
	Male.	Female.	Under Sixteen.	Sixteen and over.	Subject for hospital.	Under Sixteen.	Sixteen and over.	Subject for hospital.
Blandford, . . .	5	1	1	4	–	1	–	–
Brimfield, . . .	2	–	–	–	–	1	–	–
Chester, . . .	2	2	–	2	–	1	1	1
Chicopee, . . .	1	1	2	–	–	–	–	–
Granville, . . .	–	–	–	–	–	–	–	–
Holland, . . .	–	–	–	–	–	–	–	–
Holyoke, . . .	–	–	–	–	–	–	–	–
Longmeadow, . .	1	2	–	–	–	–	3	–
Ludlow, . . .	1	–	1	–	–	–	–	–
Monson, . . .	2	1	–	1	–	1	1	–
Montgomery, . .	–	–	–	–	–	–	–	–
Palmer, . . .	–	1	1	–	–	–	–	–
Russell, . . .	–	–	–	–	–	–	–	–
Southwick, . . .	–	1	1	–	–	–	–	–
Springfield, . . .	6	1	1	6	–	–	–	–
Tolland, . . .	–	1	–	–	–	–	1	–
Wales, ...	1	–	1	–	–	–	–	–
Westfield, . . .	–	–	–	–	–	–	–	–
West Springfield, . .	3	–	–	1	–	–	2	–
Wilbraham, . . .	2	–	–	2	–	–	–	–

WORCESTER COUNTY.

TOWNS.	SEX.		INDEPENDENT.			PAUPER.		
	Male.	Female.	Under Sixteen.	Sixteen and over.	Subject for hospital.	Under Sixteen.	Sixteen and over.	Subject for hospital.
Ashburnham, . . .	2	2	1	2	–	–	1	–
Athol, ...	2	3	2	3	–	–	–	–
Auburn, . . .	1	–	–	1	–	–	–	–
Barre, ...	3	3	1	1	–	1	3	–
Berlin, ...	–	–	–	–	–	–	–	–
Blackstone, . . .	4	1	1	2	1	–	2	–
Bolton, ...	5	1	–	3	–	–	–	–
Boylston, . . .	–	1	–	–	–	1	–	–
Brookfield, . . .	3	3	–	2	–	–	4	–
Charlton, . . .	2	–	–	1	–	–	1	1
Clinton, . . .	1	1	–	–	–	–	2	–
Dana, ...	1	4	1	2	–	–	2	–
Douglas, . . .	7	3	1	6	–	1	2	–
Dudley, . . .	–	1	–	–	–	–	1	–
Fitchburg, . . .	–	1	–	–	–	–	1	–
Gardner, . . .	–	4	1	2	–	–	1	1
Grafton, . . .	1	1	2	1	2	–	–	–
Hardwick, . . .	2	3	–	2	–	–	3	–
Harvard, . . .	2	3	–	2	–	–	3	–
Holden, . . .	2	1	1	–	–	–	2	–
Hubbardston, . .	3	4	5	1	–	–	1	–
Lancaster, . . .	3	1	1	1	–	–	2	–
Leicester, . . .	3	–	2	1	–	–	–	–

WORCESTER—Continued.

TOWNS.	Sex.		Independent.			Pauper.		
	Male.	Female.	Under Sixteen.	Sixteen and over.	Subject for hospital.	Under Sixteen.	Sixteen and over.	Subject for hospital.
Leominster, . . .	1	3	–	2	–	–	2	–
Lunenburg, . . .	4	–	–	2	–	–	2	–
Mendon, . . .	1	3	2	1	–	–	1	–
Milford, . . .	–	2	–	2	–	–	–	–
Millbury, . . .	–	–	–	–	–	–	–	–
New Braintree, . .	–	–	–	–	–	–	–	–
Northboro', . . .	1	1	–	1	–	–	1	1
Northbridge, . . .	4	–	–	4	–	–	–	–
North Brookfield, . .	1	2	–	3	–	–	–	–
Oakham, . . .	3	–	1	2	–	–	–	–
Oxford, ...	1	6	–	4	–	–	3	–
Paxton, ...	–	1	–	–	–	–	1	–
Petersham, . . .	5	7	1	4	–	–	1	–
Phillipston, . . .	1	3	–	4	–	–	–	–
Princeton, . . .	–	–	–	–	–	–	–	–
Royalston, . . .	1	3	–	3	–	–	1	–
Rutland, . . .	1	2	–	2	–	–	1	–
Shrewsbury, . . .	4	3	–	3	–	1	1	–
Southboro', . . .	–	5	–	2	–	–	3	–
Southbridge, . . .	5	4	4	5	–	–	–	–
Spencer, . . .	6	–	1	5	–	–	–	–
Sterling, . . .	1	1	–	–	–	–	2	–
Sturbridge, . . .	–	5	–	2	–	1	2	–

WORCESTER—Continued.

TOWNS.	SEX.		INDEPENDENT.			PAUPER.		
	Male.	Female.	Under Sixteen.	Sixteen and over.	Subject for hospital.	Under Sixteen.	Sixteen and over.	Subject for hospital.
Sutton, .	3	3	–	2	–	–	4	–
Templeton, .	2	3	–	2	–	–	3	–
Upton, .	–	–	–	–	–	–	–	–
Uxbridge, .	5	-	3	1	–	–	1	–
Warren, .	5	–	3	2	–	–	–	–
Webster, .	–	4	–	–	–	–	4	–
Westboro', .	2	1	–	–	–	2	1	–
West Boylston, .	–	–	–	–	–	–	–	–
West Brookfield, .	–	2	–	1	1	–	–	–
Westminster, .	1	2	1	–	–	–	2	–
Winchendon, .	1	1	1	–	–	1	–	–
Worcester, .	5	4	4	2	–	1	2	1

MIDDLESEX COUNTY.

Acton, .	–	–	–	–	–	–	–	–
Ashby, .	–	–	–	–	–	–	–	–
Ashland, .	–	–	–	–	–	–	–	–
Bedford, .	–	–	–	–	–	–	–	–
Billerica, .	2	–	–	2	–	–	–	–
Boxboro', .	–	–	–	–	–	–	–	–
Brighton, .	–	–	–	–	–	–	–	–

MIDDLESEX—Continued.

TOWNS.	SEX.		INDEPENDENT.			PAUPER.		
	Male.	Female.	Under Sixteen.	Sixteen and over.	Subject for hospital.	Under Sixteen.	Sixteen and over.	Subject for hospital.
Burlington, . . .	1	–	–	1	–	–	–	–
Cambridge, . . .	5	1	3	3	–	–	–	–
Carlisle, . . .	–	–	–	–	–	–	–	–
Charlestown, . . .	2	1	1	1	–	–	1	–
Chelmsford, . . .	3	3	–	2	–	–	4	–
Concord, . . .	–	–	–	–	–	–	–	–
Dracut, ...	2	4	–	1	–	–	5	–
Dunstable, . . .	–	–	–	–	–	–	–	–
Framingham, . .	–	1	–	–	–	–	1	–
Groton, . . .	3	3	–	5	–	–	1	–
Holliston, . . .	4	2	2	3	–	–	–	–
Hopkinton, . . .	2	2	–	1	–	–	3	–
Lexington, . . .	4	1	–	4	1	–	1	–
Lincoln, . . .	1	–	–	1	–	–	–	–
Littleton, . . .	–	–	–	–	–	–	–	–
Lowell, ...	1	3	4	–	–	–	–	–
Malden, . . .	3	–	1	2	–	–	–	–
Marlboro', . . .	1	–	–	–	–	–	1	–
Medford, . . .	10	4	4	10	1	–	–	–
Melrose, . . .	3	–	–	1	–	–	2	1
Natick, ...	1	–	–	1	–	–	–	–
Newton, . . .	1	–	–	–	–	–	–	–
North Reading, . .	–	–	–	–	–	–	–	–

MIDDLESEX—Continued.

TOWNS.	Sex.		Independent.			Pauper.		
	Male.	Female.	Under Sixteen.	Sixteen and over.	Subject for hospital.	Under Sixteen.	Sixteen and over.	Subject for hospital.
Pepperell, . . .	1	1	–	1	–	–	1	–
Reading, . . .	1	1	–	1	–	–	1	–
Sherborn, . . .	5	4	–	7	–	–	2	–
Shirley, . . .	5	–	1	2	–	–	2	–
Somerville, . . .	–	–	–	–	–	–	–	–
South Reading, . .	1	–	–	1	–	–	–	–
Stoneham, . . .	–	–	–	–	–	–	–	–
Stowe, ...	–	–	–	–	–	–	–	–
Sudbury, . . .	3	3	1	2	–	–	3	–
Tewksbury, . . .	–	1	–	–	–	–	1	–
Townsend, . . .	2	1	1	–	–	–	2	–
Tyngsboro', . . .	–	–	–	–	–	–	–	–
Waltham, . . .	3	–	1	1	–	–	1	–
Watertown, . . .	1	–	–	1	1	–	–	–
Wayland, . . .	–	2	1	1	–	–	–	–
West Cambridge, . .	1	1	–	2	–	–	–	–
Westford, . . .	3	–	2	1	–	–	–	–
Weston, . . .	–	1	1	–	–	–	–	–
Wilmington, . . .	1	–	–	1	–	–	–	–
Winchester, . . .	–	1	–	1	–	–	–	–
Woburn, . . .	4	4	1	3	–	–	4	–

ESSEX COUNTY.

TOWNS.	SEX.		INDEPENDENT.			PAUPER.		
	Male.	Female.	Under Sixteen.	Sixteen and over.	Subject for hospital.	Under Sixteen.	Sixteen and over.	Subject for hospital.
Amesbury, . . .	2	3	–	2	–	–	3	–
Andover, . . .	3	–	–	1	1	–	2	–
Beverly, . . .	10	2	4	6	1	1	1	1
Boxford, . . .	–	1	–	–	–	–	1	–
Bradford, . . .	1	–	–	–	–	–	1	–
Danvers, . . .	2	6	2	1	–	1	4	–
Essex, ...	1	–	–	1	–	–	–	–
Georgetown, . . .	–	–	–	–	–	–	–	–
Gloucester, . . .	9	2	4	4	1	–	3	–
Groveland, . . .	2	–	1	1	1	–	–	–
Hamilton, . . .	1	–	–	–	–	–	1	–
Haverhill, . . .	3	1	–	1	–	–	3	–
Ipswich, . . .	5	2	2	4	1	–	1	1
Lawrence, . . .	–	1	–	–	–	–	1	1
Lynn, ...	–	–	–	–	–	–	–	–
Lynnfield, . . .	–	–	–	–	–	–	–	–
Manchester, . . .	3	1	–	3	–	–	1	–
Marblehead, . . .	–	1	–	–	–	–	1	–
Methuen, . . .	2	1	1	1	–	–	1	–
Middleton, . . .	–	1	–	1	–	–	–	–
Nahant, . . .	–	–	–	–	–	–	–	–
Newbury, . . .	–	–	–	–	–	–	–	–
Newburyport, . .	2	2	–	4	–	–	–	–

ESSEX—Continued.

TOWNS.	SEX.		INDEPENDENT.			PAUPER.		
	Male.	Female.	Under Sixteen.	Sixteen and over.	Subject for hospital.	Under Sixteen.	Sixteen and over.	Subject for hospital.
Rockport, . . .	4	2	1	–	–	–	5	–
Rowley, . . .	2	1	–	2	–	–	1	–
Salem, ...	11	8	–	6	1	2	11	–
Salisbury, . . .	6	1	–	2	–	–	5	–
Saugus, . . .	–	–	–	–	–	–	–	–
Swampscott, . . .	–	–	–	–	–	–	–	–
Topsfield, . . .	2	2	–	2	–	–	2	–
Wenham, . . .	1	–	1	–	–	–	–	–
West Newbury, . .	4	6	1	5	–	–	4	–

SUFFOLK COUNTY.

	Male.	Female.	Under Sixteen.	Sixteen and over.	Subject for hospital.	Under Sixteen.	Sixteen and over.	Subject for hospital.
Boston, ...	15	6	4	2	1	9	6	–
Chelsea, . . .	4	–	1	1	–	1	1	–

NORFOLK COUNTY.

	Male.	Female.	Under Sixteen.	Sixteen and over.	Subject for hospital.	Under Sixteen.	Sixteen and over.	Subject for hospital.
Bellingham, . . .	1	–	–	–	–	–	1	–
Braintree, . . .	2	1	–	2	–	–	1	1
Brookline, . . .	–	1	1	–	–	–	–	–
Canton, ...	1	3	3	–	–	⌐	1	–
Cohasset, . . .	1	–	–	1	1	–	–	–

NORFOLK—Continued.

TOWNS.	SEX.		INDEPENDENT.			PAUPER.		
	Male.	Female.	Under Sixteen.	Sixteen and over.	Subject for hospital.	Under Sixteen.	Sixteen and over.	Subject for hospital.
Dedham, . . .	–	2	2	–	–	–	–	–
Dorchester, . . .	1	1	–	1	–	–	1	–
Dover, ...	1	–	–	1	–	–	¬	–
Foxboro', . . .	–	–	–	–	–	–	–	–
Franklin, . . .	1	1	1	1	–	–	–	–
Medfield, . . .	1	1	–	–	–	–	–	–
Medway, . . .	1	1	–	1	1	–	1	–
Milton, ...	1	–	–	1	1	–	–	–
Needham, . . .	–	–	–	–	–	–	–	–
Quincy, . . .	2	2	2	2	–	–	–	–
Randolph, . . .	3	2	–	5	–	–	–	–
Roxbury, . . .	2	2	3	1	–	–	–	–
Sharon, ...	1	–	–	1	–	–	–	–
Stoughton, . . .	2	–	1	–	–	–	–	–
Walpole, . . .	2	1	1	1	–	–	1	–
West Roxbury, . .	1	–	–	1	–	–	–	–
Weymouth, . . .	14	9	9	7	–	–	6	–
Wrentham, . . .	3	2	2	1	–	–	2	–

BRISTOL COUNTY.

Attleboro', . . .	1	–	–	1	1	–	–	–
Berkley, . . .	5	3	–	4	–	–	4	–

BISTOL—Continued.

TOWNS.	Sex.		Independent.			Pauper.		
	Male.	Female.	Under Sixteen.	Sixteen and over.	Subject for hospital.	Under Sixteen.	Sixteen and over.	Subject for hospital.
Dartmouth, . . .	6	2	2	4	1	–	2	–
Dighton, . . .	4	1	2	3	1	–	–	–
Easton, ...	8	2	1	7	1	1	1	–
Fairhaven, . . .	5	5	2	7	1	–	1	–
Fall River, . . .	–	1	–	1	–	–	–	–
Freetown, . . .	1	3	1	2	1	–	1	–
Mansfield, . . .	5	5	4	4	–	–	2	–
New Bedford, . .	8	8	8	3	–	1	4	–
Norton, ...	–	–	–	–	–	–	–	–
Pawtucket, . . .	2	–	–	1	–	–	1	–
Raynham, . . .	–	1	1	–	–	–	–	–
Rehoboth, . . .	–	1	–	–	–	–	1	–
Seekonk, . . .	1	–	–	–	–	–	1	–
Somerset, . . .	2	–	–	–	–	–	–	–
Swanzey, . . .	2	2	–	4	–	–	–	–
Taunton, . . .	7	2	1	5	–	–	3	–
Westport, . . .	4	4	1	5	–	–	2	–

PLYMOUTH COUNTY.

Abington, . . .	2	2	2	2	–	–	–	–
Bridgewater, . . .	–	1	–	–	–	–	1	1
Carver, ...	4	1	–	4	–	–	1	–

PLYMOUTH—Continued.

TOWNS.	Sex.		Independent.			Pauper.		
	Male.	Female.	Under Sixteen.	Sixteen and over.	Subject for hospital.	Under Sixteen.	Sixteen and over.	Subject for hospital.
Duxbury, . . .	1	5	–	3	2	–	2	–
East Bridgewater, . .	–	–	–	–	–	–	–	–
Halifax, . . .	–		–	–	–	–	–	–
Hanover, . . .	–	–	–	–	–	–	–	–
Hanson, . . .	–	1	–	–	–	–	1	–
Hingham, . . .	2	–	–	–	–	1	1	1
Kingston, . . .	2	2	2	1	–	–	1	–
Lakeville, . . .	1	–	1	–	–	–	–	–
Marion, . . .	–	1	–	–	–	–	1	–
Marshfield, . . .	2	–	–	2	–	–	–	–
Middleboro', . .	4	4	2	5	–	–	1	–
North Bridgewater, .	–	–	–	–	–	–	–	–
Pembroke, . . .	5	2	–	2	–	–	5	–
Plymouth, . . .	2	2	1	–	–	–	3	1
Plympton, . . .	1	2	–	1	–	–	2	–
Rochester, . . .	2	7	1	5	1	–	3	–
Scituate, . . .	–	1	–	1	–	–	–	–
South Scituate, . .	5	2	–	7	–	–	–	–
Wareham, . . .	1	2	–	–	–	–	3	–
West Bridgewater, .	–	–	–	–	–	–	–	–

BARNSTABLE COUNTY.

TOWNS.	SEX.		INDEPENDENT.			PAUPER.		
	Male.	Female.	Under Sixteen.	Sixteen and over.	Subject for hospital.	Under Sixteen.	Sixteen and over.	Subject for hospital.
Barnstable, . . .	10	15	–	17	1	–	8	–
Brewster, . . .	1	–	1	–	–	–	–	–
Chatham, . . .	1	–	–	–	–	–	1	–
Dennis, ...	1	2	–	–	–	1	2	–
Eastham, . . .	–	2	–	–	–	–	2	–
Falmouth, . . .	1	1	–	2	–	–	–	–
Harwich, . . .	5	3	1	7	–	–	–	–
Orleans, . . .	4	4	–	5	–	–	3	–
Provincetown, . .	1	–	–	–	–	–	1	–
Sandwich, . . .	4	4	3	2	–	–	3	–
Truro, ...	6	2	3	2	–	–	3	–
Wellfleet, . . .	3	–	1	2	–	–	–	–
Yarmouth, . . .	1	1	–	–	–	1	1	1

NANTUCKET COUNTY.

TOWNS.	Male.	Female.	Under Sixteen.	Sixteen and over.	Subject for hospital.	Under Sixteen.	Sixteen and over.	Subject for hospital.
Nantucket, . . .	2	10	2	7	–	–	3	–

DUKES COUNTY.

TOWNS.	Male.	Female.	Under Sixteen.	Sixteen and over.	Subject for hospital.	Under Sixteen.	Sixteen and over.	Subject for hospital.
Chilmark, . . .	1	–	–	1	–	–	–	–
Edgartown, . . .	5	–	–	5	–	–	–	–
Tisbury, . . .	2	3	–	3	–	–	2	–

TABLE XIX.—NATIVE IDIOTS IN COUNTIES.

Social Position, Age, and Residence.

| COUNTIES. | INDEPENDENT. | | | | | PAUPER. | | | | |
| | AGE. | | | | | AGE. | | | | |
	Under Sixteen.	Sixteen and over.	Not stated.	Total.	Subject for hospital.	Under Sixteen.	Sixteen and over.	Not stated.	Total.	Subject for hospital.
Berkshire, . . .	6	34	–	40	3	7	26	–	33	6
Franklin, . . .	8	26	2	36	1	3	15	–	18	–
Hampshire, . . .	3	28	1	32	2	1	12	1	14	2
Hampden, . . .	6	15	1	22	–	6	8	–	14	–
Worcester, . . .	41	96	3	140	4	10	61	8	79	4
Middlesex, . . .	21	60	1	82	3	6	31	1	38	1
Essex, ...	17	44	1	62	5	4	50	7	61	3
Suffolk, . . .	5	3	–	8	1	10	3	–	13	1
Norfolk, . . .	23	25	4	52	3	4	16	–	20	1
Bristol, . . .	21	47	2	70	6	3	27	–	30	2
Plymouth, . . .	8	32	1	41	3	3	25	–	28	2
Barnstable, . . .	9	37	–	46	1	2	24	–	26	1
Nantucket, . . .	2	7	–	9	–	–	3	–	3	–
Dukes, ...	–	9	–	9	–	–	2	–	2	–
Monson State Almshouse,	–	–	–	–	–	3	7	–	10	–
Tewksbury S. "	–	–	–	–	–	1	–	1	2	–
Bridgewater S. "	–	–	–	–	–	2	1	–	3	–
Totals, . . .	170	463	16	651	32	65	311	18	394	23

13

TABLE XX.—NATIVE IDIOTS OF ALL CLASSES.

Age and Residence.

COUNTIES.	AGE.			Total.	Subject for hospital.
	Under Sixteen.	Sixteen and over.	Not stated.		
Berkshire, ...	13	60	–	73	9
Franklin, ...	11	41	2	54	1
Hampshire, ...	4	40	2	46	4
Hampden, ...	12	23	1	36	–
Worcester, ...	51	157	11	219	8
Middlesex, ...	27	91	2	120	4
Essex, ...	21	94	8	123	8
Suffolk, ...	15	6	–	21	2
Norfolk, ...	27	41	4	72	4
Bristol, ...	24	74	2	100	8
Plymouth, ...	11	57	1	69	5
Barnstable, ...	11	61	–	72	2
Nantucket, ...	2	10	–	12	–
Dukes, ...	–	11	–	11	–
State Almshouses, ...	6	8	1	15	–
Totals, ...	235	774	34	1,043	55

TABLE XXI.—FOREIGN IDIOTS.

Social Position, Age, and Residence.

COUNTIES.	SEX.		INDEPENDENT.		PAUPER.		BOTH CLASSES.	
			Age.		Age.		Age.	
	Male.	Female.	Under Sixteen.	Sixteen and over.	Under Sixteen.	Sixteen and over.	Under Sixteen.	Sixteen and over.
Berkshire, . . .	1	–	1	–	–	–	1	–
Franklin, . . .	–	–	–	–	–	–	–	–
Hampshire, . . .	1	–	1	–	–	–	1	–
Hampden, . . .	–	2	1	–	1	–	2	–
Worcester, . . .	6	–	4	1	–	1	4	2
Middlesex, . . .	3	6	4	–	1	4	5	4
Essex, ...	2	1	–	2	–	1	–	3
Suffolk, . . .	3	2	1	–	4	–	5	–
Norfolk, . . .	1	2	2	1	–	–	2	1
Bristol, . . .	2	-	1	1	–	–	1	1
Plymouth, . . .	–	2	–	–	1	1	1	1
Barnstable, . . .	–	–	–	–	–	–	–	–
Nantucket, . . .	–	–	–	–	–	–	–	–
Dukes, ...	–	–	–	–	–	–	–	–
State Almshouses, .	5	5	–	–	3	7	3	7
Totals, . . .	24	20	15	5	10	14	25	19

Of the total of those referred to in the preceding Table, (forty-four,) six are violent and should be confined in a hospital.

It is a noticeable fact, that a larger proportion of the idiots than of the lunatics are of the independent or self-sustaining classes; 61 per cent. of idiots, and only 42 per cent. of the lunatics, are supported by their friends or their own estates.

There were only forty-four idiots found in the State who were born in foreign lands and brought to live in Massachusetts, and twenty of these were of the independent class, and only twenty-four were paupers; and ten of these paupers were children under sixteen years of age, and probably were brought with their parents, who were naturally unwilling to leave them behind. Only fourteen of these paupers were over sixteen years old. And these are all that could by any means be supposed to be sent to this country from poorhouses abroad to be supported by public charity here; and there is no ground for suspicion that any of these were sent here for this purpose.

The idiots bear a much larger proportion to the lunatics among the natives than among the foreigners, being in the ratio of fifty-one native and seven foreign idiots for one hundred lunatics in each class respectively.

Although the foreign constitute so small a proportion of all the idiots in Massachusetts, and although the idiots constitute so small a proportion of the foreigners whose minds are defective or deranged, there is probably a large proportion of these native idiots who are children of foreigners, though born in this country.

The whole of the idiots, both native and foreign, independent and pauper, are shown in table XXII.

TABLE XXII.—IDIOTS OF ALL NATIONS.

Sex, Age, and Residence.

COUNTIES.	SEX.		AGE.			Subject for hospital.
	Male.	Female.	Under Sixteen.	Sixteen and over.	Not stated.	
Berkshire, ...	39	35	14	60	–	9
Franklin, ...	27	27	11	41	2	1
Hampshire, ...	28	19	5	40	2	4
Hampden, ...	28	10	14	23	1	1
Worcester, ...	116	109	55	159	11	9
Middlesex, ...	85	50	32	101	2	4
Essex, ...	79	47	21	97	8	10
Suffolk, ...	14	6	14	6	–	2
Norfolk, ...	43	32	29	42	4	4
Bristol, ...	65	37	25	75	2	9
Plymouth, ...	37	34	12	58	1	6
Barnstable, ...	38	34	11	61	–	2
Nantucket, ...	2	10	2	10	–	–
Dukes, ...	8	3	–	11	–	–
State Almshouses, . . .	13	12	9	15	1	–
Totals, ...	622	465	254	799	34	61

The two hundred and fifty-four under sixteen years of age are presumed to be capable of improvement by the training now offered by the State in the Idiot School, and are proper candidates for that institution. It is not to be assumed that those who are over this age have passed the period of improvement, but that, unless the means of education have been applied in the earlier years, it becomes of little avail afterwards; and therefore the Massachusetts school very properly limits its candidates to those within the age above specified.

COLORED INSANE AND IDIOTS.

There were found nine colored lunatics and ten colored idiots within the State; these were distributed through the counties as in the following table :—

TABLE XXIII.—COLORED LUNATICS AND IDIOTS.

COUNTIES.	Lunatics.	Idiots.	COUNTIES.	Lunatics.	Idiots.
Berkshire, . . .	1	–	Suffolk, . . .	–	1
Franklin, . . .	–	1	Norfolk, . . .	–	1
Hampshire, . .	1	2	Plymouth, . .	3	–
Hampden, . . .	–	2	Barnstable, . .	–	1
Middlesex, . .	1	1	Nantucket, . .	1	–
Essex, . . .	2	1	Totals, . .	9	10

RATIO OF LUNATICS AND IDIOTS TO POPULATION.

It is a matter of interest to know the proportion of persons of diseased or defective minds to the whole population, both for the sake of determining as nearly as possible, by such a calculation, the general liability of the people to become insane or idiotic, and the degree of responsibility for their support. It is also desirable to have these data as grounds of comparison of the several counties with each other, and the State with other States or countries.

TABLE XXIV.—RATIO OF LUNATICS AND IDIOTS TO POPULATION.

COUNTIES.	Calculated Population.	NUMBER.			RATIO TO POPULATION.		
		Lunatics.	Idiots.	Both.	Lunatics—one in	Idiots—onel n	Both—one in
Berkshire, . .	53,123	119	74	193	446	717	275
Franklin, . . .	31,735	84	54	138	377	587	229
Hampshire, . .	37,872	94	47	141	402	805	268
Hampden, . .	58,208	105	38	143	554	1,531	407
Worcester, . .	148,421	351	225	576	422	659	258
Middlesex, . .	190,462	357	135	492	533	1,410	387
Essex, . . .	149,486	377	126	503	396	1,186	297
Suffolk, . . .	170,351	458	20	478	371	8,517	356
Norfolk, . . .	92,400	241	75	316	383	1,232	292
Bristol, . . .	83,741	158	102	260	530	820	322
Plymouth, . .	59,416	139	71	210	427	836	282
Barnstable, . .	36,427	78	72	150	467	505	242
Nantucket, . .	8,238	12	12	24	686	686	343
Dukes, . . .	4,796	19	11	30	252	436	159
State Almshouses, .	–	40	25	65	–	–	–
Massachusetts, .	1,124,676	2,632	1,087	3,719	427	1,034	302

There is, then, one lunatic among every four hundred and twenty-seven, and one idiot among every one thousand and thirty-four, and one of either of these classes among every three hundred and two of the people of Massachusetts.

Regarding the nativity of the people and patients,—among the natives, the lunatics were one in four hundred and forty-six, and the idiots one in eight hundred and eighty-nine, and one of both in two hundred and ninety-five of the Americans. And among the foreigners, the lunatics were one in three hundred and eighty-four, and the idiots one in seven thousand nine hundred and thirty-one, and one of both in three hundred and sixty-seven of the strangers. Among the colored population, the lunatics were one in one thousand and twenty-five, the idiots one in nine hundred and twenty-two, and both classes one in four hundred and eighty-five of this race.

This is the measure and the kind of burden of lunacy and idiocy resting upon the State of Massachusetts. We have two thousand six hundred and thirty-two lunatics, and one thousand and eighty-seven idiots, and three thousand seven hundred and nineteen of both. Of the lunatics, two thousand and seven are natives, and six hundred and twenty-five are foreigners ; one thousand one hundred and ten are independent, or supported by their own or their friends' income or capital ; one thousand five hundred and twenty-two are paupers; and of these, eight hundred and twenty-nine are supported by the cities or towns to which they belong, and six hundred and ninety-three by the State. Four hundred and thirty-five are supposed to be curable, or at least there is no evidence that they cannot be restored ; two thousand and eighteen are supposed to be incurable, and these must be supported for life.

In whatever way we look at them, these lunatics are a burden upon the Commonwealth. The curable during their limited period of disease, and the incurable during the remainder of their lives, not only cease to produce, but they must eat the bread they do not earn, and consume the substance they do not create, receiving their sustenance from the treasury of the Commonwealth or of some of its towns, or from the income or capital of some of its members.

There is no escape from this position. Whatever and

wherever these lunatics may be, whether native or foreign, independent or pauper, curable or incurable, the Commonwealth
is not only deprived of that amount which by their earnings in
health they contributed to its income, but more is now needed
for their support than when they were able to earn it.

There being, then, no question whether the State and its
people will bear this burden and support these lunatics, still
the question may be asked, whether the weight may not be
diminished in part and sustained in part with more ease to the
Commonwealth, and to the towns, and to the friends of the
patients.

It has already been stated (page 69) that insanity, if not
cured in its early stages, becomes more and more difficult to
be removed, and, in course of a longer or shorter period, varying mostly from two to five years, becomes fixed and incurable.
Then the patient is to be supported for life. On the other
hand, if the disease be submitted to proper remedial measures,
three-fourths or nine-tenths may be restored, and this proportion
of the patients made again self-supporting members of society.

The time required for the cure of different patients, in different forms or degrees of disease, varies from a few months in
most cases to a few years in extreme cases.*

The question, then, in regard to the curable cases, which
constitute three-fourths or nine-tenths of all when attacked, is
between the effort and the expenditure needed for their support
and the restorative means during the healing process through
a few months, or their support during their lives. Between the
cost of supporting for a few months and that of supporting for
life, no private economist, and certainly no political economist
or statesman, should hesitate.

The cost of restoring a lunatic to health, and enjoyment,
and power of self-sustenance, and of contributing to the support of his family, and also of bearing his part of the burden of
the State, is limited, and easily paid in money; the gain is
unmeasured. But the cost of lifelong lunacy, distressing and

* The reports of five American hospitals show that the average time required
for the recovery of the patients who had been deranged less than one year, was
about five and a half months, and for all patients a little less than seven months.
See Appendix, A.

14

oppressive to the friends who have the patient in charge, is
immeasurable, and not to be paid in money.

Humanity would admit of no choice between these; and the
State, which is the guardian of the weak and the friendless,
should surely not entertain a moment's doubt as to which it
should choose.

NECESSITY OF UNUSUAL MEANS FOR THE CURE OF INSANITY.

As the disordered stomach cannot ordinarily bear the common food that others in health enjoy and digest, but needs
some change of diet in order to be restored, so the deranged
mind is generally troubled by the common ideas and thoughts
which it found agreeable when in health, and cannot regain
its former tone unless a different set of ideas is presented to it.
The associates and the scenes of home, the common affairs of
the family, and neighborhood and business amidst which the
mind became disturbed, furnish most of the ideas and suggest
most of the thoughts to those who are among them; and
therefore, if an insane person is to be relieved of the thoughts
and ideas that troubled him, and have a change in his mental
action, he must be removed from his home and friends, and
have a change in his associates and in the objects of his attention and interest.

Men of disordered mind, when they need a change of air or
scene, cannot go to a hotel, a boarding-house, or even a friend's
private house, as those can who are merely invalids in body.
They require more caution, forbearance and oversight, and
many of them are annoying to those who are about them.
They must, therefore, go to houses, places, or people devoted
to their care and prepared to give them the needful attention
and watchfulness.

INTEREST OF THE COMMONWEALTH IN, AND ITS RESPONSIBILITY FOR, THE PROPER CARE OF THE INSANE.

In this matter the Commonwealth and its cities and towns
have more than a general interest; and this, if not immediate
and visible, is sure and unavoidable. Insanity arrests production; the lunatic ceases to be a self-supporter, and is thrown
upon his own estate, or upon his friends, or upon the public,
for sustenance. For the town or the state is the responsible

indorser for every man who becomes insane, to pay the expenses of his sickness, however long it may be; and if the friends fail of this payment in any stage of the malady, the general treasury necessarily assumes and bears the remaining responsibility.

This liability of the state and towns to be called upon to support the insane is very great. It is precisely in proportion to the number of people who are living without capital upon their daily or yearly income, or whose property may become exhausted by life-enduring insanity. It has been found to be a most expensive responsibility for the towns and the state. Within the last year they supported nine hundred and twenty-five insane and idiotic persons, who would have sustained themselves if their diseased or defective minds had not deprived them of the power to do so.

It is, then, worthy of careful attention to see whether this burden of insane pauperism may not be anticipated and prevented, partially at least, if not entirely.

In regard to other forms or sources of pauperism the law exercises a wise forecast, and allows the municipal authorities to anticipate and prevent any threatening burden upon the public, by stopping the very fountain whence it may issue. " When any person by excessive drinking, gaming, idleness or debauchery of any kind shall so spend, waste or lessen his estate as to expose himself or his family to want or suffering, or to expose the town to charge or expense for the support of himself or his family," the selectmen of the towns can place him under guardianship for the care and custody of his person and the management of his estate, so that thereby his family may be saved from want and the town from charge on his account.*

The boards of health are authorized to interfere with the condition of unsatisfactory dwellings and grounds, and to cleanse and put them in order, and thus prevent the spread and continuance of disease.

The law requires the municipal authorities to look up and force truant and vagabond children into school, to prevent their growing up in ignorance and becoming burdens upon the

---

* Rev. Stat. chap. 79, sect. 11.

State, or less able to contribute to the support of the Commonwealth.

In these cases the principle is clearly recognized, that the body politic shall be empowered and required to assume a responsibility and a burden of care or expense in regard to individuals, in the first instance, in order that they may not otherwise become a greater burden of care and of cost.

COST OF INSANE PAUPERISM.

The management of the insane presents a wider and richer field for the same foresight, the same liberal economy, that spends a little now to save much in the future. Taking the cost of maintaining those who are in hospitals, receptacles, &c., at the average price, $2.08 per week, paid by the town or state for them, and supposing the expense of supporting the others in the poorhouses and at home to be no more than the average cost of supporting all the other paupers in the various almshouses in the cities and towns, $1.48 per week, the whole cost of insane pauperism, that is, of supporting the fifteen hundred and twenty-two pauper lunatics in Massachusetts, is more than one hundred and forty-six thousand dollars ($146,897) a year.

It is impossible to determine from the reports, how many of the nine hundred and twenty-five paupers who have been thrown upon the public for support, by disordered or defective mind, were lunatics, and how many were idiots; but if they are in the proportion of the whole number of these classes who are paupers, six hundred and seventy-two are of the former class ; and their support, being the proportion of the whole, amounts to more than seventy-two thousand dollars ($72,683) a year, as the tax which the State pays for pauperism which is directly caused by insanity.

INCREASE OF INSANE PAUPERISM MAY BE PREVENTED.

It is, then, worth the consideration of the Legislature to see whether some action may not be taken to prevent the constant accession of paupers from this cause, by requiring the towns to take early measures for the cure of their pauper lunatics who are curable, and also of all others who, though independent, yet, by reason of their lunacy, are likely to become chargeable to the public treasury.

In England the law requires that recent cases of insanity be promptly transferred from the workhouse to some curative hospital.   It prohibits "the detention in any workhouse of any dangerous lunatic, insane person or idiot, for a longer period than fourteen days," and declares that "every person wilfully detaining in any workhouse any such lunatic, insane person or idiot, for more than fourteen days, shall be deemed guilty of a misdemeanor." *

" The detention of any curable lunatic in a workhouse is highly objectionable, on the score both of humanity and economy." †

In order to secure for every new patient an opportunity of restoration, if possible, the law also provides that, after an asylum shall be established for any county or borough, " no pauper, who shall have *lately* become lunatic, shall be received or lodged or detained in any house or place other than a county or borough lunatic asylum, or public hospital, or licensed house, for a longer period than shall be requisite for obtaining an order for his removal to such asylum." ‡   Not trusting to the thoughtfulness of friends, and looking solely to the good of the patient, the law still further says : " Constables, as well as relieving officers and overseers, are directed to give information on oath to justices of *any* lunatics who shall not be under proper care and control, or shall be cruelly treated or neglected by the persons having charge of them;" and "justices are empowered to order such to be removed to an asylum, hospital or licensed house." §

Moreover, in order to " furnish a safeguard against neglect and abuse in case of chargeable lunatics who are kept in workhouses, and such as are residing with relatives and friends, and who have not the advantage of the supervision and care provided in the regular lunatic establishments," the benevolent law of England directs the " medical officer of each workhouse, once in three months, to visit all the pauper lunatics detained in it, and after personal examination, to insert their names,

* Report of Commissioners in Lunacy, 1847, p. 241.   † Ibid. p. 242.   ‡ Ibid. p. 245.   § Report, 1854, p. 6.

together with a variety of particulars, as to their age, sex and condition, in a list in the form set forth in the schedule, with a declaration under his hand attached to it that the persons enumerated are properly taken care of and fit to be at large, and to transmit such list to the office of the commissioners in lunacy." *

Besides all the motives of humanity, and the hope of restoring lost men to themselves and to society, Massachusetts may take example of the older nation in her wise care of her insane children, and prevent their becoming chargeable to the public treasury from any neglect of the best means for their restoration to mental health.

But for this purpose it will be first necessary that sufficient hospitals be provided, and that they be placed within the reach, the means and the motives of the people, and that both the overseers of the poor and the friends of the patients be induced or required to send all recent cases of insanity to them.

The public hospitals, and some private establishments adapted to the purpose, offer the only home in which most lunatics can be comfortably managed and properly treated. In these they are separated from the scenes and companions, the interests and the suggestions of thought, that were burdensome at home, and sometimes causes of mental disturbance, and interfered with the curative process.

NUMBER OF LUNATICS AND IDIOTS TO BE PROVIDED FOR.

Although there are two thousand six hundred and thirty-two lunatics in the State, it is not to be supposed that all of these need to be removed from their homes, or can derive any benefit from the curative or custodial means offered in the hospitals or elsewhere. Many of them have not only been so long deranged as to be past restoration, but they are mild and harmless, and can be kept as well at their homes or in the town poorhouse as in a public institution. These constitute about nine hundred, for whom nothing more is required.

But there are one thousand seven hundred and thirteen (table II., page 39) reported by the physicians who should

---

* Report of Commissioners in Lunacy, 1847, p. 277-8.

enjoy the advantages of a hospital, either for their healing or for their protection, or for the safety of the public.

These include all the recent cases which present any prospect of restoration, and are deemed curable, or at least not incurable, and also all the violent and furious cases, and most of the excitable and troublesome lunatics; they include even some of the mild but incurable cases whose disposition to wander and become vagabonds makes them, if not dangerous, at least troublesome, and sources of anxiety to their friends, and renders a more strict guardianship necessary than would be obtained at home. To these one thousand seven hundred and thirteen lunatics there should be added the sixty-one violent and dangerous idiots who need the same restraints—making one thousand seven hundred and seventy-four for whom the accommodations or the restoring powers of a hospital should be provided.

Having thus ascertained how much was wanted for the insane in the State, the next step was to learn, how far this want is already supplied.

EXAMINATION OF HOSPITALS AND PRISONS.

In obedience to the requirements of the Legislature, the Commission examined every public establishment within the Commonwealth where the insane are or may be confined under the sanction of the law, including the four lunatic hospitals, the receptacles for the insane, the houses of correction, all the jails except that at Provincetown, the State prison and the State almshouses, and also two private establishments where the insane are received and treated. The Commission visited some and corresponded with all the hospitals in the other Northern and the Middle States, where it is supposed that any lunatics belonging to Massachusetts might be.

The following table shows the number of Massachusetts patients in each of these hospitals.

Table XXV.—LUNATICS

Belonging to Massachusetts in Hospitals.

HOSPITALS.	SEX.		NATIVE.			FOREIGN.			ALL NATIONS.		
	Male.	Female.	Curable.	Incurable.	Total.	Curable.	Incurable.	Total.	Curable.	Incurable.	Total.
Worcester, . .	175	189	27	204	231	28	105	133	55	309	364
Taunton, . .	118	134	32	113	145	35	72	107	67	185	252
Boston, . . .	107	155	9	67	76	14	172	186	23	239	262
McLean, . .	70	83	39	106	145	2	6	8	41	112	153
Pepperell, . .	6	13	8	11	19	–	–	–	8	11	19
Brattleboro', Vt., .	33	21	1	51	52	–	2	2	1	53	54
Providence, R. I., .	7	18	7	18	25	–	–	–	7	18	25
Hartford, Ct., . .	3	3	3	3	6	–	–	–	3	3	6
Concord, N. H., .	1	3	–	4	4	–	–	–	–	4	4
Augusta, Me., .	2	–	1	1	2	–	–	–	1	1	2
Totals, . .	522	619	127	578	705	79	357	436	206	935	1141

HOSPITAL AT WORCESTER.

The Hospital at Worcester has accommodations for three hundred and twenty-seven patients, besides the solitary and strong-rooms, or cells, which are designed for an occasional, and not a permanent, use; but when the house is crowded, as it is now, and as it has been excessively for several years, the officers feel compelled to make constant use of some or all of these strong-rooms. Although this institution contains now three hundred and sixty-four, and did contain five hundred and sixty-seven, previous to the opening of the Hospital at Taunton, yet, regarding the best good of the patients, three hundred and twenty-seven is the utmost that can be received.

This Hospital was planned and the greater part built before most of the modern improvements were made in institutions for the insane, and the subsequent additions have been built in style and form corresponding to the original structure.

HOSPITAL AT TAUNTON.

The Hospital at Taunton was finished in the spring of 1854; and the trustees, on receiving it from the hands of the building commission, immediately altered the structure by removing the solitary strong-rooms, and adding others more advantageous to the purposes of the institution. In other respects the Hospital would be improved and rendered more available by alteration and arrangement according to the modern improvements; yet such changes would be very difficult and costly, and therefore inexpedient at the present time.

This Hospital was intended for two hundred and fifty patients; but the pressure for admission has compelled it to receive two hundred and fifty-six.

HOSPITAL AT BOSTON.

The Hospital at South Boston was built in conformity with the law of 1836, requiring the counties to provide apartments in the Houses of Correction for the idiots and insane not furiously mad, and in accordance with some other legislation for this especial purpose. It is placed between the House of Correction and House of Industry, with a very limited extent of grounds, insufficient for the purposes of the establishment, and affording little or no room or opportunity for labor or recreation abroad.

The house is crowded, having two hundred and sixty-seven patients, with only rooms for two hundred, and no spare rooms for workshops or gatherings of the patients for any other purpose.

In view of this crowded state of this establishment, the city government is agitating the question of building a new Hospital on a more ample and commodious site, where all the accommodations and conveniences for the patients may be offered to them.

15

McLean Asylum.

The McLean Asylum was projected before the construction of lunatic hospitals had attracted much attention, and it has grown by the addition of parts from time to time until it has arrived at its present capacity. The form and condition of the site and local circumstances have been necessarily regarded in the arrangements of the several wings and parts of the establishment, so that the form and construction of the building, as it is now, are very different from what they would be were it planned and built according to the ideas of the present time. It is built on a peninsula, where their grounds must be limited, and therefore cannot be made so useful to the establishment and to the patients who reside there as is desirable. Nevertheless, with its abundant and appropriate provisions for the comfort and management of the patients, and with the various convenient and graceful means of occupation and amusement, it affords an excellent and desirable home for two hundred patients; and to this its numbers are limited.

This institution is open to all patients whose friends may apply for their admission and can afford to pay the necessary cost. Its high character and reputation for successful management through nearly forty years, and its elegant accommodations, render it especially attractive to the wealthy, and draw many from abroad. There were forty-seven patients from other States.

There are private establishments at Pepperell and Dorchester. These can accommodate about forty patients, and have now twenty-five belonging to Massachusetts.

These are all the Hospitals within this State.

The following table shows the proper accommodations in each, and the number of Massachusetts patients now resident in them:—

Table XXVI.—HOSPITAL ACCOMMODATIONS AND MASSACHUSETTS PATIENTS RESIDENT.

HOSPITALS.	Accommodations for	Massachusetts patients resident.
Worcester,	327	364
Taunton,	250	256
McLean,	200	153
Boston,	200	267
Pepperell, &c.,	40	19
Totals,	1,017	1,059

All our own public institutions are more than full. That at Worcester has thirty-seven, that at Taunton six, and that at Boston sixty-seven more than they can well accommodate. The officers of the McLean Asylum, for want of room, reject a large number of those who ask for admission ; but the State Hospitals and that at Boston are obliged to receive all that are sent to them through the courts, who supply them with the great majority of their patients.

LUNATIC RECEPTACLES CONNECTED WITH HOUSES OF CORRECTION.

The law of 1836, Supplement to Revised Statutes, page 4, chapter 223, requires,—

Sect. 1. " That there shall be within the precincts of the House of Correction, in each county in this Commonwealth, a suitable and convenient apartment or receptacle for idiots and lunatics or insane persons not furiously mad, to be confined therein as hereinafter provided."

Sect. 2. " When it shall be made to appear, on application made in writing to any two justices of the peace, one of whom shall be of the quorum, or any police court, that any person being within the jurisdiction of such justices or courts is an idiot or lunatic not furiously mad, the said justices or courts are hereby authorized to order the confinement of such persons in the receptacle provided for the purpose."

Only three counties, Suffolk, Middlesex and Essex, have complied with the requirements of this law and made this provision for their insane.

The Boston Hospital, already described, meets the condition of this law.

IPSWICH RECEPTACLE.

The receptacle for lunatics at Ipswich, in Essex County, is connected with the House of Correction, and under the same roof; yet it is entirely separated from the prison by the centre building, which contains the dwelling of the superintendent and family, the offices connected with the establishment, and by the kitchen and eating-room for the patients. A closed brick wall, also, prevents all access from one to the other. The yards are at the opposite ends of the building; that of the prison is surrounded by a high brick wall, and that of the lunatics by a high fence, so that no communication can take place between them.

The lunatic department is a single wing, three stories high, besides the basement.

The internal arrangements of the several stories are similar to those usually found in the wings of lunatic hospitals. There is a hall in each, sixty-three feet long, twelve feet wide, and ten feet high, running the entire length, with lodging-rooms on each side. These rooms are ten feet long and six feet wide, and of the same height as the hall. There is a large window at the end of each hall, and a smaller one in each lodging-room, all with iron sashes, and glazed with seven by nine glass.

The doors are all thick and heavy, and fastened with strong locks.

Besides these rooms, there are several strong-rooms or cells in the basement story for the excited and furious patients. These have grated windows like those of a prison, and some of them are provided with strong shutters, to prevent the violent inmates from breaking the glass, and to furnish more effectual security against any attempts to escape. There are also very heavy doors, which are secured with bolts and locks, to resist the destructive efforts of the furious.

Besides these means of security there are provided hand straps, mittens, muffs, &c., to restrain those who need them; and these are occasionally used.

There are eighteen rooms in each story, and also, bathing-rooms, and water-closets sufficient for each sex in the building.

The whole is warmed by hot-air furnaces in the basement, and imperfectly ventilated by Emerson's apparatus. There is an aperture for the passage of air from the lodging-rooms to the halls, and the air ducts open from the halls to the ventilators.

There are yards or airing courts for the patients contiguous to the building, and also several acres of land connected with the establishment, on which some of the men work in the summer. Some of the women are employed in the kitchen and in doing some of the other work about the establishment.

There were forty-nine male patients in two of these halls, and nineteen females in the other.

As there were only thirty-six lodging-rooms in the male wards, and two of these were occupied by the attendants, it was necessary that fifteen of these rooms, only six feet by ten, should receive two lodgers each; and in the female ward it was necessary that two rooms should do the same.

Throughout the whole establishment neatness and order prevail.

There were three attendants to take the charge of those sixty-eight patients, one in each hall.

All these patients were orderly and quiet at the time of visitation. Although the whole forty-nine male patients were then crowded into one hall, on account of the temporary cleaning of the other, yet there was no disorder, no apparent discontent. They were mostly old cases, and demented. Yet there were some whose diseases were not of very long standing, and were probably susceptible of restoration under proper remedial influences.

EAST CAMBRIDGE RECEPTACLE.

The county commissioners of Middlesex have provided apartments at East Cambridge for their lunatics within the precincts of, and connected with, the House of Correction.

The whole establishment consists of the Jail, the House of Correction proper, the workshop, the kitchen, the store-house, and the receptacles for the insane, which are all in and around the small yard or open ground in several separate buildings. The convicts march across this yard beetween their prison-house and the workshop several times a day.

There are two houses for the insane, one for each sex, both thirty feet by forty. They are on opposite sides of the yard, and unconnected with the other buildings of the establishment. The house for the males is two stories high, and that for the females is three stories. In each of these stories there is a middle hall, about eight feet wide, running through the whole length of the building, with rooms for sleeping on each side. There are seventeen of these small lodging-rooms in the house for males, and twenty-six in that for females. The attics are also occupied as dormitories.

These buildings are heated by steam, and ventilated by a system depending on the movement of the external air. The warmth was satisfactory; but in the main building the means of ventilation were "insufficient to prevent disagreeable smells pervading the whole building." *

There is an airing court connected with the females' building, about sixty feet in length and forty in width, surrounded by a high wall. A smaller airing court is connected with the males' building, and similarly guarded against the escape of the inmates.

The building for females is near to the street, and they are subject to the observation of, and conversation with, the passers by; and the noise of the patients, especially of the excited ones, can be heard abroad.

Both of these buildings are very much crowded. In two halls, forty feet by eight or ten, there were thirty-five male patients during the day, and at night they were as uncomfortably situated. Twelve of them sleep in the attic, "which is lighted by a single window in each end, and high enough to stand upright in the middle, and sloping to the eaves," * the beds being under the low roof, with no supply of air. The other twenty-one occupy the few small sleeping-rooms below,

* Letter to the Commission from Hon. John S. Keyes, Sheriff of Middlesex.

and in many of them two were obliged to sleep. " The basement story or cellar is used for an eating-room." *

The building occupied by females, having three stories, has
more room, yet not enough for the thirty-five patients. Six of
these occupy the attic, and the other twenty-nine sleep in the
small bed-rooms arranged on the sides of the halls in the other
stories.

This establishment is under the charge of the master of the
House of Correction, who has the superintendence of a very
large number of convicts, with all the responsibility for their
security, labor and board, and has therefore as much to do in
the management of the affairs and inmates of the prison as
should be required of one officer. He, of course, must delegate
the care of the insane to an under officer, or principal attend-
ant for each sex. Such persons, male and female, are employed
to oversee each building and the inmates, but all their assistants are convicts. Most of these assistant attendants were
sent to the House of Correction for intemperance, and probably
are selected as the best in the whole convict population of the
prison for the care of lunatics.

Except walking in these small yards, there is no opportunity
of obtaining any exercise in the open air in the mild and clear
weather, and none at all when storms or cold prevent their
going abroad. Within the house there are no means of employment or occupation, labor or amusement. The patients
have nothing to do but lounge listlessly about the yard without or the halls within the house.

This receptacle is provided with the means of restraining
and confining the excited and furious in strong-rooms and with
mittens, straps, &c. Most of the patients of both sexes are
natives of other countries, and incurable. About half are mild
and harmless—" not furiously mad," as described in the law.
Nearly as many are excitable and troublesome ; some are turbulent, some furious, and some very noisy.

In the female building one patient was vociferating so loudly
that she was heard in the street, and was offensive to the people who were passing by.

* Mr. Sheriff Keyes' Letter.

The Commission visited and examined all the other Houses of Correction and all the Jails in the State excepting that at Provincetown, and ascertained the extent and the kind of accommodations which were provided in them for the idiots and insane not furiously mad, in conformity with the law of 1836.

LENOX PRISON.

In Lenox, the Jail and House of Correction for Berkshire County were in one building—a prison of the modern form, one within another, with ranges of small cells side by side for the convicts. But there is another apartment, about twelve or fifteen feet square, with a range of cells on one side opening into it. These cells are small, like those in the principal prison, and made strong with iron doors and all the means of security from escape.

Until recently, there have been three lunatics confined in these cells for about twelve or fifteen years. They were separated from the convicts, no others being confined in these cells or in this room. They had no means of exercise, no occupation, and were always retained in their cells, except that one at a time, when peaceable, was allowed to be in the larger room, but they went no farther.

These three lunatics have recently been removed to the Hospital at Worcester.

These cells were not originally prepared for the lunatics, but for debtors and for female prisoners.

There were no lunatics there at the time of the visit.

SPRINGFIELD PRISON.

This single prison includes both the House of Correction and the Jail for Hampden County. This is arranged in the modern form, one prison within another, with the galleries and small cells side by side contiguously, and no other room or place for confinement or lodgment of those committed to this establishment.

There is no workshop; but the area in front of the cells and between the inner prison and the outer walls is appropriated for this purpose. There were no lunatics in the prison at the time of the visit, nor had there been any since the present master of the house commenced his administration.

But if any one should be committed to this prison, he must be confined in one of these stone-walled, iron-grated cells, by the side of those containing convicts, during the night when they are not at work, and he must be before them, and can see them at any time while they are at work during the day.

NORTHAMPTON PRISON.

This is a new, spacious establishment, including both Jail and House of Correction for Hampshire county under one roof. The whole is built on the latest improved plan. On one side of the inner prison are galleries running in front of ranges of small cells for close confinement. This is called the House of Correction, and is appropriated for the convicts. On the other side are ranges of larger rooms, ten or eleven feet square, but equally strong, with stone walls, and iron-grated doors. This is called the Jail, and is used to confine those who are accused of crime, but not yet tried or sentenced.

There is no special provision made for lunatics, and no place to keep them, except in the rooms provided for the accused or the convicted prisoner.

There were no lunatics at this House of Correction at the time of the visit, but there had recently been four committed to its charge. One was found in the streets at Ware, noisy and troublesome. He was supposed to be a recent case, although his history could not be ascertained. After a detention of four months, becoming very difficult to be managed, this patient was removed to Worcester. Another, who was sent there for similar reasons by the magistrates, was afterwards also sent to Worcester. Both of these were supposed to be dangerous to the public peace and safety, and were confined in the House of Correction for the public security, and not for their own good.

GREENFIELD JAIL.

This is the only prison in Franklin County. It is a small building of the old fashion, with a few stone rooms, sufficiently large, but dark, cold and cheerless. This is the Jail exclusively. There being no House of Correction, an arrangement is made

16

with the authorities of Hampshire to receive into the prison at Northampton such convicts as should in their county be sentenced to confinement and labor.

There are no suitable apartments provided for lunatics; and if they are sent to the House of Correction by the justices or other authorities, they must be confined in this common jail, or sent to the House of Correction at. Northampton.

There are now no lunatics confined in this prison, and there has been but one since the present jailer has had charge of it. There was a female lunatic within the year confined for some months, awaiting trial on the charge of homicide. She was acquitted on the ground of insanity, and sent to the State Hospital at Worcester.

WORCESTER PRISON.

The House of Correction at Worcester is of the modern form, with galleries and ranges of cells, but with no especial accommodations for the insane. There are none now in this prison; but some months ago, and for some time previously, nine lunatics were confined there. Having no other place for them, the lower range of cells on one side of the prison was given up to them.

CONCORD JAIL.

The Jail for Middlesex County, at Concord, is one of the old-est prisons in the State. It is a heavy stone building of the old form, with large and separated rooms, all with stone floors, heavily grated windows looking abroad, and very strong doors. Here are two lunatics confined, and have been for eighteen years. They occupy the lower rooms in the building; and one of them, on account of his noisy disposition, was put in a back or inner room, which was formerly the dungeon for the confinement of the most refractory convicts. It is now lighted in some degree, though it is yet the most uncomfortable room in the jail.

These lunatics are both State paupers. One is colored, and supposed to be an American, and the other is a Swede. Both are usually mild. The negro has generally been allowed to go about the village at will, and has spent much of his time in day labor, sawing wood, &c., for the people in the vicinity.

At other times he is very troublesome; and now for several months he has been very noisy, disturbing the neighborhood with his outcries. The Swede is " generally quite harmless, and to some extent useful in and about the jail, attending church regularly, and more foolish " (demented) " than insane, unless aroused to anger by some provocation." *

LOWELL JAIL.

This is the third jail in Middlesex; it is a small building, with an inner prison, with the galleries and ranges of small contiguous cells, and no other rooms. There are no lunatics confined there, nor have there been any, except for temporary security while waiting to be transferred to Cambridge. But when they are there they are placed in these cells by the side of those occupied by the criminals. During the visit these prisoners were very noisy, talking loudly; the sound of their voices was distinctly heard even in the neighboring office of the jailer, and would unavoidably reach and disturb the lunatics if confined with them.

LAWRENCE PRISON.

The Lawrence Prison is new, just completed by the county of Essex, after the best model of the time. It contains a House of Correction and Jail in the same building. The cells are large, eight feet square, arranged along the galleries for the security of criminals, but there are no apartments for the insane. There have as yet been no lunatics admitted here even for a temporary lodgment.

NEWBURYPORT JAIL.

This is one of the old prisons of Essex. It is built with entries and large rooms to contain one or more prisoners. One lunatic is now confined there, and he has been an inmate of that jail for many years. He is harmless, and allowed to go about the prison and the house at will, and to ride abroad, and makes himself useful to the jailer by carrying food to prisoners, &c. He is a native of Newburyport, and was, until lately, a man of property, but is now supported by the city. His room in the jail, like the others, is

---

* Letter to the Commission from Hon. John S. Keyes, Sheriff of Middlesex.

guarded with grates, a thick oaken door, and very heavy bolts.
Yet the door stands open and he is free to move abroad. His
room is comfortably furnished, and he prefers to stay there.
He has been at the Hospital in Worcester; but, being incurable,
his friends prefer to have him at the jail, where he is contented
and very kindly treated, and where they can easily visit him.

SALEM JAIL.

The old Essex Jail in Salem is like that in Newburyport;
but it contains no lunatics, nor have any been received there,
except, perhaps, for temporary custody while waiting to be
transferred to Ipswich.

BOSTON JAIL.

The new Jail at Boston has no place for the insane in the
main part. But in the lockup there are several rooms in which
prisoners under the excitement of delirium tremens, and vagabond or turbulent and troublesome lunatics are confined while
waiting for their friends to come for them, or to be transferred
to the Hospital at South Boston. These are often found
strolling in the streets, or disturbing the peace in some houses,
and are brought here by the police for safe keeping and for the
adjudication of the courts. For this purpose there was one
female lunatic here who was found strolling in the streets in
the night. Her room was sufficiently comfortable for her short
detention.

BOSTON HOUSE OF CORRECTION.

In the House of Correction at South Boston there is a very
comfortable Hospital, where every thing is provided for the
criminal patients that their disease can require and their position admit. Here were three insane convicts, who had become
deranged since they had been in prison. They are under the
immediate charge of Dr. Walker, the Physician of the Lunatic
Hospital, and receive all the appropriate treatment they need.
Whenever the criminal lunatics can be better treated in the
Lunatic Hospital they are removed to that place, where they
enjoy all the advantages that are given to any other patients
in that institution.

DEDHAM PRISON.

This Prison, for Norfolk County, is of the modern form, and embraces both the Jail and House of Correction in one building. The cells are all small and alike along the galleries, and looking into the areas.

There are no apartments provided for lunatics, no place for them, except in the narrow and strong cells by the side of the criminals.

There are three lunatics in this prison. One from Dover was committed by the magistrates under the law of 1836. He is boarded here by his friends, from his own substance, for custody. He was clothed in the party-colored garments worn by the convicts of the prison.

Another, a colored female, more idiotic than lunatic, who set fire to a barn many years ago, as she is supposed to be a dangerous person to be at large, she has been detained here ever since. She is mild, and apparently harmless, but the jailer thinks still unsafe to be abroad.

Another, an Irishman, confined for crime, became insane in prison, and is supposed to be dangerous and unsafe to be at large.

TAUNTON JAIL.

The old Bristol Jail in Taunton is of the old form, with large and very strong rooms of stone, built to resist violent efforts for escape. There are no lunatics in this prison, nor have there been any, except for temporary lodgment while waiting to be sent to the House of Correction in New Bedford.

NEW BEDFORD PRISON.

In New Bedford the Jail and the House of Correction for Bristol are in one establishment. There are several buildings around one yard, and are of both the old and the modern form, for the confinement of criminals. But there is no especial provision for the insane.

There were eight lunatics in this prison. One was constantly furious. Another, who had recently been there, could not be clothed. Some were excitable, others were quiet and easily managed. One was a recent and curable case.

These are confined in various rooms, as seems to be for their advantage and the convenience of the administration of the prison. One was in a cell five feet wide. Some of these are in a room appropriated for a hospital where others were sick.

This room, like the others, is strong, with grated windows, and thick bolted doors. It was crowded and uncomfortable, and very unfit for the insane. The beds in this hospital were in boxes or bunks, one above another, as in soldiers' barracks.

The whole aspect of the place was miserable, gloomy and forbidding, especially to persons of diseased mind.

PLYMOUTH PRISON.

In Plymouth the House of Correction and Jail were both in one establishment and one yard, though separate buildings. The Jail is of the old form, with entries and large rooms. The House of Correction is modern, with galleries and small cells within the outer walls.

There is no provision for the insane, and no place for them, except in the strong and grated rooms of the Jail, or in the narrow cells of the House of Correction.

One lunatic is confined there. He is a man of property, but violent and dangerous at home and in his own neighborhood; and even here he is very troublesome, and sometimes unmanageable. At the time of the visit he was mild and at work in the field or garden. His room was in the Jail.

BARNSTABLE JAIL.

The Prison in Barnstable is one small building, and is called both House of Correction and Jail. It is of stone, and has a few large rooms, and no cells, and no proper apartments for the insane.

There was an insane man confined in this prison at the time of the visit. He was generally mild and manageable. Yet he was easily disturbed, and might be excited suddenly, and without apparent cause. He was sometimes even furious, and was therefore unsafe to be at large, though unfit to be in prison.

NANTUCKET JAIL.

In Nantucket there is no House of Correction, and only a wooden Jail. There were four rooms in this building, furnished as comfortably as the dwellings of the laboring poor, and having more the appearance of a private dwelling than of a prison. There were no insane persons at the time of the visit, and there had been none confined in the Jail within the memory of the jailer who has had charge of it for many years.

EDGARTOWN JAIL.

In Edgartown the Prison for Dukes County is an extremely small stone building, with four rooms, nine feet square. One end is called the Jail and the other the House of Correction. There are no rooms for the insane, nor were any insane or any other inmates in this prison.

STATE PRISON.

In the State Prison at Charlestown there is a very comfortable and commodious hospital, with good and airy rooms for the sick, where they can have all the facilities for attention that their cases demand and their condition admits.

Three of the convicts are now insane. They are mild and at work, their delusions not preventing their attending to the labors required of them under the watchful care of the officers.

The lunatics in this prison are under the care of the physician of the establishment, and when occasion calls for it, they are examined by a commission of high character, and if need be, transferred to one of the State Lunatic Hospitals.

The Jail at Provincetown, in Barnstable County, was not examined.

It appears, then, from these personal examinations and this review, that there are Houses of Correction in only ten of the fourteen counties, that in Essex there are two, and in the other four counties there are only Jails. Besides these, there are seven other Jails in the counties of Middlesex, Essex, Suffolk, Bristol and Barnstable, making eleven Houses of Correction and eleven separate Jails within this Commonwealth, besides the State Prison at Charlestown.

Except at Boston and Ipswich, there are no suitable apartments provided " for the idiots and the insane persons not furiously mad " in connection with any of the Houses of Correction in the State; nor are any provisions whatever made, under the law of 1836, except in Suffolk, Essex and Middlesex. Yet lunatics who are not convicts are found in seven of these prisons, and they have been or may be, under the law of 1836, confined in any or all of the others, notwithstanding their entire unfitness for such purposes.

Table XXVII.—LUNATICS

In Receptacles, Prisons, &c.

	SEX.		NATIVITY.		CONDITION.					Convicts.	Sent from hospital at Worcester.
	Male.	Female.	American.	Foreign.	Mild—manageable.	Excitable—troublesome	Furious—dangerous.	Not stated.			
RECEPTACLES.											
Ipswich, . . .	64	22	41	45	22	63	1	–		8	9
Cambridge, . . .	28	32	13	47	29	24	5	2		–	7
Totals, . . .	92	54	54	92	51	87	6	2		–	16
HOUSES OF CORRECTION.											
Boston, ...	2	1	–	3	–	3	–	–		3	–
Dedham, . . .	2	1	2	1	–	1	2	–		2	1
New Bedford, . .	3	3	3	3	4	1	1	–		–	3
Plymouth, . . .	1	–	1	–	–	–	1	–		–	–
JAILS.											
Concord, . . .	2	–	1	1	1	–	1	–		–	2
Newburyport, . .	1	–	1	–	1	–	–	–		–	1
Boston, ...	1	–	–	1	–	–	1	–		–	–
Barnstable, . . .	1	–	1	–	1	–	–	–		–	–
State Prison, . . .	3	–	1	2	3	–	–	–		3	–
Total Jails & Prisons,	16	5	10	11	10	5	6	–		8	7
Total of all, . .	108	59	64	103	61	92	12	2		16	23

STATE ALMSHOUSES.

The Commissioners visited and examined the State Alms-houses at Monson, Tewksbury and Bridgewater, in reference to their means of accommodating the insane and their fitness for the residence of these patients. These establishments were originally intended exclusively for paupers that were presumed to be sound in mind at least. It was, therefore, no part of the plan of the architect to provide for the insane. In the external and internal arrangements and structure of the buildings there are none of the means or conveniences for them. The houses are principally divided into large wards, capable of accommo-dating about fifty paupers in each, and are all needed for the sane. The large dormitories are also appropriated to the same classes.

Underneath one of the wings of these houses is a basement story, which is sunk five feet below the surface of the ground. There are four rooms in this subterranean place. One of these rooms has a stove and is made comfortably warm. By the side of this is another room which is used for bathing and has tubs and a tank, which is usually filled with water and is sufficiently large for many boys to bathe and even swim in, at the same time.

One of the other two rooms by the side of the warmed room is fitted with cells for the use of the males. The other on the opposite corner from the heated room is fitted with cells for the females. These cells are narrow like those of prisons. They are made strong with plank partitions. Some of the doors are made of plank bars, and others of iron bars, fixed in a heavy frame-work of wood. They all are secured with heavy prison locks or iron bolts.

These cells are all dimly and indirectly lighted, and at best are dark and gloomy. There are no means whatever for ven-tilation except by opening the windows of the area in front of some of these lock-ups, and at the side of the others. There are no means of warming except by what heat may chance to pass from the stove-room through the door into the passage way, around these cells.

In the coldest weather of the winter, the water was frozen so that it could not be used in the bathing-room, which is by

17

the side of, and contiguous to, the stove-room. The room which contains the cells for the females still colder, as it is farther from the fire, and touches only upon the corner of that which is heated.

These cells were provided for the punishment of the disobedient and refractory paupers, who sometimes need discipline.

Besides the cells, which are in all these establishments, there are in Monson "five cells in a building recently erected, which are more pleasant and healthy." *

These are all the means of separating the lunatics from the rest of the household. Ordinarily they are kept in the wards with the other paupers; but when they are excited, or are troubled by, or troublesome to, the other inmates, so that it is requisite to remove them, the only resort is to send them to these cells, for there are no other rooms to which they can be sent.

The number and condition of the insane and idiots in each of these establishments is shown in the following table:—

TABLE XXVIII.—LUNATICS AND IDIOTS. †

In State Almshouses.

LOCATION.	SEX.		NATIVITY.		CONDITION.			
	Male.	Female.	American.	Foreign.	Mild — manageable.	Excitable — troublesome.	Furious—dangerous.	Total.
Monson, ...	4	2	3	3	3	3	–	6
Tewksbury, . . .	7	12	5	14	5	7	7	19
Bridgewater, . . .	7	8	1	14	6	8	1	15
Totals, . . .	18	22	9	31	14	18	8	40

* Letter of Dr. S. D. Brooks, Superintendent of the Monson Almshouse, to the Commission.

† These were the numbers in October, 1854, when the returns were made. Since that time many have been removed from Ipswich and East Cambridge receptacles, and some from the hospitals to these almshouses, so that there are now (April, 1855) about a hundred at Bridgewater, and in the others the numbers are increased.

Of the forty reported, eight are stated to be furious or dangerous, eighteen excitable and troublesome, and only fourteen, about one-third, are always mild and proper members of the general household.

SUMMARY OF ACCOMMODATIONS FOR THE INSANE.

These Hospitals, Receptacles, Prisons and State Almshouses are all the places in the Commonwealth where lunatics can be accommodated or confined, except at their homes in private dwellings, or in the city and town poorhouses.

Suitable accommodations are provided in the four hospitals and in the private establishments for one thousand and seventeen of the curable and the incurable patients who need custody or separation from home. Good custodial accommodations are provided at Ipswich for sixty-nine of the old, incurable and mild patients. Means of confinement are provided at Cambridge for sixty of the same.

Sufficient provision is made for the criminal lunatics now in the State Prison and in the Boston House of Correction. In all the establishments in the State provision of various kinds is made for eleven hundred and forty-six patients.

As the McLean and the private asylums are open to patients of every State, and as there are always some who prefer to send their insane friends to distant places, it is probable that these will always receive some, perhaps as many as they now do, from abroad. For similar reasons, and on account of the greater convenience of access to some parts of the Commonwealth, it is probable that as many will be sent from Massachusetts to the hospitals in the neighboring States, making those that come into the State about equal to those who go out.

FURTHER WANTS OF THE INSANE.

The returns received show that, in the opinion of the physicians and hospital superintendents and others, there were one thousand seven hundred and thirteen insane persons and sixty-one idiots who should enjoy the advantages of, or be confined in, some hospital or other; six hundred and ten of these are at their homes or in poorhouses; add to these one hundred and nine, the excess of patients in the hospitals at

Worcester, Taunton and Boston, and we have seven hundred and nineteen who now need, but have not, these advantages. Now, it is not to be supposed that the relations and the overseers, the friends and the guardians, would send all, or nearly all, their patients to a hospital, however excellent its accommodations, and however accessible it might be to them. It is not, therefore, deemed advisable that the State or the people should make provision for so many in addition to that which is already made. But it is well known that there are many whose friends and guardians desire them to be admitted ; but who cannot be received for want of room. Three of the public hospitals are crowded with more than they can accommodate ; and the McLean Asylum would be, if, like the other hospitals, it were obliged to receive all who were sent to it, or for whom application is made. Many of our patients now in the asylums in Brattleboro', Providence, Concord and Hartford, are sent there on account of the difficulty of getting into the hospitals at home, and the greater facilities of doing so abroad. But these institutions, which have hitherto invited patients from this and other States in order to fill their vacant wards, are now becoming filled with those of their own States, and receive strangers with more hesitation. This difficulty will necessarily increase ; and those institutions which are created by, and belong to, their respective States, will, of course, be compelled to confine their admissions to their own citizens, and exclude all others, as ours have done. The others can hardly be expected to receive more of our patients than we shall receive from abroad. Massachusetts, then, must expect to provide for, and take care of, at least as many patients as belong to the State.

Admitting, however, that many who should be in hospitals will be retained at home, whatever may be the inducements to send them to a hospital, still there can be no question that there is now a necessity of further action ; and the time is ripe for a new effort for those lunatic patients who are yet at their homes, to save those who are curable from permanent insanity, and give to the others who cannot be saved such an asylum of protection as their own good and the interests of the State demand.

Besides these six hundred and ten lunatics and idiots now at their homes, and needing hospital accommodations, the question of selling the Hospital at Worcester is proposed by the Legislature to this Commission for consideration. If this sale should be deemed expedient, it would leave three hundred and sixty-four patients to be provided for. The city government of Boston are convinced of the necessity of giving up their present Hospital, which is now inconvenient and too small for their wants, and of providing a more ample and satisfactory establishment. The County Commissioners of Middlesex are convinced that the Receptacle at Cambridge is entirely insufficient and unsatisfactory, and would have provided another if the policy of the State as to the method of supporting the State pauper lunatics were not yet in doubt. But they are certain that some other provision must be made for those insane persons now on their hands. The probability or possibility of changing these three establishments, requiring new provisions to be made for the six hundred and ninety-seven patients now in them, and the wants of six hundred and ten other lunatics and idiots now at home, whom the physicians think should be in some hospital, leaves the whole subject of the distribution of, and providing for, the insane, open for consideration.

GENERAL PLANS FOR THE FUTURE.

In view of this state of things, the Commission deemed that it would be for the interest of the State, and for the advantage of humanity, that the best plan should be devised for distributing and providing for the insane; and for this purpose the wisdom and experience of those engaged in the management and cure of this disease should be sought and made available for the use of Massachusetts.

Accordingly, letters were addressed to the superintendents of the most successful hospitals in the United States, and to the same and others familiar with the administration of hospitals and the care of insane in Great Britain.

These gentlemen were asked to advise as to the best method of distributing and providing for the insane.

Whether it were best to provide in one hospital for all classes and kinds of insane persons, male and female, independent and pauper, foreign and native, curable and incurable, innocent and criminal, as is generally done in the United States,

Or in separate establishments,

For the males and for the females; or

For the independent and the pauper; or

For the foreigners and natives; or

For the curable and incurable; or

For the criminals, as proposed by Mr. Ley, of the Oxford and Berks Asylum, and sustained by the English Commissioners in Lunacy.

They were also asked to advise as to the number that, " regarding the comfort and improvement of the patients," can properly be accommodated in one institution, and what number in reference to each of the preceding classifications which should be advised.

They were asked to give their ideas of the best plan of a hospital for lunatics for each of the above classifications.

These letters were sent to the following superintendents of hospitals:—

Dr. Luther V. Bell, of the McLean, Somerville; Dr. George Chandler, Worcester; Dr. Clement A. Walker, Boston; Dr. George C. S. Choate, Taunton; Dr. Henry M. Harlow, Augusta, Me.; Dr. John E. Tyler, Concord, N. H.; Dr. William H. Rockwell, Brattleboro', Vt.; Dr. Isaac Ray, Providence, R. I.; Dr. John S. Butler, Hartford, Ct.; Dr. John H. Gray, Utica, N. Y.; Dr. N. D. Benedict, late of Utica, N. Y.; Dr. D. Tilden Brown, Bloomingdale, N. Y.; Dr. M. H. Ranney, Blackwell's Island, N. Y. city; Dr. Horace A. Buttolph, Trenton, N. J.; Dr. Joshua Worthington, Friends' Asylum, Frankford, Pa.; Dr. Thomas S. Kirkbride, Philadelphia, Pa.; Dr. John Curwen, Harrisburg, Pa.; Dr. John Fonerden, Baltimore, Md.; Dr. Charles C. Nichols, Washington, D. C; Dr. Francis Stribbling, Staunton, Western Virginia; Dr. William M. Awl, late of Columbus, Ohio.

Similar letters of inquiry were sent to England, to Dr. Samuel Gaskell, Superintendent of the Lancaster Lunatic Hospital; Dr. John Thurnam, Wiltshire Asylum, Devizes; Dr. William Ley, Oxford and Berks, Littlemore; Dr. Daniel H. Tuke, York Retreat; Dr. W. A. F. Brown, Critchton Asylum,

Dumfries, Scotland; Dr. Forbes Winslow, editor of the Psychological Journal, London; Edwin Chadwick, Esq., Secretary of the Poor Law Commissioners; the Commissioners in Lunacy for Great Britain.

It is due to the gentlemen to say, that all of those in America whose counsel was thus asked, except two, and most of those in Europe, answered all the questions proposed to them, and several of them at great length, giving statements and opinions very important to the work of this Commission, and the purposes of the Commonwealth in connection with it. These will be used in course of this Report.

SIZE OF A HOSPITAL.

It is the unanimous opinion of the American Association of Medical Superintendents of Insane Asylums that not more than two hundred and fifty patients should be gathered into one establishment, and that two hundred is a better number. When this matter was discussed, there was no dissent as to the maximum; yet those who had the charge of the largest hospitals, and knew the disadvantages of larger numbers, thought that a lower number should be adopted.

Taking the average of the patients that now present themselves in Massachusetts, of whom eighteen per cent. are supposed to be curable, and need active treatment, and eighty-two per cent. incurable, and require principally general management and soothing custodial guardianship, and having " due regard to the comfort and improvement of the patients," this limit of two hundred and fifty should not be exceeded.

The principal physician is the responsible manager of every case, and should therefore be personally acquainted with the character and condition of his patients, the peculiarities of the diseased mind, as manifested in each one, and the sources of trouble and depression, or exaltation and perversity. This knowledge is necessary, in order that he should be able to adapt his means of medical or of moral influence with the best hope of success.

The superintendents of hospitals, in their correspondence with this Commission, generally gave their opinions on this point.   Two hundred and fifty is proposed by Drs. Bell, Chandler, Choate, Walker, Ray, Brown and Gray, Kirkbride, Curwen and Worthington, and also by the Commissioners in Lunacy in England.* Dr. Butler, of Hartford, proposes two hundred. Dr. Fonerden, of Baltimore proposes one hundred and fifty to two hundred. Dr. Thurnam proposes two to three hundred if the hospital is for the independent class exclusively, and four hundred to four hundred and fifty if for paupers.

These gentlemen individually concur in the opinion given by the association; or if they differ from that rule, it is by assigning a smaller number, on the ground stated by Dr. Bell, that it gives " every advantage of that classification of diseases, dispositions and manners which secures the most comfort, and that mutual attrition of mind upon mind which is so beneficial, and at the same time, permits one head to acquire and retain that intimate personal knowledge of each case, in all its history and relations, which is so essential to the best application of moral and medical treatment." †

With a large number, then, a less effective work must be produced, and the patients cannot be managed with that " due regard to their comfort and improvement" specified in the law.

DISADVANTAGES OF LARGE HOSPITALS.

The policy which has built large establishments for the insane is a questionable one as applied to economy. After having built a house sufficiently large, and gathered a sufficient number of patients for their proper classification and for the employment of a competent corps of officers and attendants, and allowing each to receive just as much attention as his case requires, and providing no more, any increase of numbers will either crowd the house, or create the necessity of building more rooms; and their management must be either at the cost of that attention which is due to others, or create

---

* " No asylum for curable lunatics should contain more than two hundred and fifty patients; and two hundred is, perhaps, as large a number as can be managed with the most benefit to themselves and the public in one establishment." *—Report of Metropolitan Commissioners in Lunacy for 1844, p. 23.

† Report for 1844, page 14.

* The Legislature has recognized the expediency of limiting the size of asylums, by enacting (1 and 2 Geo. IV., c. 33) that the District Asylums of Ireland " shall be sufficient to contain not more than one hundred and fifty patients."—*Note to the above.*

the necessity of employing more persons to superintend and to watch them.

If the house be crowded beyond the appropriate numbers, or if the needful attention and the healing influences due to each individual are diminished, the restorative process is retarded, and the recovery is rendered more doubtful. And if additional provision, both of accommodations and professional and subsidiary attendance, is made to meet the increase of patients beyond the best standard, it would cost at least as much per head as for the original number. Dr. Kirkbride thinks it would cost more, and that the actual recoveries of the curable and the comfortable guardianship of the incurable are not so easily attained in large hospitals as in such as come within the description herein proposed. "It might be supposed that institutions for a much larger number of patients than has been recommended could be supported at a less relative cost; but this is not found to be the case. There is always more difficulty in superintending details in a very large hospital; there are more sources of waste and loss; improvements are apt to be relatively more costly; and, without great care on the part of the officers, the patients will be less comfortable." [*]

Besides the increased cost of maintaining and the diminished efficiency of a large establishment, there is the strong objection of distance and difficulty of access, which must limit the usefulness of a large hospital in the country, and prevent its diffusing its benefits equally over any considerable extent of territory to whose people it may open its doors.

THE INFLUENCE OF DISTANCE ON THE USE OF HOSPITALS BY THE PEOPLE.

From a careful examination of the number of patients sent from the several counties to all the State hospitals in the United States which kept and published such a record, and a comparison of those with the average number of people in these counties through all the recorded periods of the operations of the institutions, it is shown that the ratio of patients to the

---

[*] Kirkbride on Hospitals for Insane; American Journal of Insanity, July, 1854, p. 11.

population, sent to the hospital, diminishes constantly with the increase of distance from it.

The following table was prepared in 1850. The counties in the several States are divided into classes. The first is the single and central county in which the hospital is situated. The second includes the next circle of counties, and the third class the second circle from the centre, &c. The population of these several classes of counties is taken from the statements of the national census, and calculated to show the average number of people existing in them in each of the years for which the observation was made; and the several columns show the proportion of patients sent to the hospitals, during that period, to the average annual population, or the number of people in each that sent one patient.

TABLE XXIX.—NUMBER OF PEOPLE IN VARIOUS DISTRICTS TO EACH PATIENT SENT TO THE LUNATIC, HOSPITAL.

HOSPITAL.	Period within which patients were sent.	Counties or Districts at various Distances from the Hospital.				
		Co'nty of Hospital.	Next District.	Third District.	Fourth District.	Fifth District.
Augusta, Me.,	1840 to 1849	263	519	856	–	–
Concord, N. H.,	1842 to 1849	248	412	900	–	–
Worcester, Mass.,	1833 to 1853	100	176	223	292	–
Providence, R. I.,	1848	406	5,710	–	–	–
Hartford, Conn.,	1844 to 1848	424	705	1,418	–	–
Utica, N. Y.,	1843 to 1849	361	680	812	1,523	–
Trenton, N. J.,	1848	1,956	3,077	6,781	–	–
Baltimore, Md.,	1843 to 1849	500	689	2,680	–	–
Staunton, Va.,	1828 to 1849	300	420	658	916	1,534
Columbus, O.,	1839 to 1849	582	994	1,093	1,168	–
Lexington, Ky.,	1824 to 1842	89	314	625	1,185	1,635
Nashville, Tenn.,	1844 to 1849	349	1,374	3,251	4,529	–

These facts are taken for various periods in various States ; no comparison is, therefore, to be made of one State with another, but only of the different classes of counties in the same State, at different distances from its hospital, in respect to the use which their people make of it.

This calculation was made in 1850.   Want of time prevents the making it for the four subsequent years, except as to Massachusetts ; but as this corroborates the previous calculations, and as they all originally agree in this matter, it is presumed that no further facts will be needed to establish the principle.

The proportion of lunatics which each county in Massachusetts sent to the State Hospital at Worcester, from 1833 to 1853, inclusive, as seen in table XXX., shows the effect of the same principle :—

TABLE XXX.—RATIO OF PATIENTS SENT TO THE LU-
NATIC HOSPITAL, AT WORCESTER, TO THE AVERAGE
POPULATION OF EACH COUNTY, DURING TWENTY-
ONE YEARS—1833 TO 1853, INCLUSIVE.

COUNTIES.	Calculated aver-age population twenty-one years.	Number of patients sent.	Population to one sent.	Population to one lunatic at home and else-where in 1854.
Worcester, . . .	107,654	1,067	100.8	422
Middlesex, . . .	124,384	524	237.3	533
Norfolk, ...	61,779	541	114.1	383
Hampden, . . .	42,114	236	178.8	554
Hampshire, . . .	32,775	181	181	402
	261,052	1,482	176	475
Franklin, . . .	29,814	102	290.5	377
Essex, ...	107,943	535	201.7	396
Bristol, ...	64,833	275	235.7	530
Plymouth, . . .	49,977	217	230.4	427
	252,567	1,129	223	427
Berkshire, . . .	44,228	144	307.1	446
Nantucket, . . .	8,409	30	283.3	686
Dukes, ...	4,111	17	241.8	252
Barnstable, . . .	32,854	115	285.6	467
	89,602	306	292	449
Suffolk, ...	110,041	464	237.1	371

It thus appears that, while Worcester County sent one in
100.8 of its people to the hospital, Hampden sent one in 178.8,
Barnstable one in 285, Frankin one in 290, and Berkshire one
in 307; showing that, in ratio of its population, the central

county, where the hospital is, and to whose people it is the most accessible and is best known, has had nearly three times as much advantage from it as the remote counties.

Taking the ratio of the insane to population in the several counties in 1854, table XXXI., there was some inequality in the distribution of the insane among them: six counties had a larger, and seven a smaller, proportion to their population than Worcester. Yet all sent a smaller proportion of patients to the Hospital.

The following table shows the exact relation of the want and the use of the hospital to the population of the several counties.

TABLE XXXI.

COUNTIES.	Lunatics in 1854.		Patients sent to Hospital in twenty-one years.	
	Population to one lunatic.	Lunatics in ten thousand people.	Average population to one patient.	Patients in ten thousand people.
Berkshire, ...	446	22	307	32
Franklin, ...	377	26	290	34
Hampshire, ...	402	24.8	181	55
Hampden, ...	554	18	178.8	56
Worcester, ...	422	23.6	100.8	99
Middlesex, ...	533	18.7	237	42
Essex, ...	396	25	201.7	49
Suffolk, ...	371	26.8	237	42
Norfolk, ...	383	26	114	87
Bristol, ...	530	18.8	235.7	42
Plymouth, ...	427	23	230	43
Barnstable, ...	467	21	285.6	35
Nantucket, ...	686	14	283	35
Dukes, ...	252	39.6	241.8	41

The opening of the State Hospital at Taunton affords another illustration of the influence of distance. At the end of March, 1854, the counties of Suffolk, Norfolk, Bristol, Plymouth, Barnstable, Nantucket and Dukes, had two hundred and twenty-five of their patients in the State Hospital at Worcester. In April, the hospital at Taunton was opened in the midst of these seven south-eastern counties, and offered to the use of their people. In October they had two hundred and seventy-five patients in both of these public hospitals—showing an increase of fifty, or 22 per cent., within six months, in consequence of the accommodations being brought so much nearer and made so much more accessible to them.

INFLUENCE OF FACILITIES OF TRAVEL ON THE USE OF A HOSPITAL.

The difference of the use made of the hospital by the people of the near and the remote counties is not to be explained by the corresponding difference in their necessity; for several of the distant counties, both in Massachusetts and in some other States, had a larger proportion of lunatics, and yet sent less, and some less than half as many, patients to their hospitals.

This difference is probably due to the difference in the facilities of access and in the labor and cost of travel. This is corroborated by comparing the use made of hospitals by people along the line of great thoroughfares with that made by those who have not these facilities of travel. In New York, the counties along the railroad and canal sent one in 790, and those in other directions, but at the same average distance, sent one in 1,155, of their people to the hospital at Utica. In Virginia, the counties in the valley of the Shenandoah, where the Western Asylum is situated, sent one in 514, while those among and beyond the mountains, and within the same distance, sent one in 877, of their people.

The same is found in the other States where the asylum is situated on some easy line of travel.

Having received proof from every quarter, and finding no countervailing fact or argument, it must be admitted as an established principle that a hospital cannot diffuse its advantages equally to the people of any large district. Those in the neighborhood having convenient access will use it much, and those farther off will use it little, and the distant still less.

Admitting this, then, it must follow that no large central hospital for any considerable extent of territory should be established; but, on the contrary, hospitals of proper size should be scattered as much as possible, and their advantages brought near to the people who ought to use them.

SEPARATE HOSPITALS FOR MALES AND FEMALES.

All the hospitals in the United States are for both sexes. One or two private asylums receive only one of the sexes. In England, all the public hospitals, and a great majority of the private licensed houses, receive both sexes. The two military and naval hospitals, and three private asylums, receive only males, and eighteen private asylums receive only females. All the public hospitals in Scotland and Ireland are open to both sexes.

Most of the superintendents of the American hospitals advise that separate institutions should be prepared for males and for females. Drs. Bell and Chandler, in their late reports, both urge this, and with good reason.

On the contrary, Dr. Thurnham, of the Wiltshire Asylum at Devizes, in England, who has devoted much attention to this particular question, says: " Asylums for the two sexes should be united. The supervision being careful and judicious, there need be no evils which are not insignificant when compared with the disadvantages of the separate plan." * Dr. Brown, of the asylum at Dumfries, in Scotland, gives the same opinion.*

Unquestionably there are some advantages to be derived from this separation. Each sex can thus have the peculiarly appropriate accommodations more freely and comfortably arranged; and the administration can be better adapted to the wants and liabilities of either, and be carried on with more ease and success, when they are separated, than when they are together in one establishment.

But all these advantages seem to be more than counterbalanced by the increase of travel made necessary by this separation.

A hospital for two hundred and fifty of only one sex must draw its patients from double the number of people that would

---

* Letter to the Commission.

be required to supply it if it contained one hundred and twenty-five of each sex; and of course these must be drawn from a much wider extent of territory. It is plain, then, that the obstacle of distance through which the remote patients must be carried will prevent the equal diffusion of the advantages of an institution for one sex in all the rural districts where people are scattered; but in large cities, or in their immediate neighborhood, which supply sufficient patients to fill two hospitals, this objection does not hold. And if separate provision should be made for the State paupers, whom the Commonwealth must take care of, and of whom none will be kept back for any of these reasons, the division of the sexes may answer, but not for the great body of the people of Massachusetts.

SEPARATE HOSPITALS FOR THE CURABLE AND INCURABLE INSANE.

The returns of the physicians and others show that, in their opinion, of the two thousand six hundred and thirty-two insane persons in Massachusetts, four hundred and thirty-five were curable, and two thousand and eighteen incurable.

The question has been much agitated by those who study these matters, and it was asked of the correspondents of this Commission, whether it were best to provide separate establishments for these two classes; and they all with one accord, and yet separately, answered in the negative.

The plan now pursued in nearly all the hospitals of this country and elsewhere, of having both classes together, is deemed the best.

As the curable may vary more from day to day, and are more susceptible of remedial influences, they require more watching and active treatment than the incurable patients. Consequently they need more accommodations, and better arrangements, and a greater amount of attention. They are managed with more expense than those who are supposed to be hopeless; and therefore mere economy would suggest that hospitals, with all the appliances and facilities for restoration, be provided for the curable, and that other asylums, with the bare means of custody and occupation, be provided for the incurable. This is done here and elsewhere, to some extent, by sending a part of the old and hopeless cases to the prisons and other places, to make room in the hospital for those whose cases are recent and promising. But this is only the result of necessity, because the curative establishments are not large enough for all.

There are strong and sufficing objections to this plan of separation. First. It is difficult to tell when a case becomes incurable, as some are restored even after several years' duration of disease. Dr. Tyler, of Concord, N. H., Hospital, says: " I do not think it in the power of man to infallibly decide on the curability or incurability of an insane person." * And second. There is ordinarily an advantage in keeping the two classes together. They have a healthy mutual influence ; they aid in each other's purposes of residence in the hospital—the restoration of one, and the discipline and comfort of the other. Many of the incurable patients, with some delusions, are mild and manageable in the wards of these institutions. A part of them have considerable, and some much, intelligence. They are, therefore, not unacceptable companions for the more excitable and recent cases, and aid in controlling them. On the other hand, the incurable, seeing the others come diseased and go restored, feel that their malady is not hopeless, and, at least, are induced to make some more effort to overcome their delusions and to regain their health.

Dr. Bell proposes * that a separate establishment, not in connection with any prison, be provided for the lowest class of demented patients—those who lead a mere vegetative life in the curative hospitals and elsewhere, for those who are now sent to the County Receptacles and Houses of Correction, and the State paupers who are sent to the State Almshouses.

SOCIAL DISTINCTIONS IN HOSPITALS.

As, in the treatment of bodily disorder, the physician recognizes and sustains all those parts of the constitution and system that are in good health, and endeavors to extend their strength through the disordered parts, and overcome the disease, so in the treatment of insanity it is necessary to have regard to all the powers, faculties and feelings which are yet sound, and use

* Letter to the Commission.

19

their aid to restore the disordered elements to health. Therefore the manager of the insane carefully respects their habits and opinions, their inclinations and associations, so far as they are healthy, and do not interfere with the restoration ; and all of these which are correct are to be disturbed as little as possible.

Hence it is desirable that the patient, as far as is consistent with the management of his malady, either for its removal or its amelioration, should live in a style similar to that which he properly enjoyed when he was in health ; he should also have associates corresponding to his former habits and tastes ; and in all things he should not be required, in course of his treatment, to submit to any new and needless disturbance, disappointment or mortification.

In general life, people associate according to their tastes and sympathies. They select their companions from among those who are similar to themselves, and shrink from such as are of different character. Hence the refined and the coarse, the cultivated and the ignorant, the high-minded and the sensually low, the gentle and the quarrelsome,—these severally are so diverse in their habits and tastes that they are unfitting and unacceptable to each other, but instinctively separate, and do not voluntarily meet, except when business or charity, or some other extraneous motive, prevails for the time. But when they desire to satisfy the wants of their hearts and find the most happiness, they select those of their own kind with whom they can sympathize. These are natural feelings and habits; they run through all society of every kind and in every country. It is not to be supposed that a man, by becoming insane, changes his character entirely in this respect, or loses all his old and healthy desires and aversions, or that he will bear crossing and disappointment, in those which are left to him, more willingly than when in health. On this account, then, there are strong objections to making microcosms of the insane hospitals, where persons of every kind of character and degree of development shall be associated together in the same halls, and be constant and unavoidable companions, in close if not intimate connection, day after day and month after month. Such a contact of opposing and inharmonious qualities interferes with the calm and happy discipline that is necessary for the recovery of the curable and for the self-control and comfort of the permanently insane.

SEPARATE HOSPITALS FOR THE INDEPENDENT AND PAUPER.

All the State Hospitals in the United States open their doors for both the independent and pauper, and these meet together in the same wards. A few of the corporate institutions—those at Somerville, Bloomingdale, N. Y., and Philadelphia—provide elegant and expensive accommodations for the more prosperous classes, and charge a price nearly in relation to the cost. This, of course, excludes the paupers; for, with an occasional exception, none of them go to these institutions. But in all the hospitals in Massachusetts, except the McLean, the paupers constitute a majority (83 per cent.) of the whole. Some of our native town paupers have been in comfortable circumstances, and used to some of the refinements of social and domestic life. Some of the insane paupers belong to independent families. Among the native population of Massachusetts there is such an imperceptible gradation from the higher and more favored classes, through all the ranks, down to those who are supported by their towns,—the last including some that are cultivated and intelligent,—that it is not easy to draw a line between them, nor is it well to try to separate them in our State Hospitals. With one partial exception, this proposition finds no favor with any of our superintendents.

In England this separation is advised by the Commissioners in Lunacy, and by others who are concerned in the care of the insane and are received as authority in these matters; and this is the general practice there. Of the county and borough asylums, twenty-five received paupers only, and twelve both classes. Of the corporate hospitals, ten take private or independent patients only, and four both classes; and of the licensed private houses, one hundred and six receive independent patients only; one, paupers only, and twenty-three, admit all classes.

In Great Britain the poor are generally ignorant and uncultivated, with no education, and little sensibility. They live in wretched cabins or hovels, or in crowded tenements; they are little used to the comforts, still less to the luxuries and graces, of life.* The English paupers are even lower in the scale than these. Between these and the middle and the more comfortable classes there is a wide difference in respect to cultivation and refinement. The latter would enjoy and profit by many comforts or even little luxuries of living, and would be benefited by more abundant and graceful appliances for their cure, and many means of occupation and amusement, which would not be beneficial to the others ; and therefore the British establishments for paupers need not be so costly and elegant as those for the other classes. When these are brought together they are subject to the antagonisms and irritations, the retarding and disturbing causes, already described, that interfere with "the comfort and improvement of the patients," interrupt the process of recovery, and make the administration of the hospital more difficult and expensive.

HOSPITAL FOR STATE PAUPERS.

The origin, character and position of the State paupers of Massachusetts differ very materially from those of the town paupers. Of the seven hundred and thirty-seven lunatics and idiots supported by the Commonwealth, five hundred and seventy-three are natives of other countries ; and a large part of the remaining one hundred and sixty-four are natives of other States, and some are colored persons. These are not only now supported by the public treasury, but they never, even in health, had sufficient ambition, or energy, or command of circumstances to own the requisite amount of property, or pay the necessary tax, or reside long enough in one place to gain a residence, and thereby establish a claim upon the people of any local municipality for their support, as the more cultivated and favored town paupers have done.

---

* See the General Report on the Sanitary Condition of the Laboring Classes of Great Britain, prepared by Edwin Chadwick, the learned Secretary of the Poor Law Commissioners, under the direction of that Board, and presented to both Houses of Parliament by command of Her Majesty. Printed in London, 1852.

See also Report of the Commissioners on the Health of Towns of Great Britain, presented also to Parliament, and printed by order of that body.

These Reports show the personal, social and domestic condition of the laboring but independent poor to be far lower than that of similar native classes in Massachusetts.

See Mr. Chadwick's Letter to the Commission, p. 62 of this Report.

The State paupers, especially those who are aliens, resemble in character and manner the English, rather than the American, dependent upon public charity. There is, therefore, a wide difference between them and the mass of our people. This is manifested in a marked degree among the sane of these nations; the natives and the aliens do not associate together, nor live in the same families. Except as employer and laborer, they do not make component parts of the same household. This disseverance is extended even to the houses and neighborhood. Wherever several families among the poor occupy one house, they are usually of one kind—either all natives, or all foreign; and they do not willingly live in close neighborhood, although in different tenements. In social life, in their gatherings, in their religious worship, each party cleaves to those of its own people, and stands aloof from others.

These feelings of affinity for those of their own nation, and aversion to the others, are not lost in insanity; they usually continue undiminished, and are often increased. To put together, in the same wards, insane persons of these two races, with such diversity of cultivation, tastes and habits, who stood aloof from each other in all social life when they were well enough to select their own companions—to require them to live in the same halls, to eat at the same table, to bear with that which was offensive, and from which they would have shrunk in health, is not the best way to calm the excitements or soothe the irritations of this disease, and is contrary to the principles everywhere acknowledged, and herein stated, that the natural and healthy feelings of the patients should not be disturbed, nor their tastes offended, nor their inclinations nor aversions needlessly opposed.

Looking, then, at the good of the patients there seems to be reason for separating the State pauper insane from the others in Massachusetts, and of making distinct provision for their healing and their protection.

It is probable that the interests of the State would be advanced by this separation. If the division would remove any of the obstacles to the cure of either party, or facilitate the discipline of the incurable and of the whole establishment, it would save some of those who are doubtful, who are almost, but not quite, cured or curable under the present influences, but who might be restored to health, to society, and to usefulness, if this cause of disturbance were taken away.

Keeping in view that the style of life in the hospital should not differ so far from that to which the patients have been accustomed at home as to offend their tastes and disappoint them, and regarding the difference of domestic condition in the measure of comfort and convenience which they adopt when they have the means and the power to select for themselves, it is obvious that there may be, with equal advantage for the restoration of the curable, and the protection and comfort of the incurable, plainer and cheaper accommodations, and a smaller expenditure for the daily maintenance and management of the State paupers, than would be proper for the average of the other patients—the members of the families of the farmers and mechanics in Massachusetts.

Considerations of economy, then, should favor the separate provision for the State paupers, as their accommodation and support might be obtained at a less cost to the Commonwealth than would be expedient for the others, and with equal advantage to them.

The State paupers are already almost exclusively in some of the public institutions. Table XXXII. shows how largely they occupy the hospitals and the receptacles, and how few of them are at any home, or in any town or city almshouse. It would, therefore, be assuming no new burden, if the State should concentrate them in one or more institutions especially appropriated for their use.

TABLE XXXII.—STATE PAUPERS.*

Residence and Disease.

Residence.	Lunatics.	Idiots.	Residence.	Lunatics.	Idiots.
Hospitals.			*Jails.*		
Worcester, . .	157	1	Concord, . .	2	–
Taunton, . .	127	1	Boston, . . .	1	–
Boston, . . .	207	1	Dedham, . .	1	–
Receptacles.			Barnstable, . .	1	–
Cambridge, . .	57	6	*State Almshouses.*		
Ipswich, . . .	68	–	Monson, . .	6	15
House of Correction.			Tewksbury, . .	19	2
Boston, . . .	3	–	Bridgewater, . .	15	8
State Prison.			*At Home,* . .	24	10
Charlestown, . .	3	.–	Totals, . .	693	44

CRIMINAL LUNATICS.

There is a natural repugnance in innocence to associating with crime. This sensibility, which society encourages and cultivates in all its members, and is deemed one of its safe-guards, usually remains with the insane; it is sometimes exalted; and if it is ever clouded or diminished, it is from disease; and then it needs to be cherished and restored as certainly as any delusion or perversity is to be removed.

To place, then, these criminals—the insane convicts from the prisons—in the same wards with the innocent patients, and to require them to associate together,—this is offensive to those

---

* The paupers were distributed as stated in this table when the returns were received. Since the Report was written, and while passing through the press, some have been transferred to the State Almshouses.

sensibilities which remain natural and healthy, and increases the disorder of those which are perverted by disease.

Besides the restlessness that frequently is manifested in insanity, there is added in the criminal a desperate hardihood in desiring to escape. The convalescence, which awakens the patient to a sense of his condition, reconciles the innocent one to his confinement as the best means of regaining and enjoying perfect liberty, and makes him contented to remain; while, on the other hand, it opens to the criminal the prospect of another and a worse confinement after his restoration, when he shall be removed back to prison. It is necessary, therefore, that a hospital which is to receive criminal lunatics should be provided with more means of security and forcible detention, and it should be stronger, and less airy and expansive, than is needed for other patients.

In Great Britain the universal sentiment is opposed to this mingling the criminal lunatics with the ordinary inmates of hospitals. The Association of Superintendents of Asylums protest against it. The Commissioners in Lunacy, in almost every one of their annual reports, earnestly call the attention of the Parliament to this matter. In their report for 1853 * they give the following reasons for their opinions against the association of these two classes of patients :—

" 1. That such association is unjust; and that it gives pain and offence to ordinary patients, (who are generally very sensitive to any supposed degradation,) and also to their friends.

" 2. That its moral effect is bad, the language and habits of criminal patients being generally offensive, and their propensities almost invariably bad; that in cases of simulated insanity, (which seems to be not unfrequent,) the patient is generally of the worst character; and that, even where the patient is actually insane, the insanity has been often caused by vicious habits; that patients of this class frequently attempt to escape, and cause insubordination and dissatisfaction amongst the other patients.

* Seventh Annual Report of the Commissioners in Lunacy to the Lord Chancellor, page 33.

" 3. That a necessity for stricter custody exists for one class than for the other; and that this interferes with proper discipline, classification, and general treatment, and strengthens the common delusion that an asylum is a prison.

"4. That criminal patients concentrate attention on themselves, and deprive the other patients of their due share of care from the attendants.

" 5. That the effect on criminal patients themselves is bad; that they are taunted by the other patients, and are irritated on seeing such other patients discharged.

" These and other objections have been expressed by almost all the superintendents and proprietors of lunatic establishments in England."

Yet the law and the custom, both in Britain and in Massachusetts, require the criminal and the guiltless lunatics to be brought together in the same hospital now; for in the present state of things, there is no other way. So long as no separate means are provided for curing the insane convicts, humanity demands that they should be sent to such as exist; for not even the felon should be unnecessarily doomed to permanent insanity, but should enjoy the due opportunity of healing, notwithstanding the revolting companionship may pain the feelings, irritate the tempers, and even aggravate and prolong the diseases of the other patients who are thus compelled to associate with them. Yet it is a questionable humanity that does not prevent this necessity.

Among the many with whom the criminal may be brought in contact in the wards of the hospital, there may be some whose curability is so doubtful, that they can recover only under the most propitious circumstances, and in whom the recuperative force is so small that any unfavorable influence weighs in the balance against their chance of recovery and destroys their hope. The introduction of criminal lunatics among such as these may make their insanity permanent.

In Great Britain it is now proposed to establish a criminal lunatic asylum, to which all the insane convicts shall be sent, and also all that class of patients whose conduct has approached the doubtful line between insanity and criminality even before they passed it, and who, though not convicted, yet

20

had committed such acts of violence as are ordinarily considered as crime or evidence of criminal intent.

There are not enough such patients as these in Massachusetts to fill an institution; and in the present state of things it is not proposed to change the policy in respect to them. Yet, if the State paupers should be provided for in a separate establishment, it should include strong and suitable wards for the criminal insane, where they could be securely kept by themselves, and where they will do less injury to the innocent patients, whose sensibilities are less tender than those of the more cultivated.

Except this provision for the State paupers and the criminal lunatics, no other separation of classes or patients is deemed advisable to be adopted in this State; but all other insane patients, of all ranks and all manifestations of mental disease, should be received, and treated and protected as they now are, in the same establishment.

POLICY OF THE STATE IN PROVIDING FOR THE INSANE.

Of the two thousand six hundred and thirty-two insane persons belonging to Massachusetts, sixteen hundred and seventy are now provided for, either in the four hospitals, two private institutions, two county receptacles, eight prisons, or three State almshouses within the State, or in five hospitals in the other States of New England.

These several classes of houses in Massachusetts, for the insane, have already been described in detail (pp. 112 to 130); and it is now for the State to decide whether all of these shall be continued, and others like unto them shall be created, now or hereafter. to meet the existing and increasing wants of those suffering under disorders of the mind, or whether any of them shall be abandoned and their places supplied by others.

The general plan of hospitals for all patients, the curable and incurable, the mild, troublesome, and the dangerous, seems to the Commissioners to be the best for their comfort and improvement, as well as a matter of economy. For a great majority of the recent and curable cases there will be no question that, in the present state of science, the hospital offers the surest means of restoration to health. The furious and violent cases, although incurable, must be confined; and the hospital not only affords them sufficient and proper restraint, but it also calms and makes them comfortable; and the excitable and troublesome are quieted and made peaceable by the same influences. As these institutions give the patient the best opportunity of restoration, and as the cost of cure is comparatively little, while the cost of life-support is very great, it is good economy to provide such establishments for the restoration of all recent cases.

The question still remains as to the means of providing for the old and incurable patients. Excepting the hospitals, all establishments now open to the insane, under sanction of the law or the authorities of the Commonwealth, fail of their purposes, and are therefore objectionable.

LAW OF 1836—COUNTY RECEPTACLES.

The law of 1836, requiring the counties to provide suitable apartments in the Houses of Correction for the insane and idiotic persons not furiously mad, was an improvement upon the previous state of things. It offered a home to a part of the insane who were strolling as vagabonds over the country, the objects of aversion and of derision to the thoughtless, and of fear to the timid. It also ordered suitable apartments to be prepared for such others as had been hitherto confined in the common rooms built for felons.

It was supposed to be the complement of the law regulating the admission into the State Lunatic Hospital, to which the courts were authorized to send only such as were " so furiously mad as to render it manifestly dangerous to the peace and safety of the community that they should be at large." * The law then intended to provide for the furiously mad at the State Hospital, and for those who were " not furiously mad" in the county receptacles. It was intended, also, that these institutions should be in each county, and that every district should find its own means of protecting these helpless patients, and that they should be within the reach of all who needed them.

An inquiry into the history of the past in reference to the operation of this law, and consultation with those who have executed it, and a careful examination of the Houses of Cor-

* Revised Statutes, chap. 48, sect. 6, p. 380.

rection and their accommodations for the insane and idiots, show that in eleven counties it has been a dead letter and entirely inoperative, and in all the counties it has failed to answer its purpose.

These eleven counties have not fulfilled the first section of the law and provided suitable apartments for these lunatics. Nor are any of their lunatics now in any apartment within the precincts of the House of Correction, under the authority of the second section of the law, except in Norfolk, Bristol, Barnstable and Plymouth. Their other patients, if removed from home, are sent to the hospitals, and they are relieved of the responsibility for and care of them.

On the other hand, the counties of Suffolk, Essex and Middlesex assume the responsibility and the expense of providing accommodations for all such of their insane as may be sent to them through the several processes of law. All of these patients undoubtedly are found in, and are presumed to belong to, one or the other of these counties. Many of them have families or friends there, and consequently better claim for home there than elsewhere. But some of them lead vagabond lives; they float on the whirlpool of society until they are carried into the vortex of the cities, where they fall into the hands of the police, and then are committed by the magistrates to the places provided for them. In this way nearly all of the State pauper lunatics whom the law of 1836 is made to reach, and who are not in the State hospitals, find their way sooner or later into these houses of refuge in these three counties.

The law operates, therefore, very unequally; for while eleven counties are relieved from any investment of capital for its fulfilment, and from all expenditure except their share of the general tax for the board of their patients, the whole burden of providing buildings and grounds, and paying the excess of the cost of their maintenance, over and above the sum allowed by the State for this purpose, falls upon these three counties.

Besides this unequal distribution of the burden of this law in its practical operation, there are other and still more important considerations in respect to the patients themselves, and to the penal institutions with which this law connects them.

CLASSES OF PATIENTS COMMITTED TO THE RECEPTACLES AND
PRISONS.

First, as to the character of the patients. The law had in
view only the mild and harmless lunatics, " not furiously mad,"
whose diseases were established beyond hope of relief, and
limited its requirements of the counties to provide for, and
the authority of the magistrates to commit, such as these, supposing that it had thereby secured proper homes and guardianship for all that are not better provided for in the hospital,
and that this was all that their disease or condition required.

But experience has shown that there is a class of incurable
lunatics who are not mild and harmless, but furiously mad,
and who, for their own good or for that of the public, need
an asylum of security where they may be protected from excitements and prevented from disturbing or injuring others.
Some of these are at their own homes troublesome or dangerous to their families ; others are found in the streets noisy and
violent. In either case they need guardianship, and perhaps
restraint. They are taken and carried before the courts for
examination, and then sent to the receptacle. Some of them
are so furious that they are tied, bound and guarded by strong
and courageous men, when they are carried to these receptacles or to the prisons. " Within a few months one of this
class was received whose ankles were, at the time, badly exco-
riated by the manacles with which it had been found necessary to restrain him." * When they arrive there they seem to
require strong rooms, and straps and muffs to curb their violence ; but they certainly need the soothing influence of trained
and skilful officers and attendants to calm them. In these
cases the letter of the law is violated.

There is another class whose malady has its periods of excitement and quiescence. " Of these many have been sent
there who had previously been periodically insane. They were
committed, in most cases, perhaps during lucid intervals, the
paroxysm continuing to occur at longer or shorter periods,
during which, in many instances, they have been violent, noisy,
and very difficult to manage." * In their cases the letter of
the law is regarded, but the spirit is transgressed.

* Letter to the Commission from Gen. Samuel Chandler, late Sheriff of Middlesex, and for fourteen years one of the Overseers of the House of Correction.

This law presupposes that none but the old and incurable cases would be included in its description and sent under it to these places of custody; but there are some recent cases committed both to the receptacles and to the prisons under its ˙sanction. Some of these recover, and others pass over the period of hope for want of the appropriate means of healing.

The reports received from these establishments state that, without including the insane convicts, they have one patient whose disease was supposed to have been less than one year's duration, fourteen from one to two years, and nineteen from two to five years. How long these had been diseased when they were committed was not stated. At the receptacle at East Cambridge about four recent and curable cases are received a year; and such are not unfrequently sent to Ipswich.

In the first class of cases the magistrates plainly overstep the letter and the spirit of the law. Yet they do so with good intent; for the hospitals are filled, and these excited lunatics need to be restrained, and the receptacle or the prison seems to be the only recourse.

In the second and third classes these officers judge by the facts presented to them. They find the patient before them mild, and " not furiously mad," and they inquire no further. In many cases they have no means of knowing what the condition of the patient has been; and a single examination is insufficient to enable them to determine whether he is constantly mild or periodically excitable. This is a difficult matter for even the practised manager of the insane to do without knowing the history of the case in question. And several of these lunatics are strollers, whose previous lives are unknown to the officers or people where they are found.

The magistrates cannot discriminate between the curable and incurable cases; nor are they required by the law to do so. They therefore look only at the present appearance of the case, and not to the future. They find the lunatic is described in the law, and commit him, without regard to the length of his disease or the hope there may be of his restoration.

There is another point in the preliminary steps of the administration of the law which is well worthy of notice here. It grants to any two justices, one being of the quorum, the power of summarily sending to these receptacles, and practically to the prisons, in eleven of the counties, any person who may seem to them to be insane or idiotic, but not furiously mad. Now one of the most difficult things in both medical and legal practice is, to determine whether a person be insane or not. Questions of this sort are usually settled in courts with extreme difficulty and caution, and only on the evidence of the most practised experts in the disease. With all their caution in admitting patients into the hospitals on the evidence of physicians or an examination by the Judge of Probate, persons are sometimes received who are not insane. But then the error is soon detected by the medical officer of the institution, and the person discharged. For want of suitable evidence, the magistrates are still more liable to make this mistake. Mr. Worcester, of the Ipswich Receptacle, writes : " I have had six committed to this Insane Asylum, under the law of 1836, that were not insane when they were committed. They did not remain but a week or two before they were discharged." * There may be other persons of sound mind brought before the magistrates under suspicion of insanity, who, for the want of proper medical evidence to establish their mental health, are sent to the prison or receptacle ; and for the want of medical supervision the true state of their health may not have been discovered, and they remain needlessly in confinement.

In regard to the admissions of these patients the officers of the prisons have no volition ; the order of commitment is mandatory, and must be obeyed. Whatever may be the meaning of the law, they are not its interpreters, but must admit every patient that is sent to them, whether furiously or not furiously mad.

OPINIONS OF SHERIFFS AND OFFICERS OF PRISONS.

In course of this investigation the Commissioners held free conversations with the officers whose position and experience have given them the best opportunities of observation, and whose opinions are therefore of great value. These are the sheriffs, the overseers and masters of the houses of correc-

---

* Letter to the Commission.

tion, the jailers, who had the immediate charge or the general oversight of twenty of these prisons, and several of the physicians who attended upon their inmates when sick. They all expressed their convictions on this subject in personal conversation, and some of them at length in letters; and they substantiated their opinions with reasons, and most of them with facts that had come within their own observation. They all, with one modified exception, concur in the belief that the system of confining the insane in any apartments of the prisons, or the connection of the establishments for lunatics in any way with the houses of correction, was a bad one, and operated unfavorably both for the diseased patient and the criminal. The two classes of persons who are thus placed within the precincts of the houses of correction, in the same establishments and under the same general supervision, have no affinity either in their character or their liability. Except that they both need custody and government, there is no similarity between them. In the causes or the objects of their confinement, the accommodations they require, the discipline and treatment that will suit their condition, there is the widest difference. To put these classes together merely because they both need walls to keep them in and men to govern them, and they belong to the State, is as unwise as to connect a cotton factory and an iron mill, because they both need overseers and water-power and belong to the same proprietor.

The opinion and reasons given by Mr. Willis, Sheriff of Berkshire, are substantially repeated by the other officers who were consulted:—

That the lunatics were a great burden upon their care and labor; and the officers and the attendants all complain of the law that allowed them to be sent to the prison. Every thing which was necessary for the convicts—the buildings, the rooms, and the officers and the men, the general plan of administration, the system of discipline—was different from that which was most proper for the insane.

As the criminals and the criminal discipline were the primary objects of the prison, every thing is arranged for them. The rooms or cells were close and strong. The officers and attendants were selected for their power or skill in managing bad, rather than diseased, persons. They were bold and saga-

ice; but they were not skilled in the wayward workings of the disordered mind, nor prepared to meet the varieties of feeling, the delusions, excitements and depressions of insanity.

The rules of the establishment were made for criminals; and the whole administration must take the penal form, and could not be altered to suit the wants of the insane. On this account the independent and guiltless lunatic at the Dedham prison was clothed like the convicts—in the variously-colored dress.

The lunatics were in the way of the criminals. They could not be controlled with the same rigid discipline. Their excitements and their outcries disturbed the convicts; and the whole establishment could not be managed so easily, with so little force and anxiety, as it could be if all the inmates were of one class—convicts.

And on the other hand, these officers were equally convinced that they could not give to the patients the care and attention, the occupation and enjoyment, which their health and condition required.

The preceding objections relate principally to the confinement of the insane in prisons; but they bear with equal certainty, though in a modified degree, upon the receptacles. As it is no part of the intention of the law to make these curative or restorative institutions, there are no physicians employed to watch and cure the derangement of mind. The insane are subject to the law of the prison and of all custodial establishments in this respect, and are only offered the means of healing when their bodies are diseased.

The law supposed these patients were entirely passive, requiring neither healing nor forcible restraint; yet its operation has compelled the receptacles to provide the last at least, if not the first.

Mr. Keyes, the Sheriff of Middlesex, says: " Here are confined, without any means of employment or amusement, this number of patients, many of them approaching to an idiotic character, and comparatively harmless, but several of both sexes furiously mad, raving and dangerous. These last require constant watchfulness on the part of the officers, and much of

21

the time mufflers and straps, to prevent their doing mischief to other inmates, themselves and their clothing." *

The overseers and the government of these establishments endeavor, as far as possible, to correct this evil by sending these furious patients to Worcester. Gen. Chandler says: " It has not been necessary to retain those who were furiously mad when received, or those who have become so afterwards, for a very long period. After becoming satisfied that a patient was likely to remain permanently in that situation, evidence to that effect has been presented to the judge of probate, and his order obtained for his or her transfer to the State Institution at Worcester. But in this our Institution has not been very much relieved; for, owing to the crowded state of that Hospital for several years past, about as many have been transferred from it to our receptacle as have been sent from ours to Worcester, and there has generally been no very great difference in the character or condition of the patients thus exchanged." *

RECEPTACLE AT IPSWICH.

The receptacle at Ipswich has more room without and within; it has better accommodations, and is in every way better suited to the wants of the patients, than that at Cambridge; and under the excellent management of Mr. Worcester, the system of connecting an insane establishment with a prison has the best opportunity of success. Yet even there, where all the accommodations probably intended by the law, are provided, and the whole administered with kindness and discretion, it is plain that the plan is inadequate to meet the wants of those who are brought in subjection to it.

The present head of the house has had much experience in watching the insane; but his attention is primarily given to the House of Correction, which, with almost nine hundred convicts in course of the year, must be the principal interest of the establishment, and his attention must be given only secondarily to the insane department. Excepting him, there is no corps of officers and assistants trained for the employment, and by their taste, study and habit, competent to guide and control the insane. There is an absence of the means of occu-

* Letter to the Commission.

pation and amusement which should be offered to this class of patients, and which are considered necessary, and are found in hospitals prepared for them; and yet this establishment is of a higher order than can be expected of any county receptacle connected with a House of Correction.

RECEPTACLE AT CAMBRIDGE.

The receptacle at Cambridge is inferior in every point of view to that at Ipswich. The prison is on a small piece of ground, no more than sufficient for its own purposes, and so situated as to render any expansion impossible. Here are the House of Correction and one of the jails of the largest county in the State, and they had eleven hundred and eighteen prisoners in course of the last year. Here nothing but mere custody and confinement within the narrowest bounds can be offered to the lunatic.

The master of the House of Correction and the officers concerned in the administration are kind and discreet men, and manifest a deep interest in the general welfare of the insane; but they are compelled to feel that they are in a false position, where humanity expects, and they desire to do, that which neither the law nor circumstances allow them to do for these patients. The care of the penal part of the establishment, with the workshop and the general management, are as much as any one man should be required to attend to. With all this burden, which he must sustain, and which he has every means of sustaining, he finds that the care of the insane is a responsibility which he has neither the time nor the power to fulfil.

Mr. Sheriff Keyes says : " Of one thing I am quite certain— that no one can pass through either building without being sickened at the sight of so much discomfort and wretchedness where there has been no crime, and that no greater relief could be afforded to all officially connected with the institution than the removal of these to a better situation." *

General Chandler was asked, " Is the whole establishment, which you think the best for criminals—the buildings and the grounds, the corps of officers, the kind of men, the rules and

* Letter to the Commission.

regulations, and the general plan of administration which is needed for them, suitable also, in your opinion, for the insane?"

The General says, "To this question I answer unhesitatingly in the negative." *

General Chandler, when asked "whether he would advise the continuance, or the repeal, or modification of the law, and some other method adopted for the care and support of such insane persons as are sent to the receptacles," answered, " I have the fullest conviction, arising from experience and observation, that the law should be repealed, and some other method adopted." *

ECONOMY OF THE LAW OF 1836.

There is an apparent economy in keeping these patients in these receptacles and in the prisons. In these they have nothing but their board and shelter; and in the hospitals they have not only these, but also the best medical and other supervision especially appropriated to their mental condition. But the same price is paid for each.

The records of the State Auditor show that the same rates, $100 a year, and $2, $2.25 and $2.50 per week have been paid by the Commonwealth for the board and care of lunatics in the Worcester, Taunton and Boston hospitals, in the Essex and Middlesex receptacles, and in the Berkshire, Hampshire, Worcester and Norfolk Houses of Correction, since the year 1848 at least. †

It is true these rates do not cover all the expense of maintenance in the State hospitals, but only the board and attendance, and perhaps repairs; and besides this, the State pays the rent in the interest on the whole cost of the establishments, and also the salaries of the medical and superintending officers; while the rent and superintendence of the Boston hospital and the two receptacles are paid by the city and the counties to which they belong.

The annual cost of the rent, medical and other superintendence, which the State pays in the hospitals at Worcester and

* Letter to the Commission.
† Letter of the Auditor to the Commission.

Taunton, is about fifty dollars a year on each patient.* This
is saved to the State on the patients who are supported at the
hospitals in Boston and in all the receptacles and prisons; but
it is either at the cost of the city and counties which built and
own these establishments, or of the patients who receive so
much less at the hands of their guardians.

It may be reasonably supposed that the annual and weekly
rates allowed by the State pay for all that is obtained—rent,
board and attendance—in the county institutions, because these
are provided on a lower and cheaper scale, while they pay
only for attendance and board in the hospitals; and the saving
in the difference of expense is therefore at the cost of the patients themselves.

Unquestionably this class of patients may be provided for
and maintained at less expense than most of the others in the
hospitals; but, considering that there are some recent and
curable cases among them, who, for want of proper remedial
treatment, may become incurable lunatics and permanent
paupers, and that the mild may become excited, and the troublesome become furious and uncontrollable, for the same
reason, it is not good economy to diminish or deprive them
entirely of that medical and other superintendence and means
of cure and discipline which are considered the best for the
management of insanity in all its manifestations and stages.

There is at the present time a crisis in the operation of the
law of 1836, which seems to open the way for a change in the

* According to the records in the State Auditor's office, Massachusetts has in-
vested $185,000 in the Hospital at Worcester, and $185,135 in that at Taunton.
Besides this, the town gave land that cost $2,400 to the former, and the land that
cost $12,000 to the latter. The salaries of the principal officers of these Hospitals
are paid directly from the treasury of the Commonwealth,—amounting to $3,900
at Worcester, and $2,750 at Taunton. These payments, with the annual interest
on the cost of these establishments, amount to $14,372 at Worcester, and $14,678
at Taunton, being the rent and salaries, which are not charged upon the patients.

These sums, being divided among the patients, make an average of $39.15 a
year, or 75 cents a week for each one at Worcester, when there are 367 in the
house, as in October, 1854, and $43.95 a year, and 84 cents a week, when the 327
rooms are no more than properly filled. At Taunton, this average is $58.71 a
year, and $1.12 cents a week, when it is not crowded.

For both hospitals, with 577 patients, these averages are $50.34 a year, or 96
cents a week, for each.

plan of taking care of this class of lunatics. The authorities of Middlesex find it necessary to provide other and more ample accommodations, and are only waiting to see whether the State will continue its present policy; and if it does, they will build another and suitable receptacle for their patients. The authorities of Boston feel the same necessity, and are only waiting to find a suitable location for a larger and more convenient hospital which they propose to build. Here is money to be expended and two new hospitals to be created. One is to be almost exclusively, and the other principally, appropriated to the use of the wards of the State. The former will, from the conditions of the law, be unsuitable, and the other suitable, for the wants of those who are to use them.

There seems to be no propriety in requiring Middlesex and Boston to make this investment and build these establishments, which the Commonwealth can do in the one case as well, and in the other better, for itself.

From these personal examinations of all the receptacles and prisons which are open for the insane and idiots under the law of 1836, from the universal evidence and opinions of so many competent witnesses, and from the reasons which have been presented, the Commission believe,—

1. That the system proposed by that law for the management and treatment of lunatics has not been successful.

2. That it is wrong to connect insanity with crime, lunatics with criminals, or asylums with prisons.

3. That this connection is injurious to the patients and to the convicts; and neither can be managed so well, nor the purposes of confinement so completely obtained, for either class, when in the same, as they can be in separate establishments.

4. That it is not good economy for the State to deprive its insane wards of those means of healing that would restore the curable, nor of those best disciplinary influences that would keep the others in the most quiet and comfortable condition.

5. That the State should provide a suitable establishment for its own pauper lunatics, and especially for such as are now in the houses of correction and the receptacles or hospitals connected with them, and also for the criminal lunatics.

6. That this establishment should be put under the care and supervision of responsible medical and other officers, who will

understand and be able to meet and to manage all the various phases of mental derangement.

STATE ALMSHOUSES.

In the crowded condition of the hospitals and of the receptacles, and the unfitness of the prisons for the confinement of the lunatics, the State almshouses seemed to be proper resorts for a portion of the State pauper lunatics who were mild and harmless, and who could no longer profit by the curative measures, nor need the peculiar confinement or vigilant watchfulness, of the hospital. Accordingly, several of these have been transferred from Worcester and Taunton and from the receptacles to these houses in Monson, Tewksbury and Bridgewater; and their numbers have been gradually increasing, and seem likely to increase more and more.[*]

These establishments were carefully examined and their intelligent superintendents consulted as to the convenience and expediency of keeping insane paupers in them. These officials gave their opinions very freely both in conversation and in letters to the Commission. They were unanimous in their convictions that the mingling of the insane with the sane in their houses operated badly, not only for both parties, but for the administration of the whole institution.

" I am fully of the opinion, from observation and experience, that the State Almshouse under my charge is not a poper or suitable place for the demented insane or idiotic in any respect." [†]

" We have no suitable accommodation in our Almshouse for this class of insane." [‡]

" Not even in the smallest and least important requirement for their proper care are suitable accommodations provided in the building for the insane and idiotic poor." [§]

It was supposed that they could live quietly, undisturbed and undisturbing, mingling with the other inmates of these

---

[*] See Appendix, C.

[†] Dr. S. D. Brooks, Superintendent of State Almshouse at Monson, in letter to the Commission.

[‡] Isaac H. Meserve, Superintendent of State Almshouse at Tewksbury, in letter to the Commission.

[§] Levi L. Goodspeed, Superintendent of State Almshouse at Bridgewater, in letter to the Commission.

houses, and be there provided for as conveniently, as any other pauper. But the result of the experience of each of the alms-houses does not justify this expectation. It is found that, although these lunatics were quiet and easily managed at the hospitals, where all the influences are regulated by the administration of the establishment, and where no irritating causes are allowed to come in contact with them, yet this quiescence and apparent good temper are due in great measure to the constant and present discipline from without rather than to any power of self-control. They will hardly bear the ordinary trials and irritations of common life even in company with discreet and well-balanced minds; but here, in these alms-houses, their associates are less favorable to their calmness than the average of the world.

The paupers in these almshouses have less than the ordinary prudence and regard for others. They have not the discretion nor the self-sacrifice to enable them to live in harmony with those of unbalanced minds; consequently they tease, taunt and irritate the lunatic. They provoke and quarrel with him. He becomes more uneasy and less controllable.

" Under the present arrangement of our building, it is an absolute impossibility to keep the two classes separate at all times; which, from my observation and experience, I *know* to be one of the most desirable things or "helps" to be sought in promoting the comfort and well-being of both divisions of our unfortunate family. The mingling together of the sane and insane will, at times, produce much of that irritable and unpleasant effect which is so desirable and necessary absolutely to avoid." *

" They" (the patients) "come in contact every day, and at all times in the day, with a class of paupers that are very curious, and whose curiosity is easily excited, and, hearing the " comical talk" (as they term it) of the insane, leads them to merriment; and all manner of questions are asked the insane paupers, exciting them, and sometimes very furiously, which often renders it necessary to confine the lunatics; whereas, if they had not come in contact with the sane pauper, they would have remained quiet." †

* Mr. Goodspeed's letter to the Commission.
† Mr. Meserve's letter to the Commission.

" It is impossible, to any considerable extent, to keep different classes of persons, in one institution or house, separate. They must and will, under the plan of our buildings, mingle more or less." *

The attendants and servants who do the work in the wards, and take care of the sane paupers, are generally the best and the healthiest of that class; yet they have not the moral nor the mental power to control these inharmonious elements and prevent these irritations and excitements.

" The policy in supporting these paupers here is, that they shall do the labor of carrying on the work of the institution, with the aid of a few officers at the head of the different departments;" but " we cannot depend on pauper help to have the care and custody of such persons." *

By this mingling the sane and insane together both parties are more disturbed and uncontrollable, and need more watchfulness and interference on the part of the superintendent and other officers.

" It occasions frequent instances of discipline. It has a reciprocal evil effect in the management of both classes of inmates." *

The evil is not limited to breaches of order; for there is no security against violence from the attrition of the indiscreet and uneasy paupers with the excitable and irresponsible lunatics and idiots.

" Most of the demented insane, and many idiots, have eccentricities; they are easily excited, disturbed; and nothing is more common than for inmates to tease, provoke, and annoy them, in view of gratifying their sportive feelings and propensities, by which they often become excited and enraged to a degree so as to require confinement to insure the safety of life." *

" There are times when, from causes entirely beyond our control, within our present accommodations, our insane and idiotic become somewhat violent and dangerous; and to maintain a proper degree of restraint, it is necessary to resort

---

* Dr. Brooks' letter to the Commission.

22

to the mufflers, wristers, &c., sometimes confinement in the lockup." *

" I could name many instances where the demented insane have become furious and excited by coming in contact with the other paupers." †

As the patients live in the wards, and eat in the rooms with the rest of the family, and have access to the instruments which are necessarily common in such houses, and are not watched by the vigilant eye of intelligent and ever-thoughtful attendants, as they are in the hospitals, there is danger of assaults and injury from these excitable patients.

" A man whom we considered very harmless was plagued by the inmates, and caught hold of a large bread knife, and made at them with it, and no doubt, would have killed them if I had not at the moment come in and took the knife from him." †

In all these and similar troubles, the only means placed in the hands of the officers, of subduing the outbreak and restoring quiet to the wards, is to separate the antagonistic parties, and to remove the lunatic who is the apparent, though not the prime, cause of the disturbance; and then, for want of attendants to watch him, it is necessary to confine him alone. " But the places for confinement in the State almshouses are not suitable to confine insane; they are cells provided for punishing the refractory and disobedient inmates." †   They are below the surface of the earth, and cannot be warmed or ventilated. ‡ §

---

* Mr. Goodspeed's letter to the Commission.

† Mr. I. H. Meserve's letter to the Commission.

‡ See page 129 of this Report.

§ In the earlier ages, when the nature of insanity was not understood, and the insane were the objects of terror to the people, they were sometimes confined in cells similarly situated.

Esquirol says : " These unfortunate creatures, like state criminals, were thrown into the cells of the basement." *

Dr. Brown, of Scotland, in his History of Insanity and Insane Asylums, says, that at " Marèville, in France, the cages containing the patients were placed in the cellars. At Lille they were confined in what were styled subterranean holes." " Revolting as these disclosures are, I feel bound to make them, in order to show from what a degrading state of ignorance and brutality we have escaped, and from what complicated misfortunes the objects of our care have been rescued by the diffusion of knowledge." †

* Maladies Mentales, II., 400.   † Page 102.

At the visits of the Commission there were three excited lunatics confined in the cells in two of the almshouses; and in the present state of things, and with the present means of government, they are liable to be confined at any time in all of them.

The confinement of the insane in solitary and strong rooms in hospitals is one of the extreme measures. It is almost abandoned in England, and is resorted to with great caution in America, and only after careful consideration by the higher officers of the house, and is limited to the shortest possible period necessary to overcome the excitement.

With the present arrangements and means put into the hands of the officers of these establishments, it is impossible to have a divided or a flexible administration to meet the wants of such diverse parties as the sane and insane inmates.

" The government adapted to the management of sane inmates is not adapted to the management of those of an opposite state of mind; and two different forms of government cannot be carried out in one house with equally good results as they can if separated, both in point of economy, and moral and intellectual improvement of the patients. Our inmates generally are not very intelligent. We cannot vary a rule to meet the palliating condition of a demented insane or idiotic person without their taking the advantage of it, oftentimes to the serious injury of the general discipline of the house." *

It was the opinion of each of the superintendents that the mingling of the State paupers, sane and insane, in these almshouses, made the whole more difficult and expensive to manage. It cost more labor, watchfulness and anxiety to take care of them together than it would to take care of them separately. The machinery which is proper for one cannot be profitably and successfully applied to the other. If, however, it be requisite to keep the lunatics at these houses, it would be necessary to have a distinct building, entirely separated from the principal house, and surrounded by a high fence, so that the insane and idiots should not come in contact with the other and sane household. They would need separate attendants and officers

---

* Dr. S. D. Brooks' letter to the Commission.

to take charge of them, and different regulations for their government. By this means each almshouse would have a distinct lunatic hospital, which could receive and accommodate an indefinite number of these patients, according to the size of the buildings that might be erected for them.

Here, then, would be three separate establishments for the insane, and none of them would be satisfactory. As these sane and insane paupers are now mingled together, the cost of maintaining the whole is greater than it would be if they were separated; and the cost of supporting the insane paupers in the three distinct houses on the almshouse farms and under the same management, and not under the care of persons trained for and exclusively devoted to them, would be as great as in another place, and less beneficial to the patients. *

OPINIONS OF SUPERINTENDENTS OF AMERICAN HOSPITALS.

Besides the especial objection to the State Almshouses as they are now constructed and administered, there are general objections to the whole principle of connecting any lunatic asylum or receptacle with any pauper establishment, and of putting both under the same government. The several superintendents of the American hospitals were consulted as to the expediency of adopting this system; none of them advised it, and some very strongly condemned the plan. Dr. Walker, of Boston, Superintendent of the City Lunatic Hospital, says, emphatically: "No lunatics should be kept in any pauper establishment, and I trust you will not advise it." †

Dr. Ray, of Providence, says: "No friend of humanity, much acquainted with the management of poorhouses, would hesitate to condemn the idea that they can be made proper receptacles for the insane." †

Dr. Tyler, of Concord, N. H., says: "I would never keep

---

* Since this was written an arrangement has been made at Bridgewater to give one large hall up to the use of the insane and idiotic; and many have been removed there from Cambridge and Ipswich, and a few from the hospitals.

These patients occupy this room, and walk or work in the yard, in the daytime, and at night most of them sleep in a large dormitory; but it is necessary to lodge some of them in the cells, on account of their dangerous dispositions and untrustworthy habits.

† Letter to the Commission.

any insane in almshouses or in houses of correction. They will be neglected at times." *

Dr. Gray, of Utica, N. Y., says: "No insane person should be treated, or in any way taken care of, in any alms or county house, or other receptacle for paupers." *

Dr. Benedict, late superintendent of the New York State Lunatic Hospital at Utica, and formerly of the Philadelphia Almshouse Hospital, says: "As to the expediency of providing, in connection with the State Almshouses, buildings or rooms for the mild pauper lunatics, I should say *no*, decidedly. Three years' experience in the Philadelphia Almshouse Hospital enables me to speak emphatically on this head. Buildings or rooms for the insane, in an almshouse and under almshouse management, would, I think, be unavoidably subject to abuse." *

Dr. Curwen, of the Harrisburg, (Pa.) Hospital, says: "The great objection to the establishments in connection with State Almshouses would be the little attention paid to the mental and bodily state of the inmates, the careless manner in which those in charge would perform their duties, from the feeling that nothing could be done for the class intrusted to their care, and the inevitable tendency of the experiment to see how small an allowance can be made to keep soul and body together." *

ENGLISH OPINIONS AND PRACTICE.

In England a great portion of the pauper lunatics are in the workhouses; yet those in authority on these matters discourage it as far as possible, and urge the removal of such patients to some proper asylum wherever room for them can be obtained. The Commissioners in 1844 said: "We think that the detention in workhouses of not only dangerous lunatics, but of all lunatics and idiots whatever, is highly objectionable. If a necessity exists for detaining the insane poor in workhouses, care should be taken to secure for them proper treatment by persons experienced in the diseases of the insane." †

* Letter to the Commission.
† Report of Commission in Lunacy, (Eng.) pp. 99, 100.

In 1847, the same commissioners, speaking of patients afflicted with melancholia and tendency to suicide, a common form of insanity, say: " Of course persons of this class are most improper inmates of a workhouse, and ought to be sent without loss of time to a lunatic asylum."*

The insufficiency of hospitals to accommodate those who needed their aid kept many in the workhouse; yet the commissioners report, in 1854 : " The number in workhouses continues in most districts to be steadily diminishing—a result which is doubtless, in great measure, attributable to the large additional accommodations now made for them in the recently erected lunatic asylums." †

While, then, the progress of civilization and political economy in England is removing the insane from the poorhouses to hospitals, it is to be confidently hoped that the reverse will not be done in Massachusetts, and that wards will not be prepared for them in the State Almshouses, nor patients be sent to mingle with the usual pauper inmates of these establishments.

WORCESTER HOSPITAL.

Plan and Structure.—This Commission have made a careful examination of the State Lunatic Hospital at Worcester, and in all its parts, and become familiar with its internal arrangements, its advantages and disadvantages, and its defects.

The plan of the building, although the best the age afforded when it was constructed, has necessarily remained the same. Improvement has been made in all the arts and sciences; so that the machinery and the instruments which were in use twenty years ago are now abandoned, and others of better model and kind adopted, and the change has been found profitable.   Similar improvements have been made in the whole management of the insane, especially in the plan and construction of the institutions appropriated for their use and in the means of occupying them.

The Hospital at Worcester now represents the past age, while the wants of the patients are measured by the means offered in the present.   All the stories are low, being only eight

* Report of Commission in Lunacy, (Eng.,) pp. 99, 100.
† Ibid., p. 40.

and a half, nine, and nine and a half feet high in the different parts.   In the latest hospitals they are twelve feet high, which, Dr. Kirkbride says, should be the lowest, but in the centre buildings they should be higher.

The halls are long and narrow, and, having rooms on each side, can receive light only at the ends.   The windows at these ends are small; very few of these open directly to the air; some of them open into verandas, and others into smaller rooms, and in either case affording no prospect abroad.   These long halls are therefore dark and gloomy, with nothing to cheer, and with little or no opportunity of receiving the direct rays of the sun.   These are the day rooms of the patients, where they are expected to remain during all their waking hours while they are in the house.

Ventilation.—The ventilation is very unsatisfactory, and insufficient to carry off the foul air.   Originally there were only small ducts in the walls leading from the wards below into the attic above.   What foul air passed through them went to the attic, but no farther, for there was no outlet from that place; and when it was once filled with the air from the rooms, no more could be received, and they were no longer ventilated; and sometimes a current was sent downward from the attic, carrying its foul air to some of the wards.

An improvement was made by making some openings from the attic; and recently, under the direction of Hon. Jonathan Preston, of Boston, these ducts, in several of the wings, were connected by wooden pipes or boxes, with ventilating shafts or chimneys, which are heated, and have an active upward current.   By this means these wards have a purer atmosphere, and are comparatively comfortable.

But the ventilation in the other wings, which have not the advantage of a chimney to make a forced current, but depend on Collins' ventilators, remains imperfect, and the air impure and insalubrious.

Warming—Danger of Fire.—The Hospital is heated with furnaces in which wood has been hitherto burned.   This method of heating is less favorable for health, and less safe, especially in a hospital, than steam.   The air is less comfortable, and the equality of the temperature less certain.   The greatest objection to the furnaces is the danger of fire.

The furnaces are in the cellar, immediately under the wooden work of the floors, which are very near, and must be in the dryest and most combustible condition.   The smoke flues pass up in the walls.   The air ducts are also of brick, but in contact with wood.   A slight crack in the furnace would allow a spark to escape into these air chambers, and thence to reach the woodwork, and combustion take place.

Some of the old furnaces being worn out or unsatisfactory, their places have been supplied by others which are safer and more effectual in warming the house.

Means of Occupation.—Besides these positive evils, there is a want of rooms and other conveniences for the use and occupation and employment of the patients.   When the house is filled according to its estimated capacity every room is occupied, and there are none left for any variety of purposes. There are no sitting-rooms, no parlors, where the patients may retire and enjoy a quiet opportunity for reading or conversation, separated from the whole company of the wards.   There are none of these places where the females can assemble for work, and carry on any special operation, except in the clothes-room and laundry, which are constantly appropriated.   Excepting for harness-makers and carpenters, there are no shops or rooms where the men who have various mechanical tastes or kinds of skill can obtain the exercise that is best for their malady.

The English Commissioners urge, emphatically, that the patients be employed in occupations as similar as possible to those in which they were engaged before they were insane, for these give healthy action to healthy faculties.

The people of Massachusetts are so largely devoted to manufacturing of every sort, and here are so many mechanics of every kind, that there must be patients from many of these classes whose hands and minds could be advantageously employed in something that had occupied those faculties when in health.   But there are no rooms in or about the Hospital for these to work in.

There is a want of opportunities of amusement, of pleasant though trivial occupation.   There are no bowling alleys nor

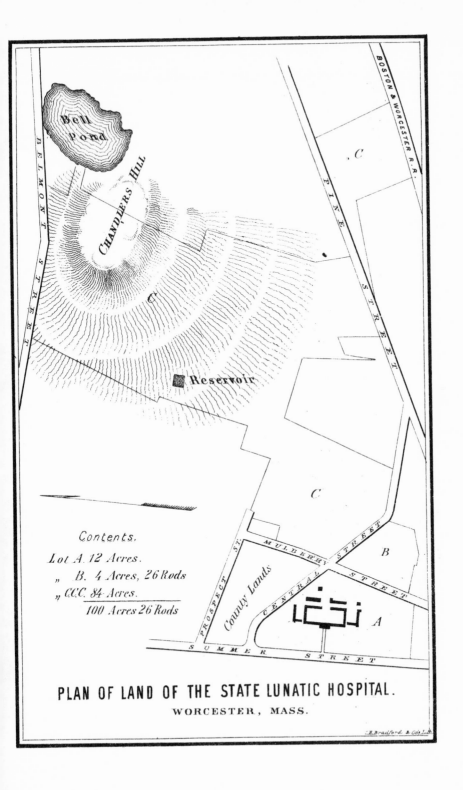

Bell Pond

CHANDLERS HILL

BOSTON & WORCESTER R.R.

PINE STREET

DELMONT STREET

C

C

Reservoir

C

Contents.

Lot A. 12 Acres.
 „ B. 4 Acres, 26 Rods
 „ C.C.C. 84 Acres.
 ─────────────────
      100 Acres 26 Rods

MULBERRY STREET

PROSPECT ST.

County Lands

CENTRAL STREET

STREET

B

A

SUMMER STREET

PLAN OF LAND OF THE STATE LUNATIC HOSPITAL.
WORCESTER, MASS.

J.H.Bradford & Co's Lith.

other means where exercise is combined with diversion, or in which the mind is agreeably and suitably employed.

The only resort for exercise is, either to walk in the public streets or in the fields of the Hospital, or to labor on the farm or in the garden, which are almost as public. Unfortunately, the original site of the Hospital is small and surrounded by streets. The other lands which have been subsequently added at various times, as opportunity offered, are necessarily separated from it.

Grounds.—The plan of the estate, which was drawn by Messrs. Boyden & Ball, of Worcester, and is herewith presented, shows that there are twelve acres in the original lot on which the buildings stand; four acres and twenty-six rods in the east garden, which is separated by Mulberry Street from the first-mentioned lot; and eighty-four acres of tillage, pasture and woodland on and about Chandler Hill, separated from both of the other lots by Central Street, and this is divided by Pine Street; and the situation of the whole estate is precisely the reverse of that compactness which is the most advantageous for a lunatic hospital.

The grounds are not only overlooked by the people in the streets, but the pasture, the great body of the land, is the common and agreeable resort for the people of the city in their hours of leisure, and for the idlers and the loungers who wish to find fresh air and enjoy a pleasant prospect. The patients cannot, therefore, exercise in that place with the privacy that is generally requisite. These lands, then are of comparatively little value except for agricultural purposes. The surface of the ground being very hilly, the steep ascents and precipitous declivities will prevent its being used for rides; the stony soil of a part will not admit of much high cultivation; and its publicity must prevent its being used for walks with the freedom that is desirable for hospital patients.

Drainage.—The drainage is unsatisfactory. Although the Hospital stands upon a hill at the foot of which runs a small stream, yet the Trustees have been unable to obtain leave to conduct the sewer and carry the waste into that channel. It was not unreasonably supposed that the pouring of the offal

23

and the waste from so large a population as live in the Hospital into a sluggish stream in the midst of the city might be detrimental to the public health. It has been necessary, therefore, to carry the sewers in another direction upon the lands belonging to the establishment; but they terminate in open pools so near to the house that the offensive effluvia of the gases reach its inmates, especially when the wind is moving from that quarter.

Great attention is now paid in England to the sewerage of the cities and compact towns, both as a sanitary and as an economical measure. Not only better and more effectual methods of draining the towns are introduced, but the matters which were formerly lost are now used as liquid manure upon the lands with the greatest advantage to crops, and in a manner not injurious to health.

As "it is a primary condition of salubrity that all ordure or town manure should be immediately removed from beneath or near habitations,"* it is a matter of the first necessity that the drainage of the Hospital should not be allowed to stop so near the house as it now does, but be carried off as far as possible, and then, both for the good of the patients and for the good of the farm, be distributed over the land. If this cannot be done, it must be an important objection to the present site of the Hospital.

Out-Buildings.—The situation of the stables and piggeries seemed particularly unfortunate. They were immediately in the rear of the building, and especially near to the female wings. They cut off the natural prospect in that direction, and presented, instead of green fields and hills, buildings that are not agreeable to all, and to some quite offensive. It is convenient to have these near to the house; they are then more accessible, and the cattle and the swine can be taken care of with greater facility and advantage. But as the State created the establishment solely for the treatment and the cure of the insane, and as the Hospital is primary, and the farm secondary, with no interest whatever to the institution excepting so far as

---

* Report of the General Board of Health to the British Parliament on sewer water and town manures, 1852.

it is subservient to the health and comfort of the patients, these buildings should be removed from the immediate vicinity of their dwelling.

There are four kitchens, all in full daily operation. By this arrangement the preparation of the food is more expensive, and the culinary department more difficult to manage, and less satisfactory, than if the whole cooking operations were done in one.

Nearness to the City.—The position of the Hospital, in the midst of an active and growing city, has some advantages, and many disadvantages. The busy scenes of life, the stir of business, the movements of passengers and carriages in the streets, the rush of railroad trains interest many patients, and stimulate at least the curiosity of some, and quicken the dormant faculties of others. And there are some who are benefited by walking in the public streets, by visits to factories, shops, and the market-places.

On the contrary, in the acute stages of insanity the excitable and violent need quiet and freedom from causes of excitement. They are disturbed and injured by the lively scenes and sounds that belong to the busy haunts of men. While, therefore, these may be presented with advantage to some classes of patients in some states of disease, they certainly should be avoided by others. It is well for a hospital that it have a city within convenient distance, that its inmates may see its sights and hear its sounds whenever it shall be profitable for them; but the whole should not be subjected at all times the necessity of seeing and hearing them. The officers should, therefore, be able to shut them out, and the Hospital should not be surrounded by, and near to, the stimulating affairs of city life.

What Improvements can be made.—The Worcester Hospital, in its present condition, cannot offer to the patients the means and facilities of cure and discipline which are found in other and more modern institutions, and to which they have a reasonable claim. Some of these defects can be removed, some modified; but others are inherent in the building and location.

The halls can be made lighter, and more airy and cheerful, by enlarging the windows at the ends and letting in as much light as possible. By cutting out some of the side-rooms, and making cross-halls, the wards will be made more airy and less monotonous. Narrow parlors and sitting-rooms for the patients to retire to, or for small parties to gather in for work or amusement, can be made by converting two or more of the lodging-rooms into one. It is easy to build shops and work-rooms for men to occupy themselves in such ways as their health may require.

The ventilation is already improved in most of the wings'; but it cannot be made satisfactory in the others without a great and radical change in the structure of the building.

Most of the strong and solitary cells that have become use-less are about to give place to other rooms which are more needed and satisfactory. The steam apparatus for heating can be introduced, and the danger of fire from the furnaces arrested.

The four kitchens can be abolished, and one suited to the wants of the whole establishment substituted.

The stables and piggeries can be removed to a proper distance from the main house.

To make these alterations and improvements would be very costly. Dr. Chandler estimated the cost of the steam apparatus for heating, ventilation of the strong-rooms, the new kitchen, removal of the barn and proper drainage, to be fifty-five thousand dollars, ($55,000.) Mr. Preston and Mr. Boyden, architects, both familiar with the construction of hospitals, estimated the cost of the heating apparatus, improved ventilation and kitchen, to be fifty-five or sixty thousand dollars, ($55,000 to $60,000.) Neither of these estimates included the cost of improving the halls, altering the rooms, providing shops, &c., which would probably cost more. A new and complete system of heating and ventilating has just been introduced into the New York Hospital, on only one side, at the cost of $100,000.

What Defects must remain.—Yet, after all shall be done that can be, other defects which cannot be amended, and other objections which cannot be removed, will remain.

The nearness to the city, the divided and interrupted grounds, which should be exclusively appropriated to the use of the patients under the entire control of the government, the low rooms, the narrow halls, the imperfect ventilation of some of the wards,—these must remain as they now are, and some of these must increase and interfere more and more with the usefulness of the institution. With all these alterations and improvements, which will require the expenditure of at least sixty thousand, and more probably seventy-five thousand, dollars, to put the Hospital in the best condition that it may be, it will still be imperfect, inadequate to its purposes, and unsatisfactory.

In view of this great cost and unsatisfactory result, the Commissioners think it not expedient to make these thorough repairs, but advise that provision be made, if possible, in some other way for the wants of the insane, more successfully for them, and more advantageously to the interests of the Commonwealth.

Value of the Hospital Estate.—Some of the circumstances and condition of the estate, its situation in the heart of the city, and the streets that run through its lands, which diminish its usefulness for its present purpose, increase its usefulness for other purposes, and give it a value in the market which would not justify the selection of this special location for a Hospital at the present time; while its intrinsic worth and increasing value afford abundant means and opportunities of escaping from these difficulties, and removing these objections hereafter, by the erection of a new structure on a cheaper and more suitable site.

Several gentlemen,* residents of, and engaged in active business in, Worcester, who represent the best commercial, manufacturing and financial talent and experience in the city, were requested to examine and appraise the whole real estate belonging to the Hospital. After careful consideration, they returned the following valuation :—

Original lot on which the buildings stand, containing the twelve acres, including the buildings, ... $70,000 00

---

* Joseph Mason, Isaac Davis, Samuel Davis, F. H. Kinnicutt, D. S. Messenger, William M. Bickford, W. A. Wheeler, William T. Merrifield, Albert Tolman, Joseph Sargent.

East garden, containing four acres and twenty-
six rods, ... $20,000 00
Residue of real estate, about eighty-four acres of
pasture, tillage and woodlands on and around
Chandler Hill, ...   30,000 00

Total, ... $120,000 00

Other gentlemen, conversant also with the value of property
in Worcester, gave different estimates, both higher and lower
than that rendered by this Commission. Taking the lowest
estimate, and adding to this the probable cost of complete
repairs, (seventy-five thousand dollars,) here is a sum almost,
if not quite, sufficient to purchase a new and suitable site, with
a large and compact farm, within the limits of the city, and to
build a new and satisfactory Hospital with all the recent improvements.

Convenient sites can be obtained in Worcester within one
or two miles of the dense part of the city and of a railroad
station, and another Hospital could be built for two hundred
and fifty patients for about two hundred thousand dollars.

As the building of a new Hospital would take at least two
years, and as the wants of the patients in the present house
are pressing, and the condition of this requires immediate relief, the Commission and the Trustees had careful consultation,
and concluded that it was best to make some temporary repairs
and alterations in this establishment, to secure the house from
danger of fire and the health of the inmates from suffering—to
provide for the immediate wants of the patients until other and
more satisfactory accommodations shall be furnished. This
work is now going on under the authority of the Trustees and
under the charge of Mr. Preston.

They are making these improvements by removing many of
the solitary and strong rooms, by opening the halls to the light,
and thus obtaining more parlors and rooms for sitting, and
giving more airy lightness and cheerfulness to the wards. They
are about to remove the barn and all the farm buildings, and
to improve the drainage. They are adding rooms for occupation, and improving the ventilation—thus rendering the whole
establishment more available in the hands of those who admin-

ister it, and more advantageous to those for whom it is administered. When these alterations shall be made, the Hospital
will necessarily afford room for a somewhat smaller number of
patients than it now does. Yet how great that reduction
must be cannot now be determined. And it will be then seen
how far they will supersede the necessity of an entire reconstruction of this establishment.*

WANTS OF THE INSANE AND PROPOSED MEANS OF RELIEF.

Here, in this stage of the progress, is an opportunity for the
Commonwealth to look the whole matter in the face, see the
full amount of the burden of insanity and dangerous idiocy
resting upon her and her people, and measure the extent of
the sacrifice she and they must make for their cure, for their
custody and guardianship, and for the public safety. The evil
is a great one, and the means of relief are correspondingly
great; but the burden is made none the less by keeping it out
of sight, and the cost is not lessened by paying it indirectly.

The expense of keeping the troublesome lunatic in the State
Almshouse is not diminished by assessing it upon the whole
household, making an average of those who need watching
and occasional restraint with the little children, and calling it
so much a head for all. Nor is this cost diminished in the
receptacles by making the counties pay a part of it.

This is not merely a present and temporary evil. A large
portion of the cases are permanent, because incurable. Others
are becoming so, although they may now be restored. Our
population is increasing rapidly; and insanity keeps pace with
it, and probably runs in the advance. The causes of insanity
are still as abundant and as efficient as they have been; and if
they are not arrested nor modified, this year and the succeeding years will produce as many lunatics as the last and those
that went before it. The next year and the next generation
will, therefore, have as large a proportion of lunatics to provide
for as we now have.

It is well, then, to look to the future as well as the present,
and lay such a plan for the administration of insanity as will

* See Appendix, C.

meet all the demands of those who suffer from it, and such as will be the best for the interests of the Commonwealth.

There are six hundred and ten lunatics and idiots who need, but have not, the advantages of a hospital for their cure or their protection.

Two hundred and five of these are said to be curable. Ninety are said to be violent and furious. Four hundred and eight are excitable and troublesome.

Besides these, who are at their homes, there are those who exceed the due numbers in the Hospitals at Worcester, Taunton and Boston.

For all of these some provision is to be made; and they demand the first attention of the State.

Without supposing that all of these would be sent to a hospital even if it were offered to them, yet, judging by the past, seeing how soon every new institution for the Insane in this and other States has been filled, there can be no doubt that another in Massachusetts would be immediately occupied.

PLAN OF FURTHER CARE OF THE INSANE.

In view of the present and future wants of the Insane in Massachusetts, the Commissioners recommend :—

1. That a new Hospital be now erected, in order to accommodate those who are not yet in any such institution, and especially the curable and furious patients.*

2. That the consideration of the sale of the Hospital at Worcester be postponed until the third Hospital shall be ready for occupancy, and then, if deemed expedient by the legislature, be sold, and another erected in its stead within the city of Worcester.

3. That the legislature take into consideration the plan of providing for the State pauper lunatics in a separate hospital suitable to their condition and wants, where the curable may be restored, and the incurable be properly and comfortably kept.

---

* *Note to Second Edition, June,* 1855.—The Legislature adopted the recommendation of this Report, and ordered a Hospital to be built in one of the western counties, and appropriated $200,000 for this purpose. See Act for this purpose, in the Report of the Committee on Charitable Institutions, at the end of this volume.

4. That the law of 1836, ordering the creation of county receptacles, be then repealed, and the counties be relieved of the responsibility of providing for the wants of the State.

5. That all the laws in respect to Insanity and Hospitals be revised, and reduced to a code more suitable to the wants and the practice of the times.

NEW HOSPITAL LOCATION.

Having come to the conclusion that the State should build a third Hospital, the Commission examined the returns from the several towns and those from all the asylums; and comparing the numbers of the Insane who were in need of such an Institution in the various sections of the Commonwealth, they became convinced that, for statistical as well as for geographical reasons, it should be placed in the western part of the State. For convenience of the people who are to use it, it should be on one of the great thoroughfares, as the Western or the Connecticut River Railroad, in a place the most accessible to the whole body of the population of those four counties.

It should be near to some large town or village, where provisions, mechanics, and other aids could be obtained if needed, and near to a railroad station, certainly not over two miles from it.

SITE AND LAND.

If possible, there should be not less than two hundred and fifty acres of land, certainly not less than two hundred, all in one body, unbroken and undisturbed by any road, or streets, or impassable stream, so that the patients may obtain all kinds of exercise within their own enclosure, and so that the whole may be constantly under the eye and the control of the officers and attendants.

The ground should be high, and susceptible of drainage; and the soil porous, to absorb the surface water. There should be an unfailing supply of pure, soft water, to the amount of not less than ten thousand gallons a day in the dryest season. It is better that this should be spring water running directly from the earth than surface water, whether in running streams or in ponds.

24

SIZE AND PLAN.

The Hospital should be built for not over two hundred and fifty patients; though one for two hundred would be probably more advantageous to its great purpose,—the healing and the management of insanity,—and consequently more profitable to the State.

By the kindness of several of the Superintendents of Hospitals in the United States, this Commission have received many plans of asylums which they have designed for this purpose. They have also received some from England. These all have high merit; and probably each one would be found convenient and useful, and satisfactory for its purpose.

A very admirable plan of the Lunatic Hospital of Wiltshire, at Devizes, in England, was sent by its author, the able and learned Dr. John Thurnham, who originally designed, and now superintends, the establishment. Mr. Chadwick and the Commission in Lunacy both write that great improvements have been made in Great Britain in the management and the construction of Hospitals for the Insane, and they offer any further aid that may be needed to secure for Massachusetts the best plan that the present time has produced.*

The Commission examined many sites for a Hospital in the Western Counties, and found several that offered all the requisites for such an establishment; they include land sufficient for all its purposes unbroken by roads; the soil is a sandy loam, that absorbs the rains, and leaves no water to rest on the surface; they have facilities of easy drainage; there is pure and soft water running from springs to the amount of twenty thousand gallons and more a day even in the summer. All of these are within convenient distance of large towns and of railroad stations. Nevertheless, it would not be advisable to make a definite selection without a further and more minute examination.

* " Our management of the lunatics has been vastly improved. In the new Asylums there have been great structural improvements. Of these the reports will inform you. You should come over and see them yourself. Given your numbers, I think it might be worth your while to send over here to Mr. R. Rawlinson, or some other architect conversant with that class of structures, for a plan of internal arrangements—you taking such elevations as might suit the taste of the country. Our lunacy inspectors would give you every facility in their power." —*Mr. Chadwick's Letter to Commission.*

The whole time of some of this Commission has been given to the work assigned them by the legislature; yet the lunacy survey, the collateral inquiries, the digestion and preparation of the facts that were learned, and the principles that were involved, have consumed the whole, and allowed this Board to do no more than is here presented. They have, therefore, omitted to select a definite site for, and plan of, a Hospital; and, inasmuch as both of them demand time for further inquiry, it is inexpedient to delay this Report for that purpose.

As the Commonwealth would not create such an Institution as herein proposed without obtaining assurance of every possible advantage and immunity from every avoidable danger, therefore, before making a definite location, it will be necessary to determine the healthiness and endemic influences of any town or district that may be proposed. This can be easily done by examining the reports of disease and mortality which have been sent from every town in each of the last twelve years to the Secretary of State, and are now preserved in his office. These annual reports will show to what extent any district or locality is subject to, or exempt from, the peculiar diseases that most frequently fall upon the insane.

This Commission has not had time to make this examination, nor have the Superintendents of Registration been able to furnish them with the requisite information in regard to this matter.

If the suggestions which are herein presented shall be adopted by the legislature, it will be necessary that another Commission be appointed, who will take the charge of the whole work of building a Hospital. It is better, then, that the responsibility of selecting both a location for the establishment and the plan for the building should be devolved on them.

They will have better opportunity in the spring to make the further inquiries that may be needed for this purpose. To that future Commission the present Board would leave this duty, with only the suggestion, that, as the buildings and grounds are the instruments in the hands of the officers and attendants for the production of health, as a factory and machinery are in the hands of the manufacturer and the workmen for the production of their articles, therefore that practical wisdom which is applied to common and private affairs should be used in selecting a site and adopting a plan, regarding present cost not so much as the advantage and success with which they may be afterwards used in the management and cure of the insane.

This Commission would advise, therefore, that in selecting a location no regard be paid to inducements that may be held out by towns, by the offer of lands or of subscriptions, to aid in the purchase, and that no gifts be accepted that will imply any obligation of the State to continue the Institution in a place when it may seem expedient to remove it, and no lesser present interest be allowed in any way to compromise the greater and future interests of the State and the lunatics for whom the whole Institution is to be created.

Like discreet individuals, the State should go into the market, make its selection with the sole view of effecting the final purpose, purchase its lands and pay the usual price, and then be independent of all further obligations.

With these suggestions, the Commissioners respectfully submit the whole matter to the wisdom of the legislature, not doubting that they will do the best that the claims of humanity for her suffering children and the interests of the intelligent and liberal Commonwealth require.

Accompanying this Report will be found all the papers referred to therein, the plans and descriptions of Hospitals, the correspondence and the returns of the physicians and others concerning the insane and idiots within or belonging to Massachusetts. The Commissioners respectfully suggest that these be deposited in the State Library, for the use of the legislature and of any future Commission which may be appointed for this or a similar work.

LEVI LINCOLN.
EDWARD JARVIS.
INCREASE SUMNER.

MARCH 1, 1855.

It is due to the intelligence, ability and fidelity of our laborious and indefatigable associate, Doctor JARVIS, to state, that the very extensive correspondence with professional gentlemen, in this country and Europe, which elicited many of the facts and much of the important and instructive information contained in this Report, was exclusively conducted by him. He directed and superintended, also, the preparation of the numerous tabular statements and illustrations which are herewith presented, and the draft of the Report is from his pen. It must be obvious that such service could be performed most connectedly and efficiently, and with greatest economy, both of time and expense, by one of the Commissioners, acting under the authority of the Commission; and the professional character of Doctor Jarvis, his personal experience and habits of observation, and his long-continued and devoted attention to the treatment of insanity and the subject of Hospitals generally, eminently recommended him for this delicate and difficult task. We hardly need add, that he has executed it in a manner most satisfactory to his associates, and, we trust, beneficially and acceptably to the government.

The other Commissioners coöperated freely in the general attention due to the objects and assigned duties of the Commission; in the direction given to the course of inquiry; in the personal visitation and examination of the public hospitals and places of confinement for the insane within the State, and in frequent consultations; and they fully concur in the opinions and recommendations which are expressed, and the results presented, in the Report.

LEVI LINCOLN.
INCREASE SUMNER.

APPENDIX.

A.

[Note to page 105.]

The Reports of the Worcester and the Western Virginia Hospitals through all of their years, and those of the New Hampshire, Kentucky, and Ohio Hospitals, through several of their years, state both the duration of the insanity before entrance into the hospital, when it was known, and the time required for recovery of each patient who was restored. The records of the McLean Asylum state the latter fact since 1840. The sum of their experience shows that the time required for recovery of all whose cases are thus stated, was less than seven months.

Duration of disease before treatment.	Cases.	Average time required for recovery.		
Less than one year, ...	2,775	5 months		19 days.
One year and over, ...	720	10	"	13 "
Unknown, ...	230	11	"	10 "
All who recovered at the McLean Asylum, . .	1,075	5	"	2 "
Totals, ...	4,800	6	"	16 "

The average time required for the recovery of all who were restored at the Worcester Hospital was five months and three days.

Dr. Chandler, twenty-first Report, p. 69, states that the average duration of insanity, of those who had died unrestored in the Worcester Hospital, was, of 201 males, six years and three days, and of 205 females, four years eleven months and five days. These include only those patients whose friends or guardians retained them in the hospital until their death. There were many others whose diseases were of sufficiently mild form to allow them to be removed to, and retained at, their homes. Although these were never restored, yet they en-

25

joyed a longer life than those who died in the hospital. If these had been included in the calculation they would have shown a greater average longevity of the incurably insane than is shown by Dr. Chandler's calculation.

Mr. John Le Cappelain, Actuary of the Albion Life Assurance Company of London, Eng., made a calculation of the expectation of life in the irrecoverable insane, founded on Dr. Thurnam's Statistics of Insanity, and has sent the result to the Commission, which is here given.

Probable duration of life in irrecoverably Insane Persons.

Age.	Males.	Females.
20	21.31 years.	28.66 years.
30	20.64 "	26.33 "
40	17.65 "	21.53 "
50	13.53 "	17.67 "
60	11.91 "	12.51 "
70	9.15 "	8.87 "

The difference of cost of time and expense of restoring, and of life support of lunacy, is largely in favor of the former.

B.

[Note to the second edition, page 167.]

The Tables and Statements presented in this Report show the distribution of the insane and idiots as they were when the inquiry was made in the autumn of 1854, and probably they are still the same, or represent similar facts now existing in Massachusetts, with the exception of some of the State Paupers.

Since the 1st of January several of the insane and idiots who were supported by the Commonwealth, have been transferred from the County Receptacles, &c., to the State Almshouses. A second inquiry was accordingly made of the superintendents of these several establishments, in respect to the number and condition of those persons under their care. The following table shows the facts as they were at the end of May, 1855.

Number and condition of the Insane and Idiots in the State Alms-houses and County Receptacles.

	Insane.	Idiots.	Both Classes.	SEX.		NATIVITY.			CONDITION.		
				Male.	Female.	American.	Foreign.	Irish.	Mild—manageable.	Excitable—troublesome	Furious—dangerous
ALMSHOUSES.											
Monson, . . .	30	17	47	24	23	10	37	29	18	28	1
Tewksbury, . .	22	5	27	10	17	6	21	16	7	11	9
Bridgewater, . .	–	–	99	60	39	6	93	87	54	40	5
Totals, . .	–	–	173	94	79	22	151	132	79	79	15
RECEPTACLES.											
Cambridge, . .	24	–	24	13	11	7	17	16	–	–	24
Ipswich, . . .	55	–	55	–	–	21	34	14	5	40	10
Totals,. . .	–	–	79	–	–	28	51	30	5	40	34

In the receptacle at Ipswich there are six insane persons whose disorders are of less than one year's standing, and all these supposed to be curable.

Some of the lunatics have been removed to other States, where they had a legal residence, and a few have been returned to Europe.

Beside these changes in location and distribution, there have undoubtedly been changes in the individual patients. Some have died and some have recovered. But, as the causes of insanity still prevail, and as like causes under like circumstances always produce the same results, others have become deranged, and taken the places of those who were removed by recovery or by death. There may also be some changes as to their numbers in the hospitals, the poor-houses, the private dwellings, and even the towns, where the insane are found. There are probably some changes in the smaller classes; but in the greater classes of society, in the State and its great divisions, the numbers of the insane, and their proportion to the population, are not, and will not, be materially altered, until the character and habits of the people, their condition, exposures, and circumstances which excite or disturb the brain are changed, and the causes of insanity shall be removed, or at least diminished.

E. J.

DORCHESTER, June 12, 1855.

C.

[Note to the second edition, page 182.]

The improvements which are indicated in this Report, page 182, are now in progress, and doubtless will be completed before the close of this season.

Dr. Chandler, in reply to an inquiry as to the present state, answers as follows :—

STATE LUNATIC HOSPITAL, }
Worcester, Mass., May 30, 1855. }

Dr. EDWARD JARVIS, *Dorchester, Mass. :—*

Dear Sir :—Very extensive changes are being made in the internal structure of this hospital under the direction of the Trustees. The halls are made more light and airy by throwing two rooms in each ward into the halls. Many of the dormitories are made larger by taking out the partition between two adjoining rooms. All but twelve of the strong rooms are being removed, and parlors made in the place of them. The piggeries have been removed to the East garden, and the barn is under way. Two ten-pin alleys have been constructed in place of one of the kitchens.

Yours, &c.,

GEORGE CHANDLER.

INDEX.

HOUSE....No. 282.

Commonwealth of Massachusetts.

House of Representatives, April 26, 1855.

The Joint Standing Committee on Charitable Institutions, to whom was referred the Report of the Commissioners on Lunacy, have considered the same, and

REPORT:

The Commission on Lunacy was created by the Resolve of the Legislature of 1854. The Commissioners were required,—

To ascertain the number and condition of all the insane and idiots in or belonging to Massachusetts;

To examine the present accommodations for them, and determine how far they were suitable for their present and immediate wants; whether any more were needed;

To ascertain and propose the best plans for the general management of insanity and the insane in this Commonwealth;

To examine the State Hospital at Worcester, and see whether it should be repaired or sold, and another be built in its stead.

It appears that the Commission attended to all the duties enjoined upon them by the government; and we have now the results of their labors, the facts they ascertained, and the conclusions they arrived at, in the Report* which is before the Legislature.

In obtaining facts, the Commission sought the aid of all the physicians in the State: and it is creditable to their high intelligence and generous devotion, that only two of these gentlemen, whose testimony was desirable, refused to answer the inquiry, and only two others neglected to do so; and the Commonwealth owes a debt of gratitude to those members of the medical profession, superintendents of hospitals, clergymen, and municipal officers, and all others who so liberally assisted the Commissioners in this important work.

In acknowledgment of these services rendered to the State, and to distribute as far as possible the valuable information contained in the Report of the Commission, this Committee recommend that the Legislature direct that one copy of that document be sent to every one who aided in gathering the facts and forming the opinions therein contained, by the Secretary of State, when he distributes the documents to the several towns, or in such other manner as may be more convenient.

There are two thousand six hundred and thirty-two insane persons, and one thousand and eighty-seven idiots, in and belonging to Massachusetts—making three thousand seven hundred and nineteen who cannot take care of themselves, but must be taken care of by their friends or the public authorities.

Of the insane,—
1,141 were in hospitals.
207 in the county receptacles, prisons and State almshouses.
1,284 at their homes, or in town or city almshouses.
2,018 are incurable.

In the opinion of the witnesses, who knew their condition, one thousand seven hundred and thirteen of the insane should be in hospitals, either because their diseases are recent and

* House Document 144, March, 1855.

curable, or because they are so excitable, or furious and dangerous, as to need confinement for the good of others. Besides these, there are sixty-one violent idiots who need restraint—making one thousand seven hundred and seventy-four for whom the accommodations of a hospital should be provided.

605 of these, who should be in hospitals, are at their homes or in the local almshouses.

Of those at their homes—

210 are recent and curable cases.

90 are violent and dangerous.

408 are excitable and troublesome.

All of these six hundred and five should enjoy the advantages of a hospital for their healing or their protection or for the good of the public; but they cannot be admitted, for want of room.

All the hospitals in Massachusetts are filled to their utmost capacity, and three of them are overflowing.

The whole experience of the world shows that insanity is one of the most curable among severe diseases, if it be properly attended to in its early stages. About four-fifths can be restored within the first year; about half, if delayed to the second year; and at about the fifth year the restoration becomes hopeless; then their disorder is permanent, and the patient must be supported for life.

A part of the two thousand and eighteen incurable lunatics were sent to a hospital in the early stages of their malady, but could not be restored. A much larger part were not sent until their day and susceptibility of cure were past. And many of them have not been in any hospital, and have never enjoyed the suitable means of restoration.

There are now in the State eight hundred and forty insane persons who have never been sent to any hospital; eight hundred and twenty-four of these are Americans, and sixteen are foreigners. Some of these were diseased beyond hope of cure before any appropriate institution was opened for them. There are several whose malady has been of twenty, thirty, forty, fifty, or even more, years' standing. None were in a hospital before 1818, when the McLean Asylum was opened, and but few before 1832, when that at Worcester was ready to receive them.

It is reasonable to suppose, that four-fifths of the eight hundred and forty who have never been in any hospital might have been healed with the proper means. Without doubt, an equally large portion of those who were sent to a hospital, but not until their day of healing was past, might have been restored if they had been sent in season.

Considering, then, the great number of the insane now in this Commonwealth, and the large proportion of these who are incurable and must be supported for life, your Committee thought it proper to inquire into, and worthy the attention of the Legislature to see, the full extent of this burden of insanity, and of its bearing upon the State, the towns, and the people. It is important to know how much of it has been produced or perpetuated by causes or circumstances that might have been avoided in past time, or may be avoided in future, and whether this, in its present degree, is a necessary evil, and whether it may not be diminished, if not now, at least hereafter.

The cost of supporting an insane person is necessarily greater than that of one who is sound in mind. His food must be always good, otherwise he becomes more excitable and difficult to be managed. He requires more personal attention and watching; and many of them require much, and even constant, attendance. But even admitting that the expense of supporting the lunatics who are at their homes, or in the almshouses, is no more than that of the sane members of the same families, this, with the known cost of supporting those who are in the public establishments, will make the expense of maintaining the two thousand six hundred and thirty-two insane in the State a matter worthy of the anxious consideration of the political economist and of the government.

Two dollars and a half a week is the lowest that any one can be supported for, even in the rural districts.

The average cost of supporting the paupers in 1854, in all the towns in the State, including children, was one dollar and forty-eight cents a week.

The State paid for the support of its insane paupers, in the hospitals, prisons, &c., an average of two dollars and eight cents a week. Besides this, the interest on the cost of the establishments and the salaries, which were paid in another manner, amounted to about sixty cents a week for each patient—making two dollars and sixty-eight cents as the average cost. But, to be on the safe side, two dollars and a half is assumed in this calculation.

The support of the independent patients in hospitals, including those at the McLean Asylum and those who were sent out of the State, will be not less than three dollars a week.

At these rates, the cost of supporting insanity in this State for the last year amounted to three hundred and twenty-one thousand eight hundred and sixty-eight dollars.

394 independent insane in hospitals, at $3 per week,				$61,464 00
716 " " at home, at $2.50 "		"		93,080 00
954 pauper insane in hospitals, at $2.50 "		"		124,020 00
568 " " elsewhere, at $1.50 "		"		43,304 00
				$321,868 00

This enormous tax for the support of insanity was paid last year, and will be paid this year; and if no change takes place in the administration of those who are afflicted with this disease, it will continue to be paid for years to come.

This great amount is paid in divided sums, by the several families or guardians of the independent insane, by the towns and the Commonwealth, for their paupers, and therefore has attracted no especial notice, either of the Legislature or the people. The only noticeable item is the fifty-three thousand and eighty-five dollars paid in 1854 for the support of insane State paupers, besides the salaries of the higher officers of the two State hospitals, amounting in all to about sixty thousand dollars.

The most painful feature in this matter is the two thousand and eighteen incurable cases, who now need to be supported forever. Including the eight hundred and forty who have never been in any hospital, and the large portion of the others who were not sent in season to the place of healing, it is probable that one-half of these incurables might have been restored if they had been properly attended to. If the average cost of maintaining them is the same as that of the whole two thousand six hundred and thirty-two, then the State and its people are paying one hundred and twenty-three thousand and ninety-eight dollars a year for the support of insanity that might have been removed and its burden prevented.

The causes of insanity are as prevalent and active among us as ever, and every year produces its own supply of the insane. This year will produce as many new cases of mental derangement as the last, and the next will produce as many in proportion to the population as this. Of course, those who are not healed will be added to the number of the permanently incurable. This annual addition ought not to be more than one-fifth of all who are attacked. The other four-fifths should be restored to health and power of self-sustenance and general usefulness.

However willing the people and the authorities might have been to heal all of their insane friends and wards, they could not have hitherto accomplished this purpose; nor can they now, because there have not been, nor are there now, sufficient means.

It is a well-established principle, that the insane cannot recover amidst the ordinary circumstances and influences of home as those who suffer from other diseases, but they must be removed from the familiar associations and scenes to others which are new and strange to them.

Diseases of the mind are affected by the influences that reach it. It is necessary, therefore, that these should be controlled, and that only such as are favorable should be allowed to reach the patients. This can be best done in the hospitals, where every thing is arranged for, and adapted to, the condition and the wants of those who are submitted to their care.

In these institutions the curable are healed, the violent are subdued, the excitable are controlled, and those who are elsewhere troublesome are there easily calmed and managed.

But these means of cure and of control have never been sufficient to meet the wants of all the sufferers from insanity. From the beginning our hospitals have been filled. Although the McLean Asylum and the Worcester and Boston Hospitals have been enlarged from time to time, to satisfy the pressing pemands for their accommodations, their wards have been immediately occupied by those who were near, or whose friends best understood their advantages; but at no time has the supply been sufficient for the real wants of all who could and ought to profit by them. Consequently many of the insane of Massachusetts have never been able to enjoy the influences of a hospital, and many others have been sent there only after their day of healing was past. These have, therefore, remained uncured and incurable, and their friends, or the towns, or the State have been and are obliged to support them as long as they live.

Now the hospitals are all filled, and some are overflowing; and yet there are six hundred and five insane persons in the State who are not in any such institution, but who ought to be there. Two hundred and ten of these have been deranged but a few months, and are, therefore, curable; they need the hospital to restore them to health. Ninety of these are violent and dangerous; they need the custody of a hospital for the safety of the community. Four hundred and eight of these are excitable and troublesome; they annoy their families and disturb their neighborhoods, and should be confined for the sake of the public peace.

Unless some means besides those now provided are offered for their cure, these two hundred and ten recent cases will ere long become incurable, and their support for life will be entailed upon their friends or the community. These violent and the excitable patients are now cared for at their homes, with great trouble and cost, by those who have charge of them, and with some danger and much annoyance to their families and neighborhood. These six hundred and five are the surplus over and above those for whom the means are furnished in Massachusetts for the healing or the protection of its insane people. Their claims come to us in a manner not to be resisted. The curable ask to be restored to health and usefulness and to the power of self-sustenance; the others ask to be protected from evil, and saved from the danger of injuring others. These speak not for themselves alone, but also for those who will follow in their train, and become insane in this and the succeeding years, as they have.

Insanity is produced by manifold and various causes and circumstances. Some of these are inherent in man, some are created by the customs of society, and others are allowed, and even encouraged, in the social law; all of them are, or have been, present with us; and they will continue to be active among us until the character and influences of our civilization shall be changed.

It is just and reasonable that every age and every year should meet and discharge its own responsibilities, and bear the burden which it creates or permits to be created, and transmit the world, with its privileges and advantages, unencumbered and untrammelled, to those who come after it.

There is a natural and an honorable aversion to incurring debts. It seems neither right nor generous that the people of any year or of any generation should assume an obligation by the creation of any good, or for the enjoyment of advantage, or for the endurance of any evil, and then throw the responsibility of meeting and discharging it upon their successors. This is often done; but it is never justifiable except when the advantage that is to be immediately gained is also to be transmitted to, and shared by, the succeeding generation who are to pay, or where the evil to be endured is one of great magnitude and rarely repeated, whose burden should be divided among others as well as those upon whom it first comes.

The creation or the development of insanity is practically a debt, which the friends of the sufferer or the public treasury must inevitably discharge, either by paying the cost of its removal or for his support during life. It is an obligation of the surest fulfilment; for the town or the State is necessarily the indorser of every insane person, and binds itself to pay all the expenses of his sickness and sustenance that his own estate or his friends do not, however long it may be needed.

The question, then, is, whether this obligation shall be discharged at once, by taking immediate measures for the cure of the patient and paying the due cost manfully and generously, or whether, by neglect of these measures, this obligation shall be thrown upon future years, requiring each to contribute an enormous proportion to sustain it.

The people in any year may build a hospital, and borrow

the money needed for its cost, with the engagement to pay it at a future period. In this way they throw the responsibility of payment upon another year and age; but with the debt they transfer the property, the hospital for which it is created; and those who are thus required to discharge the obligation receive also a fair equivalent, and no injustice is done.

But if the present year creates, or allows to be created, any cases of insanity, and fails to discharge its obligation of curing it, and, by neglecting to use the proper means, throws the burden of supporting the patient through life upon the future years, it transmits with this obligation no property, no value, to compensate for the payment, and those who pay it receive nothing but the ruins of humanity from the hands of those who created it.

In the creation and the payment of an ordinary debt, the year which incurs it, and the intermediate years, pay only the interest, and the last year only pays the full amount. But in the obligation of supporting permanent insanity, the first and the succeeding years, as well as the last, each and all, pay the same—almost as much as would have been required to pay it all off at once, by curing it in the beginning. In the case of the common debt it is paid only once, and the property is received with a clear title; while the other years, which pay the interest, enjoy and have the use of this property in return. But in case of the insanity, the obligation is multiplied and discharged almost as many times as there may be years in the patient's life; and they who annually pay it have suffering, anxiety, and loss, rather than enjoyment and profit.

It is, then, no more than the common wisdom that is applied to the ordinary business of life, to take such measures as will secure the early treatment of the insane, and give them the best opportunity of restoration that the age affords, and by this means reduce, in the future at least, the number of permanent lunatics to that small proportion whose malady is, from its very nature, incurable.

As there are not hospitals enough to admit all who need them, it is necessary to build more; but neither the patients who want them, nor their friends or guardians, can do this, nor is it well to leave it to private speculation to build them.

Considering that the State and its towns are the responsible

2

indorsers of every person that becomes insane, and must pay the cost of his restoration at once, or of his support during life, however long that may be, provided his friends cannot do it; considering, also, that this responsibility has become so great that the public are now supporting 1,522 insane persons in and out of hospitals, at the cost of more than one hundred and sixty-four thousand dollars ($164,724) a year; that 1,262 of these are incurable, and claim a life support from the general treasury, and that about half of them were self-supporters until they lost their mental health; considering, then, how great and unavoidable an interest the body politic has in every case of insanity, it is a reasonable economy and a good investment of capital for the Commonwealth to build all the hospitals that may be needed for the early and prompt cure and the proper management of insanity.

As the demand upon the public treasuries for the support of insanity, which the State and the towns recognize and pay, knows no other limit than the number of the insane and the length of their disease, or the duration of their lives, so the duty of providing the means for their cure and protection should be measured only by the necessities of those who should profit by them.

In view of these principles, and of the six hundred and five insane persons in Massachusetts who need, but cannot now obtain, the accommodations of a public institution suitable for their cure or their protection, the Committee advise that the State now build another hospital, and place it in one of the four western counties.

The Commissioners on Lunacy state in their Report, that they made all the other inquiries enjoined upon them by the Resolve of the Legislature of 1854; and the facts which they learned and the conclusions which they arrived at are set forth in that document.

This Committee have carefully examined the Report of the Commissioners, and they have followed their steps as far as to visit the hospitals, and the county receptacles, and the State almshouses, where the insane are kept, and they fully concur in the propositions which are therein set forth :—

That the insane whose diseases are recent, and therefore curable, and those who are troublesome, excitable, violent or dangerous, can be best managed in hospitals especially appropriated for their use;

That the county receptacles, and all establishments connected with prisons, and the prisons themselves, are improper places for the insane;

That the State almshouses are unsuitable places for the insane;

That, with one exception, all classes of patients should be kept in the same establishments as they now are in the State hospitals;

That the State paupers should be provided for by the Commonwealth in a separate hospital;

That the Worcester Hospital is unsuited for its present purposes, and has not the accommodations which the present age elsewhere affords; and it should, at the earliest suitable opportunity, be sold and replaced by another.

But as the wants of those lunatics now at their homes, and need, but have not, the means of healing and no proper protection, are more pressing than those of the patients in any of the establishments now built, it is proposed that,—

1. A hospital be now established in the western part of the State.

2. That, when this shall be finished, the Legislature then existing build another within the city of Worcester, and out of the dense part of the town, to which the independent patients and those who are supported by the towns be transferred, and that the State paupers be then removed to the present old hospital.

3. That the Legislature, then in being, build in a suitable place, in the eastern part of the State, another hospital for the State paupers, and the present hospital, with its grounds, be sold.

Looking at the present valuation of the Worcester Hospital and grounds, as set forth in the Report of the Commission on Lunacy, and at the rapid rise of property in the city of Worcester, there is no doubt that, at the time when, according to this plan, the State shall cease to need it, it can be sold for a sum much more than sufficient to build one of those institutions, with all the modern improvements, and with abundance of land for all its purposes.

Recognizing the propriety of this plan, the present Legislature can only take the first step, and establish the hospital in the western counties, and leave the rest to be finished by their successors.

They therefore report the following Bill.

BENJAMIN B. SISSON, *Chairman.*

Commonwealth of Massachusetts.

In the Year One Thousand Eight Hundred and Fifty-
Five.

AN ACT

To establish a Hospital for Insane in Western Massachusetts.

*Be it enacted by the Senate and House of Representa-
tives in General Court assembled, and by the authority of
the same, as follows :—*

1   SECT. 1. His excellency the governor, with the
2 advice and consent of the council, is hereby author-
3 ized and empowered to appoint a board of three com-
4 missioners, who shall purchase an eligible site within
5 one of the four western counties of this Common-
6 wealth, and cause to be erected thereon a suitable
7 hospital for the care and cure of the insane—the
8 accommodations of such hospital to be sufficient for
9 two hundred or two hundred and fifty patients, a su-
10 perintendent and steward, with their families, and all

11 necessary subordinate officers, attendants and assist-
12 ants.   And the said commissioners shall have power
13 to make all contracts and to employ all agents neces-
14 sary to carry into effect the powers hereinbefore
15 granted : *provided*, that the aggregate amount of ex-
16 penses and liabilities incurred by virtue of said
17 powers shall not exceed the amount of two hundred
18 thousand dollars ; and the said commissioners shall
19 present all their accounts to the auditor, to be by
20 him audited and allowed, from time to time, as he
21 shall deem proper.

1   SECT. 2.   In order to defray any expenses incurred
2 in pursuance of the preceding section, or to repay
3 any sums borrowed, as hereinafter authorized, the
4 treasurer is hereby empowered, under the direction of
5 the governor, with the advice and consent of the
6 council, to issue scrip or certificates of debt, in the
7 name and behalf of the Commonwealth, and under
8 his signature and the seal of the Commonwealth, to
9 an amount not exceeding one hundred and fifty thou-
10 sand dollars, which may be expressed in the currency
11 of Great Britain, and shall be payable to the holder
12 thereof in London, bearing an interest of five per
13 cent., payable semi-annually in London, on the first
14 days of April and October, with warrants for the
15 interest attached thereto, signed by the treasurer,
16 which scrip or certificates shall be redeemable in
17 London on the first day of April, one thousand eight
18 hundred and seventy-five, and shall be countersigned
91 by the governor of the Commonwealth, and be deemed
20 a pledge of the faith and credit of the Commonwealth
21 for the redemption thereof.   And the treasurer may

22 under the direction of the governor and council, dis-
23 pose of any portion of said scrip at any price not
24 less than its original par value.

1   SECT. 3. The treasurer, under the direction of the
2 governor and council, may borrow, in anticipation of
3 the issue of the scrip authorized as above, of any of
4 the banks of this Commonwealth, or of any corpora-
5 tions or individuals, such sums as may be necessary
6 for any of the purposes of this act: *provided*, that
7 the whole amount borrowed by authority hereof and
8 remaining unpaid shall at no time exceed the amount
9 of one hundred and fifty thousand dollars.